THE END OF A NATURAL MONOPOLY:

DEREGULATION AND COMPETITION IN THE ELECTRIC POWER INDUSTRY

THE ECONOMICS OF LEGAL RELATIONSHIPS

Series Editor: Nicholas Mercuro
Michigan State University

THE ECONOMICS OF LEGAL RELATIONSHIPS VOLUME 7

THE END OF A NATURAL MONOPOLY: DEREGULATION AND COMPETITION IN THE ELECTRIC POWER INDUSTRY

EDITED BY

PETER Z. GROSSMAN
Efroymson Chair in Economics, Butler University, USA

DANIEL H. COLE
M. Dale Palmer Professor of Law, Indiana University, USA

2003

Routledge
Taylor & Francis Group
LONDON AND NEW YORK

First edition 2003
By Elsevier Science Ltd

Reprinted 2004
By Routledge
2 Park Square, Milton Park,
Abingdon, Oxon OX14 4RN

Transferred to Digital Printing 2004

Routledge is an imprint of the Taylor & Francis Group

Library of Congress Cataloging in Publication Data
A catalog record from the Library of Congress has been applied for.

British Library Cataloguing in Publication Data
A catalogue record from the British Library has been applied for.

ISBN: 0-7623-0995-4
ISSN: 1569-4038 (Series)

∞The paper used in this publication meets the requirements of ANSI/NISO Z39.48-1992 (Permanence of Paper).

Printed and bound in Great Britain by TJI Digital, Padstow, Cornwall

CONTENTS

LIST OF CONTRIBUTORS

Robert L. Bradley, Jr.	Institute for Energy Research, University of Houston, USA
Reed W. Cearley	Mullett & Associates, Attorneys, USA
Daniel H. Cole	Indiana University, USA
Peter Z. Grossman	Butler University, USA
Andrew P. Morriss	Case Western Reserve University, USA
Jim Rossi	University Of North Carolina, USA
Joseph P. Tomain	University Of Cincinnati, USA

THE ECONOMICS OF LEGAL RELATIONSHIPS

STATEMENT OF SCOPE

The Economics of Legal Relationships monograph series is dedicated to publishing original scholarly contributions that systematically analyze legal-economic issues. As with other monograph series, each monograph can take a variety of forms:

(1) Each monograph may be comprised of a collection of original articles devoted to a single theme, edited by a guest volume editor.
(2) A monograph may be a collection of refereed articles derived from the Series Editor's "call for papers" on a particular legal-economic topic.
(3) An individual may wish to author an entire monograph.

Each monograph is published in hardback, approximately 250 pages in length and is dedicated to:

- Formulate and/or critique alternative theories of law and economics – including – the new law and economics, the economics of property rights, institutionalist and neoinstitutionalist law and economics, and public choice theory.
- Analyze a variety of public policy issues related to the interface between judicial decisions and/or statutory law and the economy.
- Explore the economic impact of political and legal changes brought on by new technologies and/or environmental concerns.
- Examine the broad array of legal/economic issues surrounding the deregulation-reregulation phenomena.
- Analyze the systematic effects of legal change on incentives and economic performance.

1. INTRODUCTION

Peter Z. Grossman and Daniel H. Cole

For a hundred years, economists, other scholars, and government officials understood, or thought they did, the electric power industry. Electric power, based on a single, large service provider, connected by wires to all of its customers, was thought to be an industry that could only operate efficiently as a monopoly; indeed it was something called a "natural monopoly." Since it *had* to be a monopoly, with all the attendant inefficiencies and potential market abuses monopoly entails, there was no question about the propriety of government regulation (Lowry, 1973).

These basic assumptions, which at times seemed to conflict with observed facts during the first decades of the industry's existence at the turn of the twentieth century, remained largely unquestioned for the better part of 75 years. Then, changing institutional and technological circumstances led economists (e.g Demsetz, 1968, Primeaux, 1986) to question the basis in fact of the theory of natural monopoly, and the regulatory system it entailed. As other industries, previously deemed natural monopolies, such as telecommunications, adjusted to the new reality of post-natural monopoly theory, the electric power industry and government regulators remained reluctant to concede that anything fundamental had changed. Movement toward a deregulated electric power system did not occur until the last decade of the twentieth century, and then it was undertaken haltingly and piecemeal.

While the U.S. electric power industry and government regulators dithered, their counterparts in other countries, notably the U.K., were, by the late 1980s, embracing more completely a competitive market-oriented model of electric power generation and, to a lesser extent, distribution (Ruff, 1989; Lester, 1991). In the U.S., the public-policy debate over marketization and other deregulatory

The End of a Natural Monopoly: Deregulation and Competition in the Electric Power Industry, Volume 7, pages 1–9.

ISBN: 0-7623-0995-4

policies aimed at the American electric power industry continued on through the decade, and only gradually did states began to make policy changes. These were intended ostensibly to deregulate the electric power industry and foster competitive markets, but the changes varied from state to state reflecting the peculiarity of the American regulatory system for electric power, which endows individual states with the bulk of regulatory responsibility. Consequently, regulatory proposals and changes varied widely from minor regulatory amendments to major overhauls of the system. However, few states instituted changes that could legitimately be described as "deregulatory." The process was largely one of *re*-regulation rather than *de*regulation.

The result of this crazy quilt of regulations, re-regulations, and deregulatory proposals has resulted in more costs than benefits for the regulated industry, consumers, and the economy as a whole. Indeed, because of the most infamous case of California's regulatory miasma, which will be examined in Chapter 10, the entire enterprise of regulatory change has been called into question. The process of de- or re-regulation in several other states has ground to a halt because of fear of repeating California's mistakes (e.g. Banerjee, 2002). And many observers have raised California as a cautionary tale, from which they extrapolate that deregulation is bad policy. In their view, the California experience proves that electric power production and distribution remain a natural monopoly, which must be heavily regulated by government (e.g. Bradley, 2001). As one energy consultant was quoted as saying, "I don't think one can have a deregulated electricity system if one wants reliable power" (Francis, 2001). These arguments are based, however, on the presumption that California had truly deregulated its electric power industry. As we will argue in Chapter 10, there was no actual "deregulation" of electric power in California. In fact, nothing that happened in California bears on the arguments about the necessity or desirability of monopoly electric power systems.

This book addresses some of the fundamental issues underlying the debate over electric power regulation and deregulation. Only by understanding these questions and exploring a variety of possible answers to them can we hope to move the debate over the proper structure of the electric power industry in the United States. This requires a comparative institutional and organizational analysis of alternative structures of electricity production and distribution. Note that we are not promoting a completely *laissez-faire* conception of electric power production and distribution, devoid of government oversight. In our economy, legal boundaries are necessary for the any market, including the power market, to operate efficiently (Eggertsson, 1989). However, the huge and unwieldy structure of the old natural monopoly approach to electric power production and distribution is plainly obsolete (if it ever did make sense). Its institutional and organizational structures are out of tune with both contemporary economic theory and the economic and technological realities of the twenty-first century.

Here are some of the questions this book will address in attempting to determine the proper institutional and organizational structure of electric power production and distribution. First, what is meant by a *natural monopoly*, and is there really any such thing? If you pick up any textbook on the principles of economics, and look in the index, you will find a reference to natural monopoly. Now flip to that page, and you will likely find a very clear and concise definition of natural monopoly, perhaps including a graph showing a single, downward-sloping average-cost curve. A firm with such a cost-curve, the book will tell you, *is* a natural monopoly.[1] But just what kind of firm has this structure? The example in the book is based on nothing but a "production function," a kind of economic black box with only hypothetical, not actual, inputs or outputs. It bears at best a stylized resemblance to any real firm operating in the real world. The text will often go on to say, however, that this kind of configuration will be determined by the technological characteristics of an industry, that is, that industrial organization is merely the inevitable outcome of scientific realities.[2]

Then the textbooks will go on to say that real-life examples of the phenomenon they've labeled natural monopolies include electric power producers, telecommunications companies, and transportation providers, particularly railroads (for example, O'Sullivan & Sheffrin, 2001). In recent years, some authors have removed these examples, recognizing that changing conceptions of industrial organization have raised serious doubts about whether they are, or ever have been, natural monopolies (for example, Case & Fair, 2002). Yet, the electric power industry remains firmly based on some conception of this often elusive, ill-defined, and poorly understood concept. And serious arguments continue to be put forward to the effect that electric power production, transmission and distribution really are of such a nature that they require extensive government regulation (see Chapter 10). In Chapter 2, we will explain what is meant by a natural monopoly, and provide a frame of reference to assess the arguments about electric power deregulation.

A second issue addressed in this book concerns the institutional structure of electric power regulation, and how that structure has evolved over time. It may seem to the casual observer that electric power production has always been the province of a single, monopolistic firm, controlling the market in its particular region of the country, and strictly regulated by state public utility commissions. For most people alive today, regulated monopoly is the only system of power production and distribution they have ever known. As we will discuss, however, the structure we take for granted did not emerge fully formed with the birth of the industry. It is a creature both of deliberate, economically and politically-motivated policy decisions and of historical contingencies or accidents. In fact, the original state of affairs when the industry first emerged was largely unregulated competition. The utilities themselves first argued in favor of monopoly control mitigated by government regulation, to prevent "ruinous competition," ostensibly for the sake of consumers. However, as discussed in Chapters 3 and 4, the utilities had other concerns besides consumer welfare, namely their own rents derived from protection against competition. In sum, the utilities relied on the natural monopoly theories of economists not to maximize social welfare but to maximize their private profits.

Of course, it takes two to create a monopoly out of a competitive environment. The utilities could not have obtained monopolistic control of electricity markets without the active participation of, first, state and local governments, and, later, the federal government. Why did governments agree to this structure? Chapter 3 will explore this question, and explain what governments had to gain from agreeing to what came to be called the "regulatory contract." Whatever the explanation, the fact of the matter is that the so-called "natural" monopoly of power production and distribution did not arise naturally, but was deliberately instituted by political agreement between governments and utilities.

The next question, addressed in Chapter 4, is what constituted the precise nature of the "regulatory contract" between electric utilities and state governments? Was this contract really designed to enhance the welfare of consumers, as some scholars have argued (Sidak & Spulber, 1997)? Historical research suggests that this was not the case. Rather, the regulatory contract appears to have been created predominantly for the benefit of certain, powerful utilities and local politicians they supported. No matter who was intended to benefit from the regulatory contract at the time it was created, the nature and composition of that contract remains a highly charged issue because of its implications for proposed changes to the regulatory system, which would, in effect, alter the terms of the "contract." Alterations to the terms of the contract – redistributing rights and duties as between utilities and governments – could give rise, in some circumstances, to legal liability. One provision of the regulatory contract is the so-called "duty to serve" – the requirement that utilities, as a *quid pro quo* for their regional monopolies, must serve the entire region, regardless of the marginal costs of providing service to outlying customers. The implications of this requirement are considered by Jim Rossi in Chapter 7. Another provision of the regulatory contract entitles utilities to a fair return on prudent and productive investments. If deregulation (or reregulation) terminates current "rate-of-return" regulation, and the competitive market "undervalues" earlier investments, the question arises whether utilities have been deprived of the benefit of past bargains. In other words, must utilities be guaranteed recovery of costs for investments undertaken under the old regulatory regime, but which become uneconomic in the new competitive market system? Reed Cearley and Daniel Cole take up this issue in Chapter 8.

If it is true, as this book will argue, that natural monopoly is not natural, and that monopoly arose through an agreement of industry and government, then the question becomes: why did that system last as long as it did? Once the natural monopoly regulatory approach was institutionalized beginning in the early years of the 1900s and codified fully in the 1930s, it persisted more or less unquestioned until the 1960s. Why did it remain largely unchallenged for more than 50 years? These questions are considered in Chapter 5. The key to the answer lies in the functionality of the natural monopoly conception. As Chapter 2 explains, the most efficient form of organization for any industry is highly contingent on a variety of technological and institutional factors. There is no reason why an industry cannot temporarily be better off, or at least as well off, as a single firm, and ostensibly have some of the characteristics of a "natural" monopoly. And given the state of the electric industry and technology generally, the form of single firm, regional monopolists was, if not ideal, at least serviceable especially during the period after World War II. The regulatory system, though never capable of actually monitoring and analyzing the details of the industry it supervised, nonetheless allowed for expansion and development of the electric system that served a rapidly growing U.S. economy. In other words, the basic institutional form was for a time at least a stable equilibrium. However, Chapter 5 shows that early on there were reasons to doubt the long-term efficacy of such a system and the assumptions on which it was based. The fact that so many in industry and government had invested in the natural monopoly system, however, guaranteed that it would prove resistant to change.

What finally led to a reexamination of the economic model and the underlying legal structure that supported it? This is an issue that Joseph Tomain takes up in Chapter 6. As he points out, regulation inevitably goes through a "life cycle," so change, be it evolutionary or revolutionary, is inevitable in any regulatory process. But the changes in perceptions about electric power also developed from exogenous forces in the larger economy. The energy crisis of the 1970s in particular led government and industry officials to reexamine some of their beliefs relating to the organization of the power industry. This, in turn, led directly to new policies that in very real ways undermined claims that monopoly was a necessary form of organization for the socially efficient production and distribution of electricity. Failures within the industry, for example the catastrophic cost overruns in power plant construction, led to tension between government and industry, and inevitably disturbed the fragile coalition supporting natural monopoly. With each change, critics argued, there were more and more reasons to doubt the assumptions of the model of a regulated natural monopoly.

Changes in industry structure and the overlying regulatory system have been numerous but incomplete. Often, they have involved the application of piecemeal reforms in response to specific, local issues or isolated problems. Only rarely, at least until the 1990s, did regulators and the regulated community contemplate wholesale changes to industry structure. Nevertheless, some of these changes have had important impacts, not all of them positive by any stretch of the imagination. Still, the changes have led to important rearrangements of political forces, legal structures, and industrial organization. These changes and their effects, which are best viewed as *re*regulatory rather than *de*regulatory, are examined in Chapters 6 through 10. For example, as discussed in Chapter 8, efforts to address utility demands for recovery of so-called "stranded costs" – unrecovered costs of investments undertaken under the old regulatory system – have led regulators to propose market prices on the one hand but guaranteed profits on the other. In other cases, state governments have loosened the single, vertical monopoly structure of utilities by forcing separation between production and distribution units. However, often the terms on which this separation has been affected require at least as much government oversight and intervention as the previous regulatory system required. For the most part, states have not proposed, let alone implemented, policies that would truly *de*regulate the electric power industry. In a few states, wholesale and retail electricity prices are now more or less determined in competitive markets, and consumers in those states can choose between power providers. But in most states, electric power production remains highly, if differently, regulated. In Chapter 9, Andrew Morriss explains why, for the most part, electric power production has been *re*regulated rather than *de*regulated, and he considers the outlook for the future of the American electric power industry. His view is pessimistic, based on his perception that public choice pressures are likely to impede true deregulation. In Chapter 10, Peter Grossman offers an alternative, and somewhat more optimistic, vision of the power industry's future, this despite his dour analysis of California's disastrous experience with regulatory reform. Like Morriss, Grossman appreciates the institutional difficulties of real deregulation; but unlike Morriss, he sees at least the possibility that efficiency-enhancing change will emerge in the long run.

Still, we do not doubt the basic difficulty that institutional change entails. As Nobel-laureate Douglass C. North (1990) has explained, institutional change is a problematic, haphazard, and usually incremental process. The result is sometimes less socially efficient than the pre-existing situation those changes were designed to improve upon. In North's work, institutions are defined strictly as "the humanly designed constraints imposed on human interactions," (North 1991). That is, institutions are the formal laws, cultural norms and the mechanisms of enforcement of both formal and informal rules that bound, structure and focus social interaction.[3] All societies by definition are bound by sets of rules ("rules of the game," to North) since human interaction requires structure. These rules create and determine political and economic incentives, reduce uncertainty for everyone in society and channel social forces in specific directions. As North points out, if a society values piracy, it will structure institutions to reward that activity and produce people adept at piracy.

But while institutions play a part in controlling human behavior, they are alterable and indeed, economic and political actors in any society might see the potential for a more favorable distribution of costs and benefits by changing the institutional framework to their own benefit. There is likely to be a tension in a social system whereby some forces act for preservation of existing institutions and others act for their change. In general the force for institutional change will predominate when there are increases in uncertainty or in the cost of transacting, arising from changes in technology, ideology and other dynamic factors confronting society. As change occurs, there are changes in relative costs and benefits, which lead to an examination of existing rules and the distribution of social and economic benefits.

But the demand for change and in fact actual change in the institutional structure does not guarantee greater efficiency of the result. Social actors may see a need for a reduction of uncertainty and hence change in the institutional structure. But uncertainty may be reduced at the expense of efficiency. So for example, free markets may be more efficient in the long run but the dislocation that is produced as a consequence of their creation may lead in turn to inefficient, but more certain, kinds of rules, for instance totalitarian dictatorship and/or centrally planned economic systems. There are many examples in human history – the Russian Revolution comes to mind – where institutional change was demanded and change affected, but the result was highly inefficient, producing a decline in living standards or long-run stagnation. In other cases, the result embodied compromises among groups for the distribution of benefits and costs such that while greater efficiency was achieved in one social or economic dimension, it was offset only by the implementation of inefficient rules elsewhere.

This picture of institutional change is certainly pertinent with respect to the electric power industry. First, at the start of the twentieth century, monopoly organization and regulation developed in response to changes in technology and the distribution of costs and benefits that the new technology presented. The organizations devised under these institutional arrangements – the monopoly utilities and the regulatory bodies that oversaw them – had a vested interest: first, in maintaining (or maximizing) the benefits that they received from those institutional and organizational arrangements, and minimizing (or externalizing) the costs; and second, in seeing that any changes in the institutional and organizational structures would yield them further net benefits. They would understandably resist efforts to alter the institutional structure in ways that might reduce their net benefits. Even as technological innovations and changing political and economic circumstances altered the conditions of electric power production and distribution, a strong status quo bias remained.

Utilities that benefited from the existing regulatory system opposed changes that, they perceived, would threaten their monopoly status. Meanwhile, however, other firms that did not benefit from the existing system, but which perceived economic opportunities from deregulation, pushed strongly for change. In addition, electricity consumers and state regulators pursued what they perceived to be their own interests, which were often at odds with both entrenched power suppliers and their would-be competitors. The multilateral, inherently political contest that ensued virtually ensured that institutional change would be contested at every step and, ultimately, incomplete.

Nothing has happened so far that would lead us to question this supposition. The implications for the future of electric power deregulation are that, at the very least, the outcome of efforts to reform the power industry are uncertain at best. It is possible, but by no means guaranteed, that the outcome will be a more efficient system. That said, the very fact that this economic, legal, and political battle is being waged indicates that the basic assumptions underlying natural monopoly theory, and the system constructed upon that theory, are obsolete. We are witnessing the end of natural monopoly. What comes next?

NOTES

1. As Baumol et al. (1988) have demonstrated, this description of a natural monopoly is exceedingly over-simplified.

2. Milton Friedman (1962), for example, has referred to natural monopoly as "a technical monopoly."

3. Institutions are distinct from organizations, which are groups of individuals that form to take advantage of the institutional structure of society (North, 1990).

REFERENCES

Banerjee, N. (2000). Dwindling Faith in Deregulation. *New York Times*. September 20, online at: http://www.nytimes.com

Baumol, W., Panzar, J., & Willig, R. (1988). *Contestable Markets and the Theory of Market Structures, Revised.* San Diego: Harcourt Brace Jovanovich.

Bradley, W. (2001). Power to the People. *The American Prospect, 12*(11)(June 25), online at: http://www.prospect.org

Case, K., & Fair, R. (2002). *Principles of Economics.* Upper Saddle River, NJ: PrenticeHall.

Demsetz, H. (1968). Why Regulate Utilities? *Journal of Law & Economics, 11*, 55–65.

Eggertsson, T. (1990). *Economic Behavior and Institutions.* Cambridge: Cambridge University Press.

Francis, D. (2001). Cooling to Electricity Deregulation. *Christian Science Monitor*, (April 3), online at: http://www.csmonitor.com

Friedman, M. (1962). *Capitalism and Freedom.* Chicago: University of Chicago Press.

Lester, T. (1991). Regions Plug Into the Market. *Management Today*, (March), 102.

Lowry, E. (1973). Justification for Regulation: The Case for Natural Monopoly. *Public Utilities Fortnightly*, (November 8), 17–23.

North, D. (1990). *Institutions, Institutional Change and Economic Performance.* Cambridge: Cambridge University Press.

North, D. (1991). Institutional Change: A Framework of Analysis. Manuscript. Washington University: St. Louis.

O'Sullivan, A., & Sheffrin, S. (2001). *Economics: Principles and Tools.* Upper Saddle River, NJ: Prentice Hall.

Primeaux, W. (1986). *Direct Electric Utility Competition: The Natural Monopoly Myth.* New York: Praeger.

Ruff, L. (1989). Electricity Restructuring in Two Nations: Different Paths to a Competitive Future. *Public Utilities Fortnightly*, (June 22), 13–17.

Sidak, J., & Spulber, D. (1997). *Deregulatory Takings and the Regulatory Contract: The Competitive Transformation of Network Industries in the United States.* Cambridge: Cambridge University Press.

2. IS ANYTHING NATURALLY A MONOPOLY?

Peter Z. Grossman

> . . . public utilities such as water and electric power companies are examples of natural monopolies.
>
> – from *Exploring Economics*, an introductory textbook by Robert L. Sexton (1999, p. 267). The definition is illustrated with a large picture of an electric light bulb.

INTRODUCTION

The title of this book refers to the economic concept of a "natural" monopoly, and as the quote above suggests, electric power has usually been considered an exemplar of this type of firm and industry structure. The importance of this concept to the development of electric power industry and government regulation in the U.S. cannot be overstated. Because electric power companies have been considered natural monopolies, it has been believed that such companies *cannot* be competitive, that they *must* be monopolies, and that they *must* be regulated by government agencies. Indeed, it is fair to say that the economic theory of natural monopoly has provided the foundation for: the establishment of monopoly power systems in the U.S.; the legal structure that exists with respect to electric power; and the regulatory system established by local, state and federal government bodies to control electric power production, distribution and consumption.

The early development of the electric power system in the U.S. will be examined in the next chapter. This chapter will consider the concept of natural monopoly itself, and what happens in a market if a firm actually displays

The End of a Natural Monopoly: Deregulation and Competition in the Electric Power Industry, Volume 7, pages 11–39.

ISBN: 0-7623-0995-4

characteristics of a natural monopoly. As we will see, if an industry is identified as an actual natural monopoly, government regulation becomes desirable and probably inevitable.

The problem, however, as this chapter will discuss, is that it is not clear that *any* industry is "naturally" a particular form of industrial organization. When an industry is typed-based on some supposed characteristics, usually technical, typology will likely obscure the subtleties of organization and technology, as well as market and government behavior. Of course, it is easier for government to identify types and regulate an industry (or not) according to some general criteria or technical characteristics. But once such a regime is established, it is very difficult to change or to permit exceptions. And as this chapter will argue, the form any industry would take in the absence of regulation, will be highly contingent to various circumstances that would lead to different industry structures in different places, as well as to different forms of industry organization in the same place at different times.

To understand this, we will, first, examine the standard version of natural monopoly theory, and the assumptions on which it is based. Then we will propose an alternative version that it will be argued more accurately reflects the nature of a firm in a dynamic technological and institutional environment. Finally, we will review the history of how this concept evolved and was applied to utilities in general and electric power in particular.

WHAT IS A NATURAL MONOPOLY?

Most introductory economics textbooks begin (and some end with) a very simple definition of natural monopoly. It goes something like this:

> A natural monopoly exists when "a single firm can supply a good or a service to an entire market at a smaller cost than could two or more firms (Mankiw 1998, p. 306).

To expand on this more completely: if one firm has lower costs than any other firm or combination of firms in producing a good or service at the full level of market demand, then the industry, operating in a free market, will become a monopoly because the one firm can always profitably underprice entrants and drive them out of business.

This definition is undoubtedly true; indeed it is so simplified as to be a truism. But mostly it begs the question: how does such a situation arise? Or perhaps even more fundamentally, *does* such a situation arise and when?

It is generally argued in the literature that a natural monopoly condition arises from persistent economies of scale, which cause average costs to fall over the entire range of market demand. This is illustrated in Fig. 1.

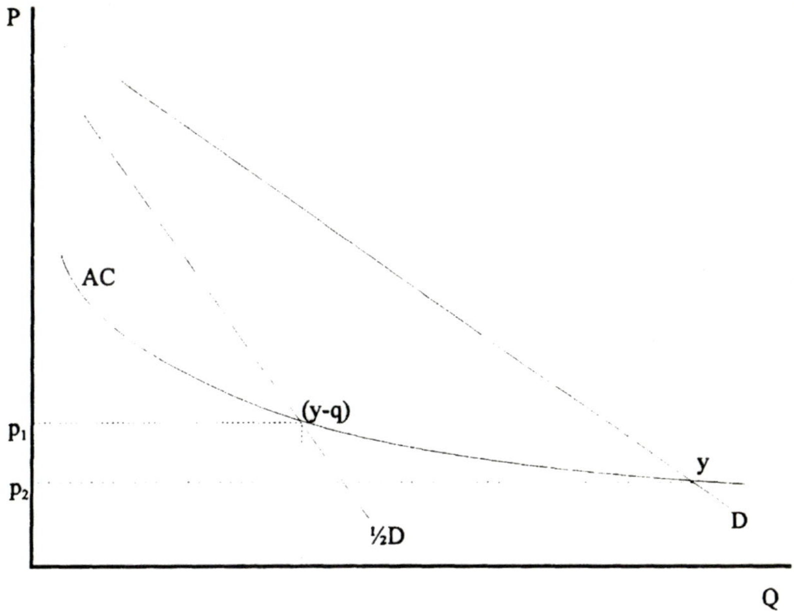

Fig. 1. Standard Textbook Illustration of Natural Monopoly.

Notes: Average costs are declining through the entire range of demand. The firm that supplies the entire market can sell as p_2, while the one serving less than the market must charge more (p_1).

This figure is the starting point for most discussions of natural monopoly. Consider the demand curve (solid line on the graph, D) to represent the market demand for a given commodity X. What price the product will sell at in a free market will usually be determined by the intersection of supply and demand. But here we depict not supply, but the average cost curve (AC) for the entire industry, which slopes downward (and bows inwards) even at the point where it intersects the demand curve.[1] Since average costs – at least long run average costs – represent the cost to firms per unit of output (including the firm's normal rate of return), then if any one firm can produce the quantity at the lowest point of the AC curve it can underprice its competition. Here, since the AC curve is still downward sloping at the point of intersection with market demand (point y), one firm producing y will be able to produce for the entire market and will drive out competition.

To illustrate, say that there are two firms, both of which can produce half of market demand. But in that case their share of the market intersects average costs at a point above y (in Fig. 1), and so they both produce a lower quantity than y (point y-a), and must both receive a price of at least P_1 – if they are to in fact cover their costs of production. But now one firm expands and in so doing can drive down the price until at y, where output is sufficient to satisfy the entire market, the price is at P_2. Clearly, the other firm producing at y-a will be unable to compete. The expanding firm will have the advantage, which will be unassailable – unless another firm is in some way able to lower its costs even further say through technological innovation and subsequently take over the market. Barring that, the expanding firm captures the entire market gaining a monopoly that cannot be overcome by competition.

Of course, as theory tells us, the monopoly firm, once it has gained an unassailable (or "natural)" monopoly does not set the price at the average cost. Rather it chooses a price that maximizes profits, which will be at the point where marginal costs equal marginal revenues, as shown in Fig. 2.[2]

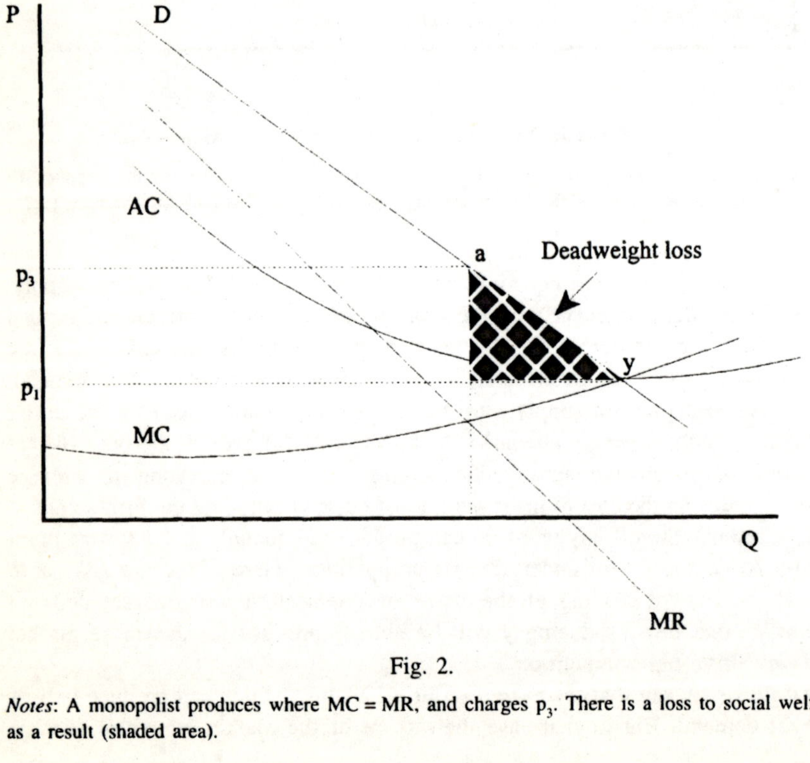

Fig. 2.

Notes: A monopolist produces where MC = MR, and charges p_3. There is a loss to social welfare as a result (shaded area).

This is socially wasteful. The amount that should be produced – that is where resources are efficiently employed and producers still make a profit – is at y, at price P_1. But instead, production is set at {a} by the monopolist, at price P_3, the point that would maximize the firm's profits. As a result, too little is produced, and it is sold at too high a price. The shaded area on the graph represents the social loss this entails, referred to as a "deadweight" loss from monopoly. In economics, this is an example of a market failure since the market acting on its own does not produce the socially optimal quantity of the good.

It might be thought that at this point another firm can enter the market and sell the product at some point below P_3, since now there seems to be an opportunity to capture a share of the market. But the monopolist can always ramp up production and lower prices back to P_1 – where it will still be profitable for the one firm to produce, but not for an entrant. Assuming entry has costs, the second firm won't enter and so the incumbent firm retains the monopoly.

Given the inability of competitive forces to curtail the firm's monopoly power and the social loss that this theoretically entails, government regulation of natural monopoly would seem highly desirable. Of course, government could choose to force a competitive market by decreeing a size limit to firms, but that – if natural monopoly in fact exists in that particular industry – would mean that each would be producing at too high a cost and so prices would have to be *too* high (so firms could make a profit); some social losses would still result. Moreover, if a single firm is the natural state of things, so the argument has gone for more than a century, better that the government enfranchise one firm, grant it monopoly power, but reduce its ability to employ monopolistic pricing power. This basic idea has been an article of faith for those who accept that some industries are indeed natural monopolies.

It should be noted that falling costs for the entire range of output are not strictly necessary for even this simple picture of natural monopoly. Figure 3 shows the case where average costs fall to a certain point but then before the entire range of market demand is satisfied, they begin to rise. (This would result when the marginal cost of production begins to exceed average costs.)

This case in an unregulated market would still lead to a monopoly outcome. While it is true that minimum cost is reached where output is at c, not y, no one can beat price P*, the price the monopolist could charge at an acceptable profit, and still satisfy market demand. No entrant can enter and capture the small portion of output where average costs have begun to rise (the portion from c to y), because to gear up its production processes the entrant would be starting at the upper end of the average cost curve. The price it would need to charge for its output would be well above P*. Consequently, the market situation illustrated in Fig. 3 still represents a natural monopoly.

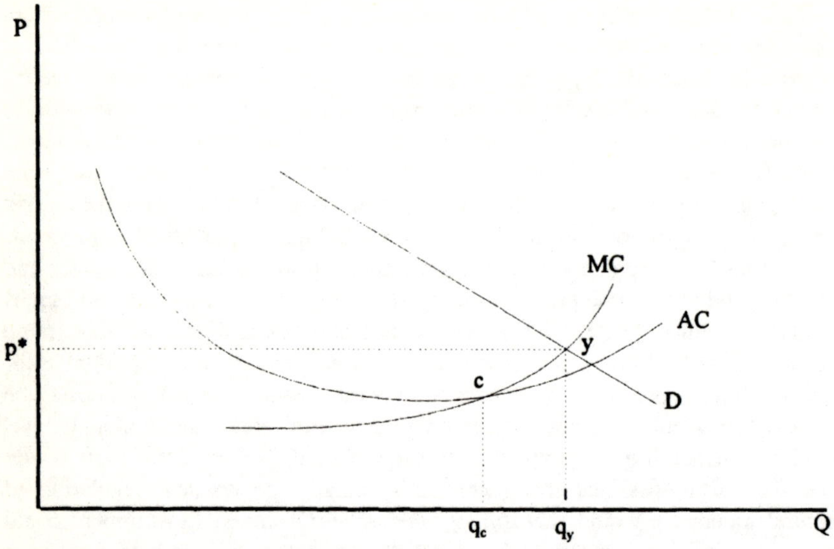

Fig. 3.

Note: In this case, firms would charge marginal cost; otherwise all sales above q_c would be at a loss. Still, this is subaddictive since any entrant would have to charge more that p*.

Sources of Falling Costs

The source of falling costs, and hence natural monopoly, is generally assumed to be pervasive "economies of scale" (Schiller, 2003, p. 76) This concept – scale economies – is even confused in the economic literature (e.g. Dranove, 1998; Train, 1991). Economies of scale are said to exist when at given set of input prices,[3] a percentage quantity increase of inputs leads to a greater percentage increase in output. In other words, economies of scale mean that by expanding production a firm can increase output more than proportionally to its input requirements. This kind of outcome can be the result of technological innovation, or it can result from, as Michael Porter (1985) notes, from greater "efficiencies in the actual operation of an activity at higher scales as well as from less than proportional increases in the infrastructure or overhead needed to support the activity as it grows." Economies of scale are not equal to, but nevertheless require, that production show "increasing returns to scale" (Truett & Truett, 1990), and that only with increasing returns will genuine scale economies emerge.[4]

There are some obvious cases of technological economies of scale: if the cylindrical area of a water pipe is increased, the volume of water the pipe can carry increases by a greater percentage than the percentage increase in materials needed to construct the pipe. In electric power, it was the case especially in the early years of the industry that a generator could be increased in size and produce proportionally more units of electricity – in kilowatt hours – than the increase in inputs of capital, labor and materials needed to generate them.

Since technological economies of scale are known to exist and since they can be a source of falling average costs, the argument has often been that a natural monopoly is entirely a technological phenomenon. Indeed, Friedman (1962, pp. 28–29) has explicitly referred to natural monopoly as a "technical" monopoly that could, by its nature, justify government regulation. Posner (1969, p. 8) similarly has argued that natural monopoly refers to the "relationship between demand and the technology of supply."

There is no doubt that scale economies from technology can lead to decreased long-run costs, but there needs to be some caution with regards to just how determinant technical characteristics actually are. Economies of scale are present in nearly all forms of production. The average cost curve even for a small competitive firm will have a range over which average costs fall (and so the curve will be u-shaped, showing economies of scale over some range and diseconomics over another). It is only in their pervasiveness that these determine a single-firm industry structure that would be considered a natural monopoly. And then it must also be the case that costs are so overwhelmingly a technical phenomenon that nothing else really matters. Or alternatively, the market must be small enough so that it only can accommodate one firm.[5]

The technological issue has a further, and important, implication: if a technology is deemed a natural monopoly, then it follows that whenever the technology is adopted the form of industry organization must follow. This may well ignore local conditions that change the nature of costs, so that even when a single firm is demonstrably efficient in one instance, it will be notably inefficient in another. Moreover, it will be argued later in this chapter that technology alone is seldom – if ever – so overwhelmingly determinate as to proscribe all but one form or organization.

Even in many technical arguments relative to natural monopoly, the sources of scale economies are not accurately identified. Or more exactly, the literature often has misidentified (and inaccurately defined) scale economies and thus the rationale for natural monopoly.

The Source of Scale Economies

The mistake most often made is to believe that economies of scale derive from high fixed costs, and that by having a larger output the costs are reduced on average across that output. As Train (1991, p. 6) puts it: "The most prevalent source of economies of scale are fixed costs. . . . When output expands, the fixed costs (in this case the costs of the [electric generating] plant) are spread over more units, such that average cost declines."

There are important – albeit commonly held – errors in this statement. Most crucially, from a long run perspective there are no fixed costs, and so this comment is by definition false. Capital costs – the costs of plant and equipment – are not fixed in the long run since most capital can be sold or put to alternative uses; capital, like labor, then varies and can be considered over time as a variable rental price. In the long run, the amount of capital can be adjusted to reflect the output that is demanded from it. If output is too great, then capital can be reduced to the appropriate level; if it is insufficient, new capital can be employed. Thus, there should be no *long run* impact of such costs on average costs generally. That is, no matter what the short run fixed costs are, the long run average cost should be unchanged. Of course as a practical matter, there are mis-forecasts or imperfect capital markets that lead to too much or too little capital and so short run constraints that may lead to excessive or insufficient capital for the needed output. But this result is not the same as arguing that fixed costs are a present condition that determines economies of scale.

Train (1991) is apparently mistaking fixed costs for sunk costs. Costs are sunk when they cannot be recouped through alternative use. In other words, if capital can not resold or leased then expenditure would entail the potential for loss in the long as well as the short run. Sunk costs may well present a barrier to entry that will keep others out of a market, but that would be true whether average costs are increasing or decreasing.[6]

Even if we were to allow fixed costs in the long term, the basic premise of Train's statement is still inaccurate, because it identifies economies of scale with the spreading of fixed costs. In fact, it confuses scale economies with capacity utilization, which again is a confusion of short run constraints for long run conditions. It must be emphasized that economies of scale involve the long run. If average costs are not falling in the long run *as production expands*, where there is merely the spreading of fixed costs, then scale economies are not demonstrably present.

To illustrate, consider a case where a factory with one machine is constructed. In all cases, the output from the machine will be expected to pay the cost of that capital as well as more obviously variable costs of labor and raw materials of production. If the machine runs at half capacity, but the full capital cost must be born anyway, then it is true that in the short run the average cost will fall as output expands toward capacity. But now let's say capacity is reached.

If there are pervasive economies of scale in this industry then when output capacity is expanded (a second machine is added), average costs must *continue to fall*. If, however, what is achieved is mere capacity utilization, then they will not fall. Indeed, adding a second machine may require the same capital and labor and materials as the first machine.[7] The *average* cost will in that case never fall below the level achieved at capacity from the production by one machine. This would mean that in fact the increased capacity utilization did not reflect continuing economies of scale in the industry, and that the production process had in the long-run constant, not increasing, returns to scale.

Now consider what this implies with respect to a natural monopoly argument. For the technological argument to be the case, the production of a particular good – and thus far we have examined the case of a single good – would be a natural monopoly only if as output were expanded to meet the entire market demand, one machine or one plant or, for some reason, one dispersed firm would have to be able to achieve reduced average long term costs. That is, costs would have to be lower per unit at higher and higher levels of output. Of course, as we noted in Figure 2, it is possible for the argument to hold even if a point is reached before full market demand is satisfied where diseconomies raise average costs slightly. But even in that case, relative to market demand scale economies would have to be pervasive enough so that entry by another firm using the same technology would be futile.

A further technological point: this monopoly might still be only temporary, unless for some reason no technological innovation were possible – a hardly tenable position – or, more possibly, one firm had absolute control of the technology.[8] Otherwise, as long as the monopoly depended on technical characteristics alone any innovation that would lower costs including ones of organizational process would mean that an entrant could come in acquire the necessary capital and take over the entire market by underpricing the original monopolist. The prospect of long-term monopoly rents should make this a very attractive proposition. However, if a firm has a government-provided monopoly franchise this kind of outcome will not occur since an entry is barred by statute. But then we could hardly consider it a "natural" monopoly.

Subadditivity and Contestability

There are a number of features of the simple natural monopoly concept that are not reflective of the real world. The most important of these is that few firms produce only one good; joint production of two or more goods is far more common. This may not seem so obvious at first glance: an electric company produces electric power, a cable tv company (also often identified as a natural monopoly) distributes television programs, and so on. But in fact, these and other firms have a measure, often a large measure, of vertical integration.

An electric company – of the type that has generally been seen in the U.S. and most other countries, a franchised (or government-owned) monopoly – is vertically integrated across a number of "outputs." First, it produces electric power. Then it distributes the power. It markets the power directly to consumers, and it also services distribution access points. The list can go on, but the point is straightforward: most firms identified as natural monopolies have more than one output so the simple model of the previous sections is clearly too simple.

In a classic work that is the starting point for much of modern theory relating to natural monopoly, Baumol, Panzar and Willig (1988) argued that both the single output and multi-output cases could be explored by abandoning the pure economies of scale definition and using instead the concept of "subadditivity." Essentially for any natural monopoly, costs in the industry must be strictly subadditive. That is, the costs of single firm must be less than the sum of the costs of all possible combinations of firms. Mathematically, for a single output, x, and cost function C(x):

$$C(x) < C(x^1) + \ldots + C(x^i),$$

where the sum of all outputs of firms $1 \ldots i$, $(x^1 \ldots x^i) = x$.

This general approach can be extended to a multi-output case. Indeed, it can be argued that without the general concept of subadditivity, it is not possible to examine coherently the multi-product case. It is in fact possible to show that two or more outputs can have increasing returns and yet there would be no gain by having them both produced by one firm (Sharkey, 1982).[9] Thus when there is a multi-product example, which in fact encompasses most industries identified as natural monopolies, including electric power, economies of scale through the range of production are not sufficient to justify a natural monopoly. At the same time, it is perfectly plausible that production in a range may not exhibit economies of scale, or that throughout the range one product may not display increasing returns, and yet strict subadditivity still obtain. Put a bit differently, it may be the case that the cost of production of two outputs may be lower if performed by one firm than any alternative arrangement, because the joint cost of production is lower than the cost of producing the products separately (Baumol et al., 1988).[10]

This would result from economies not of scale but of scope; in fact, that is how economies of scope are defined. Mathematically, economies of scope case can be illustrated for outputs x and y, by the expression:

$$C(x,y) < C(x) + C(y)$$

It is not difficult to think of examples of where joint production of two goods may be cheaper than producing the goods separately. German dye-makers of the late nineteenth century were able to use the same capital, labor and raw materials to make a variety of different dyes and even pharmaceuticals (Chandler 1990). Modern "natural" monopolies have also been able to utilize economies of scope. The old telephone monopoly provided both long distance and local calling utilizing much of the same equipment, which was believed to represent a cost savings (Train, 1991).

To summarize then, pervasive economies of scale are not sufficient to explain the existence of natural monopoly once we look beyond the single output case to the more realistic multi-product case. Here the literature looks to see if subadditivity obtains. But even when an industry exhibits subadditivity, there can still be a question of whether a natural monopoly exists or at least whether any firm can function as a monopolist requiring government intervention to prevent consumer abuse and social deadweight loss.

Baumol et al. (1988) examine the problem by exploring whether or not a market is "contestable." A perfectly contestable market (also called "perfectly competitive)" is one in which entry and exit are essentially costless. Thus there are no sunk – that is, nonrecoverable – capital or other costs to enter, and anyone can enter whenever profit opportunities appear and exit when those opportunities are gone. While this clearly applies to competitive industries, even ones that are oligopolistic or monopolistic may still be contestable. That is, the industry may have scale economies and a large firm may dominate. But if entry and exit costs are low then the threat of entry is always present and so the monopolist is always constrained in pricing (Demsetz, 1968). If prices rise above average cost, then entry will immediately occur with the entrant offering the product (or products) at a lower price. Thus the monopolist is forced to behave like a firm in a competitive industry, and keep prices at the socially optimal average cost level.

Baumol et al. (1988) have been criticized for this formulation because it is clear that most endeavors have at least some sunk costs, and, it has been argued, that this may well negate many contestability claims (Weiztman, 1983; Schwartz & Reynolds, 1983). But it can be argued that even when there are sunk costs, and there are ways for entrants to secure contracts with customers (in the event of price increases by the monopolist) the monopolist will be constrained regardless of whether there is actually ongoing competition for the market itself (Demsetz, 1968). The market will be "almost contestable," at least sufficient to keep the monopolist from exercising substantial market power.

Though pricing power may be lacking, a subadditive cost function will lead to what Baumol et al. (1988) refer to as a sustainable natural monopoly configuration. In the presence of high sunk costs that firm may also be able to exercise monopoly power. It is at least implied that public utilities were (and in some instances still are) considered natural monopolies of this sort – industries with high sunk costs and subadditive cost functions. However, as we will see later in this chapter and in the next, there has always been some lack of clarity and contradiction in the arguments presented to support this natural monopoly conclusion with respect to electric power.

The theory of contestability is a highly sophisticated view of markets and firms, and underlies much of current scholarly discussion with respect to industrial organization generally. But it is important to note that Baumol et al. have not departed very substantially from a basic technological paradigm, a view of what causes natural monopoly that is not much different from that found in the simpler form of the theory. Actually, this is not always so apparent. When Baumol et al. state conditions of production functions, they seem to make them general enough to be inclusive of all costs of production. There is no reason on the face of it that these cannot include the costs of contracting, measurement, enforcement, and so on. But when the authors seek to operationalize the concept of contestable markets, it is clear that they fall into the technologically determined view. For example, in a footnote (1988, p. 152), they observe that certain institutional factors in developing countries might result in firms that are too small, or as they put it, there must exist "strong 'impediments' to large enterprise that are unrelated to either absolute or relative input prices." Since the prices of inputs determine cost, the translation of this is that institutional factors can lead to distortions of the "true" costs of production and limits on the true size of the firm, which must be the same, presumably, whenever the given technology is applied.[11] As will be argued in the next section, that idea, as a practical matter, is incorrect except in an ideal world of perfect information and no transaction costs. And most especially, it is devoid of meaningful application in the real world.

A TRANSACTION-COST APPROACH TO NATURAL MONOPOLY[12]

In his groundbreaking 1937 article, "The Nature of the Firm," Ronald Coase asked the simple question: why do we have firms? From the standpoint of neoclassical economic theory it was not at all clear that they should exist. Consider a world in which there is complete information by all economic agents, entry and exit to any industry is free, and transacting is costless. These are assumptions of a neoclassical model of perfectly competitive markets. If they were true there would be no particular reason for firms. Let's say an individual wanted to make cloth. He or she could contract with a supplier of raw materials; contract with a transportation specialist to carry the materials; contract with a spinner to turn it into thread; contract with an owner of capital to rent a machine and a space to turn the thread into cloth; contract with a dyer or other finisher; contract with someone who would market the cloth; and so on. Each of these transactions would be costless: The cost of drawing up the contracts is zero and the prices for the services reflect competitive market equilibria of supply and demand, and the behavior of agents – contracting parties – is known in advance with certainty. Consequently, there would be no benefit to the creation of a firm. Market transactions could efficiently substitute for transactions that go on within the firm, and all people would be independent contractors since they would achieve no gains through another form of organization.

But of course we do have firms, and Coase argued that the reason is that transaction costs are not zero and information is not complete. It is costly to bargain around, write, and enforce contracts; costly to monitor agents; costly to measure performance; costly to search for information on all prices. Therefore, it must sometimes be cost effective to internalize some transactions, organizing and coordinating them within a hierarchical firm. Of course many activities are still more efficiently transacted in markets. The decision of when to use a market and when to organize a firm is determined by which form of organization is lowest cost. Put another way, it is not technology that determines the boundaries of the firm, but the cost of transacting.

As indicated by the example of an ideal neoclassical world without firms above, one way to conceptualize transaction costs for firms is to think of all functions within a firm as a set of contracts. Some scholars in the Coasean tradition have in fact defined the firm itself as a "nexus of contractual relationships" (Jensen & Meckling, 1976). The point is that every facet of a firm's operation could be seen as an explicit or implicit contract between the firm's owner and separate owners of capital, labor, services, materials, etc, with many terms of measurement and enforcement spelled out or inferred. The firm then is an organization that consolidates some of the contracts into a single defined unit as a means to lowering the cost of organization and coordination of production.

While Coase focused on the rationale for the existence of firms, his work also had important implications about firm size and organization generally. As some scholars have argued (for example, Cheung, 1983; Liu & Yang, 2000) that to talk of a particular firm size as appropriate to a particular technology, is meaningless or "irrelevant." In their view, it is entirely contingent on the degree of specialization within and between firms as well as the cost of contracting (Williamson 1979). Clearly, this same kind of analysis can be applied to natural monopoly in general and electric power in particular.

The Organization of Electric Power Systems

In the nineteenth century, the English scientist Michael Faraday demonstrated the basic principles by which electricity is produced. Faraday showed that if a coil of wires is rotated through a magnetic field (or if the field is rotated within a coil of wires) a continuous electric current is induced. The current travels at close to the speed of light and can be utilized instantaneously for various tasks provided the electric generator (and coils and the magnetic field) produces enough energy (measured in watts or more typically kilowatts or megawatts – a thousand watts and a million watts respectively) to do the job. If the generator stops turning, the current ceases instantaneously and any and all things connected to the generator cease to function as well.

Generators since the late nineteenth century have operated primarily by creating high-pressure steam in a boiler and using it to turn the blades of a turbine, which in turn spins the generator. Alternatively, moving water has been used for the same basic purpose.[13] Individual generators are capable of an electric output in some cases large enough to provide electric energy for entire cities.

Any individual can in theory provide her own electricity by acquiring all elements of power production including generation equipment. But in the 1880s, Thomas A. Edison demonstrated that one large generator connected to customers through a system of wires could in fact provide energy to a neighborhood and more. Customers joined the power network first for light, then for the various other benefits that electric devices provided. Initially, consumers paid only for the light fixtures, which were also provided by the electricity provider; later billing was on a metered use-of-energy basis.

Over time, many electric generators became interconnected so that power could be distributed over high voltage lines from community to community. This allowed companies to trade electric power and to move it instantaneously to meet fluctuations in demand – day to day, hour to hour. Though some electricity providers maintained independence from larger power grids, the electric power system today is a vast collection of interconnected generators of various sizes and primary energy sources; long distance high voltage lines; distribution nodes; and plugged-in end-use consumers. As the next chapter will detail, most electricity providers have been legal regulated monopolies, and to many, "natural" monopolies because of their technical characteristics, especially perceived economies of scale in power production and distribution.

The Source of Monopoly: A Coasean Thought Experiment

To get an idea of how problematic it is to claim that an industry is a natural monopoly on technical grounds alone, consider the following Coasean scenario:

There is a world in which there are some economies of scale in electric power production and distribution, and (as the neoclassical model of competitive markets assumes) information is complete and contracting is costless. An owner of an electric generator, a very large one that captures whatever technical scale economies are present in power production, contracts with the owner of a factory space to rent a portion of it to install the generator. He then contracts with an owner of a steam turbine to drive the generator, who in turn contracts with the owner of coal resources and with coal transporters to provide the raw materials for the process to make steam to turn the generator. Our generator-owner then contracts with someone who owns wires to distribute the electricity and with the customers who ultimately use the power. Since all of this contracting and coordination is costless, all contract terms specified, and no cost for information on performance or price, there is no reason why these independent producers need to be organized as a separate hierarchical entity that would resemble a firm. They would not need, especially, to be so vertically integrated to encompass all of the functions noted above in one commonly owned, hierarchically-managed monopolistic entity.

Of course, the picture above is not complete. With electric power, there would be a far greater network of independent contractors. One generator would not suffice. There would be a large generator for a general level of need (called "base load"). There would also have to be a smaller second generator to provide extra power for highest demand times of the day (called "peak load") and spare generating capacity of some kind for times when there would be maintenance problems with the primary generator. There would also need to be a service contractor, and so on. It would be a large web of contractual relationships to be sure, but this does not change the basic idea. That is, there is not any reason why, in a world of zero transaction costs, we would need vertically integrated electric power companies at all, much less monopoly providers. Contracting could achieve the same result without losing the scale economies of a large generator or any other technical scale economies. In this world, there would not be anything called a "natural" monopoly.

Needless to say, this ideal world doesn't and cannot exist, and in the real world of positive transactions costs, there are and will be firms because they economize over market alternatives. But when, if ever, will there be "natural" monopolies? Indeed, from a transaction cost approach, what does "natural monopoly" mean?

A Theoretical Analysis

To begin the analysis, firms are assumed to be cost minimizers, but consider what is meant in economics by "cost." A cost function, the representation of cost, has been given thus far by the simple: C(x); that is, cost is functionally related to the quantity of output (x) that is produced. But while the cost function is typically given in terms of output, this is really a decomposition of a larger function composed of a vector of factor prices **w** (w_{1-n}) and **x**, or:

$$C = C(w_1, \ldots, w_n; x).$$

Given factors of production, capital, labor, etc. (z_1), cost is commonly assumed to be linear, where $C = z_1w_1 + z_2w_2 + \ldots + z_nw_n$, and where each w is determined in competitive factor markets and x is constrained by the technology, given as a production function, $x = f(z_{1-n})$.[14] Average costs then are the sum of the cost components, which must be assumed to be a large string of factor costs, divided by x. It is assumed that, in natural monopoly, as output increases, new factors are added and total costs rise, but at a rate relative to output that leads to a decline in average costs. As noted before, and this point should be stressed, the basic model assumes that factor prices do not change with expanded output and that indeed they are set competitively and solely in factor markets. So then for example, the cost of labor is entirely the wage rate that is set by forces of supply and demand in the labor market.

Now consider a firm – any firm – as a nexus of contractual relationships in which contracting is costly (in other words transaction costs are non-zero, as in fact they are in the real world). This firm will still be assumed to minimize costs. A monopoly will exist if a single firm can minimize the overall cost of its contractual relationships such that it has a lower cost per unit of output than that achieved by any alternative arrangement of firms. Or more to the point by any alternative arrangement of contracts. Cost overall is based on the ability of the firm to contract (that is write, measure and enforce a contract) both internally and externally, with all factors of production as well as all customers, at the lowest average cost. Many contracts with factors of production are internalized within the firm, precisely to minimize cost over market alternatives.

But the cost function in this alternative approach must be conceived differently from that of the standard model. Indeed, the standard model, where cost is functionally related to output and factor wages, is oversimplified in important respects.

Most crucially costs depend on more than factor wages. There are costs of creating, measuring and enforcing the terms of each contract with all factors of production and coordinating their operations; there are also contracts and their attendant costs with customers of the firm. While it may seem that the only change then would be a different variable in the cost function, (e.g. $C = C(x,t)$, where t is some measure of transaction costs) in fact the introduction of transaction costs alters the behavior of the function in a few important ways. First, the overall *cost* of a factor will not be identical to the *wage* (or market price) of the factor. In other words, a wage rate for labor may be determined in a competitive factor market, but the cost of contracting with the labor force may be determined by the legal and social structure, by the technology of information and enforcement, by the size of the firm itself, and by other transactional factors. The cost of a factor is thus both exogenously and endogenously determined. While a wage rate may be constant for any class of workers, transaction costs may not be constant and indeed may be a functional argument in the cost function subject to a set of constraints apart from those imposed by the production function. In other words, while the average cost of physical production may fall because of scale, costs of transactions with factors may rise precisely because of scale, or may rise (or fall) because of constraints placed by government on firm behavior or because of the technology involved in carrying through a contract. Consequently, the price of all factors may rise with scale even where the firm is able to acquire factors in largely competitive markets and is producing where there are technical economies of scale in production.

Second, a transactional analysis of a cost function reveals important interdependencies among the components of that function that do not appear in the standard model. In the standard neoclassical model, there are also interdependencies; the quantities of factors will change when there are changes in relative prices, provided some alteration in production methods is possible with a given technology. In other words, it is understood that if the relative price of capital rises, assuming input ratios are not fixed in production, then a firm will add more labor or raw materials to substitute for more expensive capital.

In a transaction cost analysis interdependencies are deeper. The most important consequence of looking at the transactional side is that not only do prices affect quantities of factors, but that *quantities* can now be shown to affect *prices*. The point is this: even if we include a transactional term in the price of each factor, the quantities of factors impact the prices of other factors. For example, a firm hires supervisory personnel. The point of these factors is at least partly to monitor compliance with contractual terms on the part of labor. If the monitors fail to perform their jobs adequately or are constrained by informational barriers or other transactional problems, there is a higher probability of labor's failure to adhere to contractual terms. Shirking rises and productivity diminishes; as a result, the effective price of the labor that is to be monitored rises (and the costs to the firm go up).[15]

To see this a bit more concretely, consider the following illustration: A firm that is deemed a natural monopoly needs to hire factors of production to produce a particular level (any level) of output. The factors are purchased in competitive factor markets. Assume also from a technical standpoint the production process exhibits increasing returns to scale as output is increased. Is the cost of monitoring, supervision and enforcement also declining with scale? There is no reason to assume so, and indeed evidence suggests that hierarchical inefficiencies will lead to diseconomies. (The Soviet Union was of course the great exemplar of scale inefficiencies.) It may be that as inputs are decreased proportionately to capture technical economies of scale, the amount of monitoring and enforcement personnel and capital must increase disproportionately to prevent the price of labor and capital used in the production process from rising. It is not unreasonable to assume for transactions a rising, flat or u-shaped curve that shows diseconomies soon after some level of scale benefits are reached (see Fig. 4).

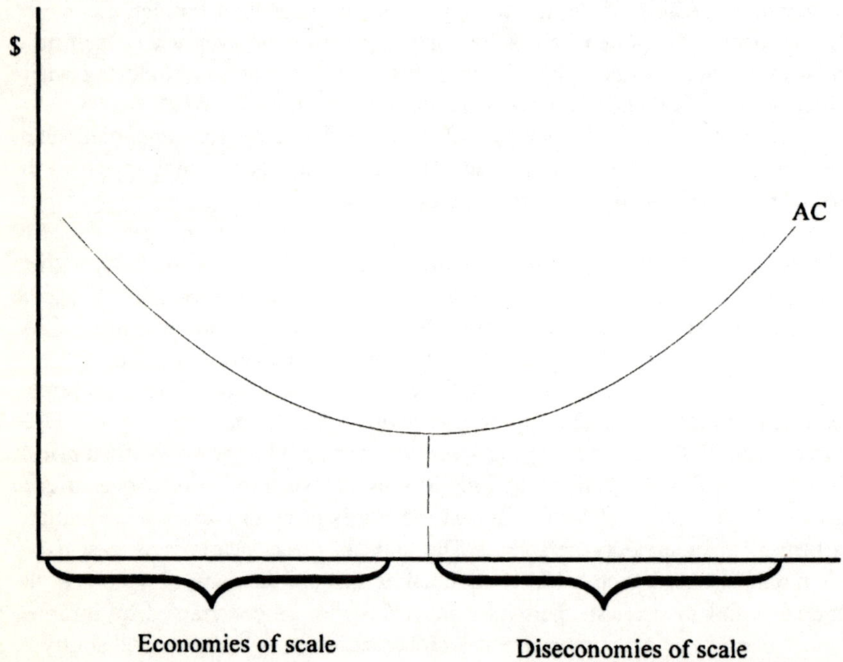

Fig. 4.

Source: Train, p. 6, Fig. 1.2.

Now assume that the firm vertically integrates because it is deemed that there are economies of scope, thus (it is hoped) achieving subadditivity, and it contracts with a new group of factors. Additionally, it incurs costs of coordination between the two types of production within the vertically integrated firm. These stem from new needs for monitoring, measuring and enforcing implicit and explicit contract terms across the various factors, and types of production. Subadditivity obtains if this new system of coordination is actually less costly than the alternative. But again, these costs will depend on the relationship between factors, and the technology and cost of contract measurement and enforcement. This will inevitably vary with institutional and market circumstances (as well as technological advance), and there may well be decreasing returns to the transactions side of the firm. Thus, in one circumstance vertical integration may lower costs; in another raise them. But in all cases, the cost of individual factors will depend on the quantities of other factors, the technology of information about those factors, and the institutional circumstances that provide the setting in which contracting for factors takes place. The efficient size of the firm will result from a comparison of the various costs of internal contracting vs. market alternatives.

To summarize: how then might we define a natural monopoly from a transaction cost perspective? Subadditivity in principles still obtains, but for any one firm, total cost is a complex of factor costs (and the contractual relationships for them) that are interdependent with one another. If we add to this picture external contracts (also costs to the firm), we have an even larger string of cost components that in sum must be smaller than any alternative arrangement. Or put another way, for any "natural" monopoly, at any given time, the *preponderance* of costs must be lowest with a single firm configuration over all other possible arrangements. But this must be highly contingent. It is unlikely to hold true in all institutional settings, all demand conditions, and all market conditions. Rather than a technologically determined fact of life, it may more accurately be said to be accidental. That is, for total costs to be less in one vertically integrated firm, like electric power monopolies, than in *any* alternative arrangement, there must be some problem with market contracting and some unusual benefit to hierarchical coordination to make it so. There is no reason why the problems will be identical or even largely similar from one institutional setting to another. As Crocker and Masten (1996, p. 35) have observed, "The fundamental lesson provided by transaction cost economics is that organization form matters and that, depending on the specifics of the environment, some modes of governance will be preferred to others."

While this analysis has been static (as is most analysis of natural monopoly), there are also important dynamic considerations. We noted above that changes in technology can alter the picture for an industry's organizational characteristics.

But changes in transactional constraints – technological or institutional – will also alter cost curves. Each individual cost curve may be subjected to differing conditions that may shift them upward (or downward) over time. For example, changes in laws may affect the cost of contracting, or changes in certain technologies may affect the cost of transacting. Inevitably, some costs will not continue to fall with expanded output even if technical characteristics of production lead to greater efficiency at higher levels of output. Others, over time, will rise (or fall) *regardless* of the quantity of output that is produced. In fact, costs will rise (or fall) independently of whether production increases, decreases or remains constant.

These considerations are based largely on exogenous changes. But if an industry is to be designated a "natural" monopoly a priori, then some thought must be given to the question: under what conditions will it remain one? This is especially important where government assumes that regulation is necessary (and a single firm industry must be enfranchised) because it has perceived that a "natural monopoly" exists. If such a monopoly is determined solely by technology, then institutional change does not matter. But if it is only a temporary condition due to particular contingent circumstances, then the industry should perhaps be allowed to assume whatever form is appropriate to those circumstances. But if an industry is designated by a broad technological typology, this often cannot happen because of path dependence, government inertia, the vested interests of the monopolists, or simply a failure of information about how changes affect the industry. This failure may be due precisely because competitive markets are unable to point to efficiency gains since such markets are not permitted to exist.

Given that institutional settings differ (and that they are subject to change), the lowest cost industry configuration – the minimum size for firm efficiency – will not necessarily be the same either across settings or over time. Average costs, in fact, will not ever be the same unless socio-political factors are identical and change identically. Where costs of internal contacting are high, it is doubtful that a monopoly will actually exist or be sustained without government help. Ironically, as we will explore later in this book, it is often the case that so-called natural monopolies are industries where government regulation prevents a competitive industry – not where it protects consumers from monopoly pricing.

What Does it Actually Mean to Call the Electric Power Industry a Natural Monopoly?

Given the argument above, we can now consider just what it must mean if it is to be claimed that electric power production and distribution is a "natural monopoly."

First, it means that the electric production and distribution is functionally subadditive; that is, a single firm produces electricity in a given market at lower cost than any alternative organization of the industry. This must be true by definition.

Second, a single provider of electricity production needs to vertically integrate for all products and services related to electric power because all functions together are subadditive. This cannot be due solely to scale economies in production or distribution. Consider again the zero transactions cost model: even if there are great economies from one big generator than from several small ones, it is never the case that one big generator alone can most efficiently provide a community with all of its power. As noted, there will be many of various sizes; and there may well be links to other power companies to arrange power purchase arrangements and affect transmission and distribution. Without significant transaction costs, there is no reason why generators must be part of a single firm, or that one company will most efficiently handle all functions of power production and distribution and so must contain all functions in a single vertically-linked enterprise. In fact, there must be a coordination problem that *prevents* these functions from efficient operation competitively or separately.

Put more generally, even if there are economies with respect to power production, these do not necessarily mean there are benefits to linking in one hierarchical firm production with distribution or transmission much less service or marketing. Indeed, it is clear that they should be linked only in the event that there are high coordination costs to market transactions among firms at different stages of production and consumption. These are conditions that must be met to say that a power provider has a natural monopoly over all phases of electric power.

Third, given that all phases of electric power production and distribution are subadditive, without regulation, the industry will *necessarily* resolve into a single firm monopoly since any other type of organization is unsustainable. Entry into a market occupied by an incumbent firm, unless the entrant has some new cost advantage (either transactional or productive) that is unavailable or hidden to the incumbent, is not just unwise, it is economically irrational. Entry might be observed in an early stage of industry development as firms vie for a stream of long run monopoly rents, but it is unlikely to persist. Initially there might be merger among early entrants; later there would be simple destruction of entrants since the incumbent firm, by dint of subadditivity, can always underprice newcomers.

In fact, the electric industry did become a network primarily of vertically integrated regional electric monopolies that provided all functions of electric production and service, with rates regulated by the government.[16] This would suggest one of two possibilities: either that the above conditions were in fact observed in the early years of the electric power industry, or that the companies were able to use the power of government to force monopolization where none was warranted.

For the former to be true, of course, means that natural monopoly was applied to electric power because clear evidence of a subadditive cost structure was evident. Was this the case? In fact, historically the above conditions were not clearly observed (see Chapter 3). Rather than demonstrated empirically, natural monopoly was mainly asserted by its proponents as the condition of the electric industry. Indeed, there has been little clear cut evidence that the industry even has had for much of its history pervasive economies of scale. In general this has merely been assumed.

In fairness, it must be admitted that there is no way to prove or disprove the proposition that at *some* times in the past and in *some* places in the U.S., the lowest cost form of organization for a regional electric system was a monopoly.[17] For technical and/or institutional reasons, internal coordination and contracting costs in a vertically integrated electric power system may have been lower than any alternative, and thus, the single firm's costs were at those times in those places, subadditive. In such instances, government enfranchisement and regulation might have seemed the best alternative to prevent market failure from monopoly pricing.

But without much evidence, there is no reason to assume that electric power is or ever was by some definition or typology, naturally anything. Moreover, the requirements for subadditivity in a vertically integrated company listed above are quite stringent and it is doubtful that it applies universally to any industry. In any case, none of the conditions listed above seemed to apply in the early years of the electric industry. Indeed the main argument for much of the monopoly formation process and the regulatory apparatus that governed it, seems not to have been based on subadditivity at all. Rather it was argued that competition was bad because it "ruinous" to existing electric providers. That is, prices in competition were "too low." Not too low to drive all providers out of business, or necessarily to disadvantage customers, but presumably to drive down profits to level that distressed company executives.[18]

It was argued that that this ruinous competition would hurt the industry and would, somehow, lead to monopoly in the long run. But this argument is tenuous at best and not at all identical to, or even consistent with, the model of natural monopoly in the economics literature. Finally, to cast further doubt on natural monopoly as an inherent technological characteristic of the electric power industry, it has been shown that competitive power production continued in some localities throughout the twentieth century with little loss to the consumer or total destruction of the competing firms (Primeaux, 1986).

"NATURAL MONOPOLY" THEORY AND PUBLIC UTILITIES

As the foregoing discussion suggests, the theory behind natural monopoly was not very solidly grounded when it was applied to the electric power industry. Yet it has been so applied, and not just by rent-seeking firms. Many economists and legal scholars have supported this idea for quite some time – supported not just the theory in the abstract but its application specifically to public utilities like electric power systems.

Some scholars (for example, Hovenkamp, 1984) accord the genesis of the idea of natural monopoly to English Lord Chief Justice Mathew Hale who in the seventeenth century noted that some that some seaport facilities were strategically located and "affected with the publick interest."[19] Hale and later Blackstone, who also commented on the legal status of businesses that had implications for public welfare, were interested mainly in specifying the nature of ventures that should face public regulation, not to specify a condition for a monopolistic outcome (Hovenkamp, 1984).

John Stuart Mill appears to be the first to have elaborated the possible benefits of regulated monopoly enterprises in the provision of public utilities. Indeed, Mill observed that local gas and water companies, if organized as legal monopolies could achieve scale economies and "make lower charges" while at the same time obtaining the then current level of profit (Mill, 1965 [1848]) – the benefits of a falling average-cost curve discussed earlier. It should be noted that monopolies did exist in Mill's time, but most monopolies persisted primarily by royal or state charter. These charters were granted for various purposes, for example, like the Hudson Bay Company to invest in colonial development, but not because of perceived economic characteristics of production.

In any case, the main impetus to natural monopoly theory came in the second half of the nineteenth century. At the time, economists were grappling with the remarkable technical advances of the Second Industrial Revolution. These seemed to indicate: first, the potential for enterprises that could be efficient on a vast scale; second, the potential for predatory behavior and monopoly pricing by those enterprises; and third, corruption and social problems that such enterprises could create by virtue of their sheer size and wealth.

Economist Richard Ely (1887), one of the founders of the American Economic Association, specifically used the term "natural monopoly" to describe vast enterprises that in particular, to use Lord Hale's phrase, were "affected with the public interest." These businesses did not include electric companies but did pertain to communications, transportation, as well as utilities supplying water and gas (Hazlett, 1985).[20] The key point for Ely was that efficiency gains from the size of enterprises were socially beneficial but that the utilities and transportation companies by virtue of their importance to society were notable "for the abuse of corporate power." (Ely, 1887). Thus they were from a technical standpoint destined to be (and best left as) a monopoly, but they needed to be regulated by the state on behalf of the public interest.

As DiLorenzo (1996) points out, Ely could be ambiguous even about how to identify a natural monopoly since, in Ely's view, vast scale alone was an insufficient criterion. But it is nevertheless true that Ely has continued to be cited well into the twentieth century (Lowry, 1973) as the first theorist to legitimize the concept of government-regulated natural monopoly. As Ely (1887) argued, "It is not true that that private corporations are a bad form of industrial organization; it is true that their sphere has been unduly extended."

Henry Carter Adams, writing at about the same time as Ely, elaborated the theory of natural monopoly and most explicitly focused on the importance of high fixed costs, increasing returns to scale, and a declining average cost curve. Industries with these characteristics could not, according to Adams, be regulated by market forces since increasing returns permitted a single firm monopoly that would inevitably be "administered for personal profit" if left to its own devices. Instead, the answer had to be government regulation to prevent monopoly abuses (Adams, 1954 [1887]). As Hazlett (1985, p. 10) notes Adams was engaged mainly in an "ad hominem attack on corporate capitalism" rather than an explication of natural monopoly theory. But Adams's basic formulation provided the underpinnings of the traditional natural monopoly argument that persisted well into the 20th century. Indeed, its basic construction is still found in introductory economics textbooks today.

In fairness to Adams, while the increasing returns argument for natural monopoly is at best overly simplified, it is the case that if a firm that can meet all of market demand at a point where average costs are decreasing, it should be able to capture the entire market. And since most production processes have some degree scale economies there may be a point at which any business can achieve a monopoly, at least in a local market. Thus we see only one (a local monopoly) general store in a small town, one gas station, one barbershop,[21] where demand is low and producers can gain the limited scale economies that are available to them. Such businesses will stay monopolies if: demand is static; they become more efficient and move to a lower average cost curve; and/or lower cost substitutes do not materialize. But they are also constrained in their ability to exploit their monopoly position as long as there is the potential for entry or innovations in other areas (such as transportation) that might make substitutes more desirable.

But as noted earlier, average cost curves for any industry are likely to be U-shaped. That is, over a certain range they will be decreasing; over another range they will be constant; and then they will rise as the scale of operation increases. Natural monopoly theory based on decreasing average costs implied that scale economies not only existed but that they were somehow inherent for a technology at any level of output. Further, demand could never rise to the point of appreciable decreasing returns; and finally that no substitutes could exist and so no one could ever enter the market and offer an alternative product.

Now it is undoubtedly the case that in the nineteenth century, economists observed that as some technologies advanced, average costs fell. Firms could operate at unprecedentedly large scale and still be on a declining portion of their average cost curves. This may have influenced some of the thinking at the time. Or alternatively, for something like the provision of water, a good "affected with the public interest," demand intersected a declining cost curve far from any recognizable minimum efficient scale and so it was pointless for competitors to attempt entry and contest a given market. Thus *de facto* monopolies were the norm and seemed likely to remain so for a long time.

But economists at the time did not empirically test the model or examine its long run implications. As in the case of Adams, much of the discussion was ideological rather than economic. And while theorists applied the basic theory widely to cover all industries in transportation, communication and public services, in fact as has been argued above, the implications of the model were so stringent few if any industries probably fit.

Some economists in the second half of the twentieth century began to point out the shortcomings in the theory of natural monopoly and a few questioned the existence, or even the idea, of natural monopoly altogether (e.g. DiLorenzo, 1996) and particularly its application to electric power (e.g. Hammond, 1986). Probably the most notable critique of natural monopoly came from economist Harold Demsetz in a classic article, "Why Regulate Utilities." Demsetz questioned whether a firm, regardless of its size and its domination of a market, could actually exercise monopoly market power given the *potential* for entry or for opportunities to contract around a large firm's market position. But this piece did not appear until 1968. By then, electric power companies as well as gas, water and telephone companies were franchised as local, regional or even national monopolies and regulated *as if* the natural monopoly model were true.[22] Whether competition was actually impossible, whether monopoly abuses were actually inevitable, whether substitutes really were unavailable were all beside the point.[23] That's the way the industry was treated and the common wisdom, natural monopoly theory, continued to support it.[24]

CONCLUSION

The rationale for a single firm has often been broader than that given by the common definition of natural monopoly. Many in politics, industry, and even public consumer advocacy claim that social welfare was and is improved by the presence of a regulated monopoly system – regardless of any justification in economic theory. This seems on the face of it self-contradictory. In economics, it can be shown that the best – socially optimal – uses of resources are most clearly determined in competitive markets. And if competition in electric power would exist in the absence of government regulation, then why would it be socially more desirable to have a regulated monopoly than a relatively unregulated competitive market?[25] The implication is that a competitive market in electric power would be notably prone to market failure but as the next chapter suggests there is little reason to believe that that was or would be the case.

And for the purposes of this book, the key question is this: even if it once seemed correct, is there still greater efficiency in a single firm than in competition for electric power – or any part of that industry? Few would argue generally that electric power is now a natural monopoly, whatever it once was. But given that natural monopoly is at best contingent and must be held highly unlikely in most circumstances, it seems that the concept was largely empty of real empirical content. The better question (discussed later in this book) then is: how why did it take so long for such a concept to unravel?

NOTES

1. Mathematically, the derivative of average costs is negative.

2. Marginal revenue declines as the monopolist expands production, and it is always less than or equal to price, because of the downward sloping demand curve. Say, for example, the monopolist sells one unit for $10. Then that is the marginal revenue. Now to sell two units, the monopolist must reduce prices to $9 each. Thus total revenue is $18, but the marginal revenue is $8 – less than the price. The monopolist gains additional profits so long as $MR \geq MC$.

3. This is important. Any consideration of economies of scale assumes constant input prices; this issue will be explored in greater detail later in this chapter.

4. Mathematically, economies of scale can be represented in terms of its effects on costs by: $C(\lambda q) < \lambda C(q)$ for all λ, where $1 \leq \lambda \leq 1 + a$, where a is a positive number. The key point here is that at the output is increased by λ, costs rise by less than when costs themselves are increased by λ. It can be easily shown from this that average costs are less as well (Sharkey, 1982).

5. In some sense virtually any firm can be a monopoly given a small enough market for their product. See the discussion on page 36.

6. This issue will be considered later with respect to contestability of markets and subadditivity.

7. And indeed it may involve higher management and oversight costs raising average costs, not lowering them.

8. Note that all of the figures represent a static picture, but all parts of these graphs are potentially dynamic: demand as well as the costs of production change over time.

9. Sharkey (1982) uses a cost function with the form for outputs x and y: $C(x,y) = x^{1/2} + y^{1/2} + (xy)^{1/2}$. This function exhibits economies of scale (as multiplying through by λ would show), but it is also possible to demonstrate for some values of x and y, the function is not subadditive.

10. Baumol et al. view a composite good as a bundle with fixed output proportions to avoid the problem of aggregating two different kinds of goods varying in quantity.

11. Of course there would be differences from the costs of transportation, as the "law of one price" would dictate.

12. For an overview of transaction cost economics with respect to regulated industries see Crocker and Masten (1996).

13. Wind is also capable of turning a turbine as is a diesel or other internal combustion engine and a gas-powered turbine like that found in jet aircraft. Solar energy may be used either to heat water for steam or to produce power directly through a process called photovoltaics (Cassedy & Grossman, 1998).

14. If the factor market is monopsonistic then purchases by the firm affect market prices, whereas in a competitive market all participants are assumed to be price takers.

15. Principal-agent literature is quite extensive (see for example, Grossman & Hart, 1983).

16. Some municipalities and various agencies of states and the federal government have in some cases taken full control and ownership of electric power production and distribution. The movement toward municipalization of power is discussed in Chapter 3.

17. Since this proposition seems to defy falsification, it calls into question whether "natural monopoly" should be considered a scientific concept.

18. There is a public policy justification against competition; that is, that competing capital investment is inherently "wasteful" because it is unnecessarily duplicative. Therefore there should be only one firm. But that is not obviously the case unless there is only one unit of capital.

19. Cited in Hovenkamp, 1984, p. 1282.

20. Some of the earliest claims for some kind of natural monopoly status were accorded to the gas-light industry in the period just after the Civil War (Platt, 1991, p. 310).

21. Mill, in fact, was pleased to see the scale of enterprise increase since it meant that many of the former local monopolists were being replaced by lower cost national producers (Hazlett, 1985).

22. An important line of argument has come from the Public Choice school of economic thought. In this view, public regulation of utilities was largely an effort on the part of the businesses themselves to seek rents through government intervention (Mueller, 1979).

23. Experimental work by Coursey et al. (1984) suggested strongly that Demsetz was correct. As the authors of the former study wrote (p. 111), "It is simply not true that monopoly pricing is a 'natural' result of a market merely because firms in the market exhibit decreasing costs and demand is sufficient to support no more than a single firm."

24. There are those who argue that natural monopoly still should be applied to electric power transmission. This point will be considered further in later chapters, especially Chapter 6.

25. Of course, there is no market that is without some degree of government role. Indeed, the more sophisticated the economy, the more it depends on basic rules of contract and property law and their (relatively) impartial enforcement. But regulated monopolies also entail government price setting and other features that make it quite apart from those industries that rely on market price setting and contracting. See also Chapter 6.

REFERENCES

Adams, H. (1954[1887]). *Relation of the State to Industrial Action and Economics and Jurisprudence (two essays).* New York: Columbia University Press [1954 reprint].

Baumol, W., Panzar, J., & Willig, R. (1988). *Contestable Markets and the Theory of Market Structures* (Revised). San Diego: Harcourt Brace Jovanovich.

Cassedy, E., & Grossman, P. (1998). *Introduction to Energy* (2nd ed.). Cambridge: Cambridge University Press.

Chandler, A. (1990). *Scale and Scope: The Dynamics of Industrial Capitalism.*Cambridge, MA: Belknap Press.

Cheung, S. (1983). The Contractual Nature of the Firm. *Journal of Law and Economics, 26,* 1–21.

Coase, R. (1937). The Nature of the Firm. *Economica, 4,* 386–405.

Coursey, D., Issac, R., & Smith, V. (1984). Natural Monopoly and Contested Markets:Some Experimental Results. *Journal of Law & Economics, 27,* 91–113.

Crocker, K., & Masten, S. (1996). Regulation and Administered Contracts Revisited:Lessons from Transaction-Cost Economics for Public Utility Regulation. *Journal of Regulatory Economics, 9,* 5–39.

Demsetz, H. (1968). Why Regulate Utilities. *Journal of Law and Economics, 11,* 55–65.

DiLorenzo, T. (1996). The Myth of Natural Monopoly. *Review of Austrian Economics, 9*(2), 43–58.

Dranove, D. (1998). Economies of Scale in Non-Revenue Producing Cost Centers:Implications for Hospital Mergers. *Journal of Health Economics, 17,* 69–83.

Ely, R. (1887). The Growth of Corporations. *Harper's,* (June), 71–79.

Friedman, M. (1962). *Capitalism and Freedom,* Chicago: University of Chicago Press.

Grossman, S., & Hart, O. (1983). An Analysis of the Principal-Agent Problem. *Econometrica, 51,* 7–45.

Hammond, C. (1986). An Overview of Electricity Regulation. In: J. Moorhouse (Ed.), *Electric Power: Deregulation and the Public Interest* (pp. 31–61). San Francisco: Pacific Research Institute for Public Policy.

Hazlett, T. (1985). The Curious Evolution of Natural Monopoly Theory. In: R. Poole (Ed.), *Unnatural Monopolies: The Case for Deregulating Public Utilities* (pp. 1–26). Lexington, MA: Lexington Books.

Hovenkamp, H. (1984). Technology, Politics and Regulated Monopoly: An American Historical Perspective. *Texas Law Review, 62,* 1263–1312.

Jensen, M., & Meckling, W. (1976). Theory of the Firm: Managerial Behavior, Agency Costs, and Capital Structure. *Journal of Financial Economics, 3,* 305–360.

Liu, P.-W., & Yang, X. (2000). The Theory of Irrelevance of the Size of the Firm. *Journal of Economic Behavior and Organization, 42,* 145–165.

Lowry, E. (1973). Justification for Regulation: The Case for Natural Monopoly. *Public Utilities Fortnightly*, (November 8), 17–23.

Mankiw, N. (1998). *Principles of Economics*. Ft. Worth: Dryden.

Mill, J. (1965[1848]). *Principles of Political Economy*. New York: A. M. Kelley.

Platt, H. (1991). *The Electric City* Chicago: Chicago University Press.

Porter, M. (1985). *Competitive Advantage: Creating and Sustaining CompetitivePerformance*. New York: The Free Press.

Posner, R. (1969). Natural Monopoly and its Regulation. *Stanford Law Review*, *21*, 548–643.

Primeaux, W. (1986). *Direct Electric Utility Competition: The Natural Monopoly Myth*. New York: Praeger.

Sexton, R. (1999). *Exploring Economics*. Ft. Worth: Dryden Press.

Shiller, B. (2003). *The Micro Economy Today* (9th ed.). New York: McGraw-Hill.

Sharkey, W. (1982). *The Theory of Natural Monopoly*. Cambridge: Cambridge University Press.

Schwartz, M., & Reynolds, R. (1983). Contestable Markets: An Uprising in the Theory of Industry Structure. *American Economic Review*, *73*, 488–490.

Train, K. (1991). *Optimal Regulation: The Economic Theory of Natural Monopoly*. Cambridge, MA: MIT Press.

Truett, L., & Truett, D. (1990). Regions of the Production Function, Returns and Economies Scale: Further Considerations. *Journal of Economic Education*, *21*(4), 411–419.

Weitzman, M. (1983). Contestable Markets: An Uprising in the Theory of Industry Structure: Comment. *American Economic Review*, *73*, 486–487.

Williamson, O. (1979). Transaction-Cost Economics: The Governance of Contractual Relations. *Journal of Law and Economics*, *22*(2), 233–262.

EDITORS' FOREWORD TO CHAPTER 3

If, as the previous chapter has argued, a "natural" monopoly is at best accidental and contingent, then how is it that the electric power industry came to be identified as one? There would seem to be two possibilities. First, contingencies at the time the industry was founded made it a natural monopoly, in which one firm truly would have been the outcome of market competition. The second alternative is that political and/or business interests wanted to create the industry as a set of government-regulated monopolies, regardless of whether institutional, technological, and economic circumstances justified such a structure.

Well into the 1970s and 1980s, representatives of the electric power industry argued that it was, and in fact had always been, a real natural monopoly (Lowry, 1973). To explain how the system of regulated monopoly firms came into being, the industry offered two different, and not entirely consistent, "creation myths," both of which incorporated aspects of natural monopoly theory.

The first story is one of natural evolution from a competitive industry towards self-regulated monopoly. The industry, according to this story, was heading towards a monopoly structure before the government ever got involved. Subsequent government regulation was intended to prevent the inevitable monopoly providers from exercising too much market power to the detriment of consumers. In this story, the government acted, after the reality of monopoly became both apparent and desirable, strictly to protect the public interest. The utilities at first worked with "unvarying consistency and stubbornness" using "all their political influence to oppose the establishment of regulatory bodies and later the extension of powers of such bodies" (Mosher & Crawford, 1933, p. 551). That is to say, the utilities wanted freedom from government regulation. But once it was clear that regulation was coming because government would not relent in its assault on free enterprise, industry firms and organizations used their influence to minimize its effects, so that the market would rule to the greatest extent possible.

According to the second "creation myth," utilities began competitively but, because of the industry's natural monopoly characteristics, competition became "ruinous."[1] In any case, on this account, it was not just the utilities that suffered from "ruinous competition," but the public. Multiple providers, with their layers upon layers of duplicate wires, were defacing cities and confusing consumers. Already poor service grew increasingly irregular as competition intensified. At this point, so the story goes, government joined together with industry, in the spirit of public interest, to bring order to the market. They agreed that a regulated monopoly structure, towards which the industry was naturally heading anyway, was preferable to current situation of too much competition. Whether anyone actually believed this nonsense is beside the point of the second "creation myth," which was to justify the monopoly status of electric power production and distribution.

One other problematic aspect of the creation stories is also noteworthy: If the industry was truly a natural monopoly, then didn't that justify "municipalization," where the government became owner, provider of electric power? This was a fear and a justification for monopoly in itself. Regulated monopoly often became, according to the stories, the preferred alternative given that the natural monopoly characteristics of the industry meant either that either a single private monopoly firm or a government-owned entity were the only possible outcomes.

As Robert Bradley, Jr. explains in this chapter, the actual history of the electric power industry and the imposition of regulated monopolies followed a path rather different from what the popular creation myths would lead one to believe.

NOTE

1. This argument starts from a theoretically untenable premise, for reasons cited in the preceding chapter: if the industry truly had natural monopoly characteristics, competition should not have been "ruinous," but should have led in due course to consolidation of the industry into a single provider.

REFERENCES

Lowry, E. D. (1973). Justification for Regulation: The Case for Natural Monopoly. *Public Utilities Fortnightly*, (November 8), 17–23.

Mosher, W. E., & Crawford, F. (1933). *Public Utility Regulation*. New York: Harper.

3. THE ORIGINS AND DEVELOPMENT OF ELECTRIC POWER REGULATION[1]

Robert L. Bradley, Jr.

INTRODUCTION

The current debate over restructuring the electric industry makes a look back at the origins of political electricity relevant. The thesis of this chapter – government intervention into electric markets was not the result of market failures but business and political opportunism – suggests that the intellectual and empirical case for market oriented reform is even stronger than would otherwise be the case.

A major theme of applied political economy is the dynamics of government intervention in the marketplace. Because interventions are often related, an analytical distinction can be made between *basis point intervention* and *cumulative intervention* (Bradley, 1996). Basis point regulation, taxation, or subsidization is the opening government intervention into a market setting; cumulative intervention is further regulation, taxation, or subsidization that is attributable to the effects of prior (basis point or cumulative) intervention. The origins and maturation of political electricity are interpretable through this theoretical framework.

The End of a Natural Monopoly: Deregulation and Competition in the Electric Power Industry, Volume 7, pages 43–75.

ISBN: 0-7623-0995-4

A NEW INDUSTRY

The commercialization of electric lighting in the U.S., successfully competing against gas lamps, kerosene lamps, and wax candles, required affordable generation, long distance transmission capabilities, and satisfactory illumination equipment. All three converged beginning in the 1870s, the most remembered being Thomas Edison's invention of the incandescent electric light bulb in 1878.

Beginning in 1879, electricity was used to light streets and selected buildings in major cities. The firms providing the new service, like the manufactured gas companies that had inaugurated lighting service several decades before, had to receive corporate charters and franchises, which often meant providing city fathers with "some kind of personal, extralegal arrangement" (McDonald, 1962).[2] This was particularly true given the prior existence of gas franchises and municipal lighting contracts in major cities, a sampling of which is shown in Table 1.

The opening era of the electric industry was characterized by competing franchises and "regulation by competition." The only "regulation" was price ceilings in long-term fixed-priced contracts for street lighting, which would not be a major constraint due to stable price levels and lower costs from improving technology (Behling, 1938; Glaeser, 1927).

The free market era was positive for consumers. Although aggregate price and quantity information is not available for the 1880–1900 period (the first comprehensive Federal Census of the industry was compiled in 1902), city- and

Table 1. Beginning Dates for Gas and Electric Service in Selected U.S. Cities.

City	Gas service	Electric service
Baltimore	1816	1881
Boston	1822	1882
New York	1823	1882
St. Louis	1836	1890
Detroit	1849	1883
San Francisco	1854	1879
Los Angeles	1867	1882
Seattle	1873	1889
San Diego	1881	1886

Source: Stotz, Louis (1938). *History of the Gas Industry* 9–10. New York: Press of Stettinfa Bros., various others.

company-specific information indicates that prices were falling and quantity supplied was rapidly increasing. Between the turn of the century and 1910, power generation surged from 4.5 million to 17.2 million megawatt hours (MWh), a 280% increase. Generation capacity rose proportionally, increasing from 2 million to 7.5 million MWh. Annual revenue from electricity sales grew from nothing to over $100 million by 1900 (Bauer & Costello, 1949).

This rate of expansion, which would not be subsequently equaled, hardly suggests the "monopolistic" practice of restricting output to maintain or increase prices. Indeed, average prices fell from 3.36 cents per kWh in 1902 to 2.89 cents in 1907, 2.48 cents in 1912, and 1.97 cents in 1917 (Gould, 1946). The "electrification of America" did not require "tearing up the streets" as with manufactured gas lighting, and the economics did not exist for consumer unrest. Consumer organization was virtually absent, in fact. The impetus for regulation and municipalization would come from elsewhere as seen in the next section.

Many factors were behind the industry's growth in its first three decades. The introduction of electric streetcars in the mid-1880s created a daytime market to complement the nighttime lighting load. Metering usage allowed differential pricing to tailor demand to supply – something the gas industry was slower to adopt due to regulatory concerns (Insull, 1924). A committee of the Institute of Electrical Engineers worked to standardize electric machinery to lower costs, improve quality, and expedite repair and replacement. Other cooperative organizations formed in the 1880s were the National Electric Light Association (NELA) and the Association of Edison Illuminating Companies. Safety procedures were developed in conjunction with the National Board of Fire Underwriters.

Market conservation came of age when usage-insensitive rates (a fixed price per lamp per month) were replaced with charges based on recorded usage. This development was simple economics for the supplier, not a public calling to conserve supply for its own sake. On the other hand, quantity discounts encouraged incremental consumption – a standard business practice not unique to electricity. The invention and application of alternating current transformers in the 1890s greatly expanded the range of power transmission to allow large central generating stations to replace "neighborhood" dynamos dependent on direct current transmission that had to be located within a mile of their market. Rotary-powered steam turbines, which came into service after the turn of the century, generated electricity more cheaply, more quietly, and in less space than reciprocating engines. As if led by an "invisible hand," progress on many fronts was turning electric lighting from a luxury for the few to a necessity for the many.

THE RISE OF STATE PUBLIC-UTILITY REGULATION

The Crusade of Samuel Insull for Public Utility Regulation

The NELA was founded on February 25, 1885, in Chicago. For much of its early history, the association (which in 1933 would become the Edison Electric Institute) focused on business and technical issues and only peripherally delved into political questions such as franchise policy and municipalization. This would change. In a landmark presidential address before the NELA on June 7, 1898, Samuel Insull, head of Chicago Edison Company, inaugurated a political agenda advocating a middle way between "municipal socialism" and "acute competition." The competitive franchise, complained Insull, "frightens the investor, and compels corporations to pay a very high price for capital." The "inevitable" consolidation then leaves the combined corporation with the economic wastes of duplicate facilities and high interest costs. The solution was the quid pro quo of exclusive franchises for rate regulation. In his words:

> The best service at the lowest possible price can only be obtained . . . by exclusive control of a given territory being placed in the hands of one undertaking . . .. In order to protect the public, exclusive franchises should be coupled with the condition of public control requiring all charges for services fixed by public bodies to be based on cost, plus a reasonable profit . . . The more certain [franchise] protection is made, the lower the rate of interest and the lower the total cost of operation will be, and, consequently, the lower the price of the service to public and private users (Insull, 1898, p. 27).

Insull was not the first to make a "natural monopoly" argument to regulate electric utilities. A decade earlier one writer concluded: "It is everywhere acknowledged that the multiplication of wires overhead is a crying evil and danger . . .. Can there be any doubt that it is the height of folly to continue [competition], and that the only rational way of entrusting electric service to incorporated companies is to permit but a single company to operate in a district and control prices by some other means than competition?" (Baker, 1889, pp. 66–67).

The majority of Insull's fellow executives favored the status quo of "home rule" over public utility regulation. While open competition was a burden to established firms, regulation that systemically governed rates and service was perceived as a threat as well. It would take a different threat than market competition – and a multi-front public relations effort[3] – to bring the majority of the industry to Insull's view.

Insull's resolve against competition would never waiver in the next decades. He denied ever having a business reason to enter into an occupied market and decried "the desire of . . . the raiding promoter . . . to possess themselves of other men's property." Smaller operations were advised to "go into the consolidation and holding-company business on your own account." Insull saw the "concentrated production" of World War I planning by the Fuel Administration as a model for peacetime. As a second-best alternative "if public regulation fails," Insull favored municipalization over competitive franchises (Insull, 1924, p. 64).

Insull's goal was to serve all of Chicago, a market that had attracted dozens of competitors.[4] Even if he consolidated the market, open entry made every new day insecure. His goal of "a greater permanency of our investment" required regulation by a state commission. It was the empowered state commission, not market competition, which Insull wanted to grade his report card: "If there is anything wrong with my business, I want to know it, and the best way for me to know it is to have a public official who has the right to lookinto my affairs .... I know of no better arrangement than a centralized regulating body covering the whole state" (Insull, 1924, p. 58).

Insull knew that commission-industry relations had to be cordial and preached to the NELA and other bodies to this end. The one thing Insull did not do, which many others did in the franchised gas, water, streetcar, and electric industries, was to bribe politicians; across-the-board campaign contributions and small favors such as employment referrals were enough to allow him political access but not controversy (McDonald, 1962).

Since the perceived alternative to public-utility regulation was municipalization, Insull used the specter of municipalization to muster support for his legislative program. The Public Policy Committee of the NELA, with Insull at the helm, issued a report in 1907 warning that the self-preservation of private companies depended on replacing competition with regulation; if not, the wastes of competition would lead the public to demand municipalization. "Properly constituted general supervision and regulation of the electric light industry," the study concluded, required exclusive franchises, nondiscriminatory cost-based rates, uniform accounting, and full public disclosure (McDonald 1962, p. 118). The report was adopted by the full association as the lesser evil.

The NELA study was joined by another study the same year that reflected a business-wide consensus favoring state regulation. The National Civic Federation (NCF), a broad-based organization with representation from business, labor, and academia, published a three-volume report esposing "a system of legalized ... monopoly ... subject to public regulation and examination under a system of uniform records and accounts and full publicity" (National Civic Federation, 1907). This position mirrored the NELA report; indeed, Insull's leadership was instrumental to both (McDonald, 1962).

The momentum created by the NELA report and particularly the NCF study directly translated into state action despite the fact that the threat of municipalization was subsequently lessened because of the collapse of the municipal bond market. Within months of the reports, New York reorganized its two-year old Commission on Gas and Electricity as a full-scale Public Service Commission, and Wisconsin established a commission to regulate the entry, rates, and service of public utilities. The enabling legislation of the Wisconsin Public Service Commission was drafted by University of Wisconsin economist John Commons, who had worked closely with Insull on the NCF report (McDonald, 1962). Commons' language would become a model for other states that rapidly followed the lead of New York and Wisconsin.[5]

A follow-up study released by the NCF in 1913, which added precision to the policy recommendations of the first report, was utilized by numerous state legislatures considering public utility commissions. A record ten states would establish commissions regulating electricity in this year alone. The rationale of the state commissions over the piecemeal legislative approach was encapsulated by the Republican platform of one state:

> We advocate a just, impartial, and unprejudiced control of public service corporations and public utilities generally in this state through incorruptible, enlightened, and non-partisan agencies; and we condemn any exemption from such supervision and control, and any other special favors to any particular enterprise or corporation (Brown, 1936, p. 104).

The belief that public service commissions would be above "big city political machines" and could "scientifically" ascertain "just and reasonable" prices characterized the honeymoon period of commission regulation. This idealistic view of regulation also existed within academia. Statewide regulation received the benefit of the doubt since as an American institution it was "democratic," and the infancy of the new organizations precluded case studies of commission failure. Questions such as "who regulates the regulators" were before their time. Experience would have to be the great teacher.

Concurrent Interest in Public-Utility Regulation

The drive for state-level public utility regulation of electricity was abetted by precedent at home and abroad. In England, gas and electricity companies had been consolidated and placed under utility regulation (Byatt, 1979) – something that Insull and other regulatory proponents did not fail to emphasize. The manufactured gas industry implemented a model state-level public utility commission in Massachusetts in 1885; two years later electric regulation was added as well. The Interstate Commerce Act of 1887, subjecting interstate railroads to standardized cost-based rates and entry certification, "indicated the path which the states were to follow in their attempts at regulation" (Brown, 1936, p. 72).

Approximately thirty states had established "weak type" railroad commissions, primarily dealing with operational and safety issues. In this period (1855–1906), only Massachusetts (1885) and New York (1905) established "strong-type" public utility commissions to regulate gas and electricity (Ruggles, 1937). Ten states regulated telephone companies as public utilities by 1909; by 1917, the number swelled to forty-two (Kolko, 1963). Beginning in 1897, Charles Yerkes, Chicago's electric streetcar magnate, worked to bring the traction industry under state commission regulation to perpetuate his franchises. And last but not least, members of the upstart economics profession, whose views were being considered as expert opinion, looked more critically at laissez faire than regulation and municipalization (High, 1991).

The Institutionalization of State Regulation

Electric utility regulation by state commissions became a very popular movement. Noted historian Forrest McDonald (1962):

> Each of the three pioneer commissions was of extraordinarily high caliber and as a result the regulatory movement was off to an auspicious start. By 1909 most people who were concerned with the subject, in and out of the industry, had begun to look favorably upon regulation by state commissions (p. 121).

High marks were given to the commissions' efforts to remove the political impurities of the prior system of franchise regulation and sooth tensions between neighboring municipal and investor-owned electric systems. A new era of stability was ushered in. Commission staffs worked diligently to formulate a uniform system of accounts and set general rate principles (McDonald, 1962, p. 121). The new fervor spread rapidly – by 1915 the number of state commissions with jurisdiction over electricity swelled from three to thirty-three. This momentum lead NELA president Carl Jackson to note that as of 1922 all states either had established a commission or were considering the same (1922). He concluded: "The necessity for regulation and supervision is no longer, I believe, an open question."[6] Another seven commissions brought the total to forty by 1934 as seen in Table 2.

Early experience reinforced Insull's belief that the regulatory covenant of franchise protection for rate and service regulation would be a net benefit over "regulation by competition" for established investor-owned utilities. In 1915

Table 2. State Public Utility Commissions Regulating Electricity.

Massachusetts	1887	Idaho	1913
New York	1905	Pennsylvania	1913
Wisconsin	1907	West Virginia	1913
Georgia	1907	Indiana	1913
Vermont	1908	Missouri	1913
Maryland	1910	Montana	1913
New Jersey	1910	North Carolina	1913
California	1911	Oklahoma	1913
Connecticut	1911	Maine	1914
Kansas	1911	Illinois	1914
Nevada	1911	Virginia	1914
New Hampshire	1911	Alabama	1915
Ohio	1911	Wyoming	1915
Oregon	1911	North Dakota	1919
Washington	1911	Utah	1911
Arizona	1912	Michigan	1919
Rhode Island	1912	Tennessee	1919
New Mexico	1912	Louisiana	1921
Colorado	1913	South Carolina	1922
District Of		Arkansas	1933
Columbia	1913	Kentucky	1934

Source: Ruggles, C. O. (1937). *Aspects of the Organization, Functions, and Financing of State Public Utility Commissions* (pp. 4–5).
As of 1940, only eight states – Delaware (enacted in 1949), Florida (1951), Lowa (1954), Minnesota, Mississippi (1956), Nebraska, South Dakota and Texas – did not have commissions authorized to regulate electric rates and service.

Insull boasted, "The greatest event that has taken place in the last ten or fifteen years in the local public-utility business is the transfer of control and regulation in most of the states from the state legislatures to state commissions which, besides exercising administrative powers, are also exercising semi-legislative and semi-judicial functions" (Insull, 1924, p. 26). He pointed to the high approval rate of rate increase applications by commissions around the country, which in 1917 was approximately 90%.

Yet just two years later, with rate regulation becoming more stringent, Insull would proclaim, "control of public utilities by means of state regulation is at a crisis in Illinois" (Insull, 1924, p. 183). The risk of regulation for business – rate reductions for their own sake – was polluting his ideal of enlightened, impartial regulation. Despite the best efforts of the father of public utility regulation of electricity, government intervention was proving to be a double-edged sword (Insull, 1924).

Municipalization in the Competitive and Regulatory Eras

Government ownership and operation of electric operations grew up alongside the investor-owned industry. Four municipalities were formed in 1882, the same year as Thomas Edison's demonstration project at Pearl Street in New York City. The number of municipalities grew to over one hundred by 1890, 728 by 1900, and 1,534 by 1910 (Schap, 1936). This growth was heavily concentrated in small towns, with the cities primarily relying on investor-owned service. Consequently, the market share of investor-owned utilities was dominant. In 1922, near the peak of the municipal population, the government entities served only 13% of the population and held only 5% of the nation's electric infrastructure (Dewey, 1934).

Relatively few municipalities were discontinued or privatized in this period – two between 1880 and 1890, 24 between 1891 and 1900, and 106 between 1901 and 1910. The growth of municipalities would continue until the early 1920s. After peaking at 3,083 entities in 1923, private holding companies (described below) began to purchase public power systems in addition to consolidating private ones. By 1931, some 1,210 municipalities (39% of the total) were either sold or deactivated from this peak (Schap, 1986).[7]

Another trend was for municipalities to purchase their power from private firms rather than generate it. In 1909, fewer than 10% of the municipalities purchased their power from investor owned companies; by 1923 over one-third did (Rudolph & Ridley, 1986). Wholesale power sales allowed private firms to expand their generation and displace the need for municipal reinvestment. This quasi-privatization left these municipalities in the transmission and distribution business only.

The political recipe for creating and maintaining municipalities, particularly in the big cities, was a time-honored one – concentrated benefits to the municipal hierarchy and dispersed costs to general citizenry. Many urban projects that could not be financed privately were financed publicly. All that was needed was a referendum, and those leading the way could find themselves with jobs with the new municipality after the election. Other beneficiaries that lobbied for municipalization were: (1) private gas firms that believed that government ownership and operation made electricity less competitive with their product; and (2) electric equipment manufacturers who did not want to wait until the private sector found electric provision in a particular local economy (McDonald, 1962).

Consumers were baited by the fact that they received service when there might have been none and enjoyed lower rates than would have otherwise been the case through tax exemptions granted to the municipality. Thus municipalities as "yardstick" enterprises protruded a false economic signal of superior economic performance compared to private utilities.

Several factors limited the spread of municipalization. The NELA formed a Committee on Municipal Ownership in 1904 to educate the public against government ownership and operation. A limit on bonded indebtedness prevented some projects. Another factor that discouraged the spread of municipalization but promoted inefficiency of existing governmental operations was prohibitions on interconnections with other public or private systems (Dewey, 1934).

The Turn to State Public Utility Regulation: Market Failure or Business Protectionism?

The rush to state-level public utility regulation represented internally-generated intervention by business interests, not external intervention imposed on business from organized consumers aided by public-spirited regulators (Bradley, 1996). The consumer gains from quasi-open competition precluded the fervor for regulatory reform among ratepayers as it did vested providers. Without industry support for regulation, marshaled through the NELA and the NCF, government interest in public utility control would have been much less. However, there was public concern over franchise corruption – a "government failure" rather than a market failure as explained below – that did contribute to the municipalization movement with electricity.

The Myth of Natural Monopoly

Insull's argument was the classic rationale for applying public-utility regulation to "natural monopoly"[8] since, in this view, economies of scale made price wars, competitive waste, and eventual monopolization inevitable. To achieve the end result of consolidation, yet avoid the wasteful means of duplication and protect the consumer, the state would grant exclusive franchises and restrict rates to the utility's cost and a normal profit on the firm's rate base. This argument was not only made by industry leaders such as Samuel Insull, who referred to public control of monopoly as "the first essential," but academic economists such as Richard Ely (see Chapter 2) of the University of Wisconsin who favored municipal ownership to solve a perceived natural monopoly problem.

An anomaly permeates Insull's (and most other) arguments for public-utility regulation. If a geographical monopoly is really more efficient than rivalry from scale economies and high capital costs, then the natural outcome should be monopoly. Natural monopoly, indeed, would be natural. An aggressive managerial philosophy of low pricing to existing customers and promotional pricing to new customers – which Insull faithfully practiced[9] – would be all that is necessary to prevent inefficient entry. The market phenomenon of natural monopoly should not require governmental involvement, and, indeed, firms would be arguing against regulation rather than for it. A true natural monopolist would have argued that:

> One firm is most efficient, and my firm is it. We beat the competition fair and square, and we should not be regulated as a result. Neither should the winning firms in other metropolitan areas be regulated from their success. Regulation only increases business costs, introduces taxpayer obligations, and distorts entrepreneurial behavior.

What was really occurring? New entry and price wars were continually making life difficult for the incumbent firms. "Natural monopoly" was not natural, and a political monopoly was sought instead. New entrants were serving wholly new markets and using their state-of-the-art technology to overcome the sunk-cost advantage of incumbents in existing markets. New entrants were not throwing bad money after the incumbent's good money; they were risking their scarce capital to meet unmet consumer wants.

Insull's agenda sought to create *unnatural monopolies*. Competition would be frozen as if technological advances could never favor a new entrant and the entire market was being efficiently served by the existing firm(s). This was rarely, if ever, the case. Actual and potential competition was still necessary.

The historical fact is that rivalry was not "over" at the time it became illegal because of exclusive franchises under public utility regulation. Given this, it is fair to ask whether rivalry would have ever been over and natural monopoly institutionalized under free market conditions.[10]

Gains from Competition

The competitive saga in Insull's own market, Chicago, hardly suggests that consumers were losing from open competition. In 1892, the year Insull became president of Chicago Edison, electricity was sold for $0.20 per kilowatt-hour (kWh). By 1897 rates had dropped to $0.10/kWh, well below other comparable cities (McDonald, 1962). After the turn of the century price competition and rate reductions continued. Actual and potential competition ensured this result; if one firm would not pass along the fruits of technological progress and scale economies, another firm would.

National statistics that were first compiled in 1902 showed a more-than-doubling of station capacity and generated power five years later, a time in which only four states had implemented public utility regulation. In the same period operating revenue per kilowatt-hour fell over 8% (Nash, 1925). Thus it is not surprising that Insull's speeches calling for regulation did not contain statistics concerning price or quantity. Evidence of "natural monopoly" would have included erratic price behavior by the monopolist, at least after the consolidation phase, restraints in the quantity supplied, and service indiscretions. Open competition, however, worked to preclude these results.

"Cut-throat" competition, "duplicative" facilities, and "monopolistic" consolidation all had a beneficial role in the market process. Price wars from new entry represented immediate ratepayer gains. "Duplicative" capacity fostered electric-on-electric competition, insurance capacity to meet peak demand, and market growth over the longer term. New entry and rivalry were expanding markets. Consolidation was not the end of competition but a stage in the competitive process that new entry could (and often did) challenge. Insull stated in 1914 that electricity provision "has not reached a point of saturation in any of the communities in which it is operated" (Insull, 1924, p. 6), confirming that the competitive process was young too. The proactive force of new entry was still needed to push new markets and discipline existing ones. There was little time for competitive holidays.

The oft-cited inconveniences of duplicate electric service were exaggerated. The analogue of "tearing up the streets" with new gas mains was the relatively innocuous "dead wires and useless poles" (Behling, 1938, p. 20) with electricity. Removing obsolete wires and poles was a simple maintenance chore for the municipality and not an important consideration for public policy. "Street brawls among the workers of the rival organizations, each seeking to prevent the other from installing its distributions system" (Behling, 1938, p. 21) were more serious, but they, too, were not a matter for public policy. It was a matter for the street owners to set conditions of entry and police their property against the initiation of force.

Whatever the above problems, evidence also exists that new entry was not duplicative. Gregg Jarrell's (1978, p. 295) study of the historical record found "many cases of competitive franchises being granted with no resulting increase in physical plant or duplication of facilities."

As was the case with manufactured gas, the electric industry in the market-raiding era was constantly innovating and improving. England, which terminated its competitive era several decades before the United States did, failed to keep up technologically with its trans-Atlantic rival (Byatt, 1979). Both the prospect and actuality of competition had an undeniable salutary effect of lowering prices for consumers. Existing providers must price electricity below what new entrants would need to charge, and situations of stranded capacity sparked "price wars" where rates were driven down to variable cost. What the provider had to give up was the consumer's gain.

Competition in these decades existed not only between electric firms but also among rival lighting fuels – kerosene and manufactured gas, in particular. One electric utility executive complained, "The Standard Oil Company is better satisfied with the profit which it makes on the sale of kerosene in Detroit than are either the Detroit Gas Company or the electric-light companies in that city with their profits" (Dow, 1898, p. 106). The introduction of the Welsbach gas mantle in the early 1890s allowed manufactured gas to leapfrog electricity in the lighting market. Although ignored by the natural monopoly model, consumers had choices in the lighting market.

If the natural monopoly model for regulation was correct, the states that first implemented statewide public-utility regulation should have been the ones that had the highest rates and the lowest quantity supplied. Conversely, the states with the lowest rates and highest quantity supplied should be the last to implement regulation. However, evidence suggests that the opposite was true with electricity, consistent with the hypothesis that regulation was more a response to protect vested business interests than to address monopolistic behavior during the free market era. Comparing statistics from 1912 (when only five states implemented state public utility regulation with electricity) and 1917, a period when twenty-five states had such regulation, Jarrell (1978) concluded:

> Utilities in early-regulated (ER) states had 46% lower prices, 38% lower gross profits, and 23% higher output than did utilities in later regulated (LR) states in 1912. By 1917, after state regulation was established in ER states, prices and profits had risen and output had fallen. These empirical results are difficult to square with the traditional explanation that state regulation was designed to minimize the undesirable social consequences of a naturally monopolistic electric utility industry . . . The electric utility interests were not acting suicidally when, around 1910, they became the main champions of the movement for state regulation (292–3, 295).

Franchised-Monopoly Failure and Government Failure

A realistic perspective of the choice between political regulation and the self-regulating market must not only account for "market failure" but also "monopoly failure" by exclusively franchised utilities and "government failure" of political control. Insull (1924) himself had pains of conscience over the "new element" of political interference in business life that he himself was so instrumental in securing:

> Sometimes I wonder whether this regulation may not check enterprise and destroy individuality in management. I sometimes ask myself whether we are not in danger of drifting to

a species of paternalism which will end in our simply fulfilling our allotted task and being satisfied with just what we have today, forgetful of the fact that the electricity-supply business is relatively a new industry (p. 31).

Future decades would give credence to Insull's early fears that his vision of "calm, scientific, and just regulation" would be contradicted by reality. State regulation, like local regulation before it, turned out not to be apolitical, peopled by altruistic, energetic, career-minded individuals. The machinery of regulation was political and peopled by quite ordinary and fallible individuals. It would also bring out the worst in the regulated industry. Executive decision-making in the regulated era would contradict the paternalistic image exhibited by Insull as the apostle for electric regulation.

Why Municipalization?

The argument for establishing municipal electric operations in place of investor owned utilities involved an economic element of lower rates and a managerial aspect of less political control. Both reasons, however, were illusory from a market viewpoint.

The rate advantage of municipalities centered around its tax advantages compared to private utilities. "In an endeavor to supply electric service at lower apparent cost than possible under private operation," explained Ernest Abrams (1940), "political expediency has decreed that public electric systems be largely relieved of the tax burdens which weigh so heavily on private enterprise today" (p. 17). Other things equal, the costs and rates of private firms subject to market competition should be lower than government firms protected from competition.

The rationale for municipalization was intertwined with the problems of private regulation, both ad hoc franchise regulation and systematic public utility regulation. Municipalization, however, was not an escape from politics as proponents advertised but a more pure form of institutionalized political control. Stated William Prendergast:

Those who clamor for public ownership and operation of the electric industry are in the same breath condemning regulation by state commissions. But if regulation is a failure – regulation by appointed and elected public officials – what chance would there be for the success of public ownership and operation with public officials in charge. The proposed task is certainly ten times as great as the present one![11] (Quoted in Hausman & Nuefeld, 1991, pp. 244–245).

Many states regulated electric municipalities to address the distortions of political control. By 1928, 17 state utility commissions regulated electric municipalities along with investor-owned utilities (Ruggles, 1937). This increased to 24 state commissions by 1940. Private ownership, particularly if unregulated, would have allowed a degree of entrepreneurial discovery and economic efficiency that bureaucratic management could not. City fathers could have entered into private contracts to support the private provision of electricity rather than create a new department to provide the same.

The Cumulative March of Early Regulation

A 1914 National Municipal League study (King, 1914) verified the sentiment for regulation:

> All now seem to assent to the proposition that municipal utilities must be regulated. The point of difference is as to the method and extent of regulation (p. 23).

This universal agreement resulted from a long process of government involvement, not a sudden distrust of market competition. Public utility control of investor-owned electric utilities is a case study of cumulative government intervention. The beginning or basis point intervention was government ownership and operation of the streets, which led to franchise agreements by city fathers for street usage and street lighting contracts.[12] These agreements had the legal status of contracts. Corporate charters, too, were an entré to government-imposed conditions (regulation). Regulation by state commissions was, in fact, a cumulative intervention to the political and administrative shortcomings of local (1879–1907) regulation.

The Politicization of Franchise Regulation

The politicization of franchise regulation was recognized in the same National Municipal League study:

> There is no side-stepping the fact that, in American cities, municipal utilities are too often the city's actual governing power. If the utilities cannot, unaided, dominate a city's governmental machinery, they dominate it through alliances with other interests. . . . Obtaining franchises invites occasional corruption and municipal subversion; the interpretation and administration of those franchises invite permanent corruption and subversion.

In their review of the period, Richard Rudolph and Scott Ridley (1986) similarly concluded:

> In major cities across the nation, journalists and government investigators turned up a steady stream of city councilors for sale and government officials acting on behalf of private interests. One of the choicest plums of public office, and one rife with corruption, was the granting of franchises for electric power, the new industrial heartblood (pp. 22–23).

Franchise Uncertainty

Limited-term franchises posed another problem that inspired replacement regulation within the industry. Explained NELA president Carl Jackson in 1922:

> A limited-term franchise is a suspended sentence or threat. . . . [It] is notice that at some future date the municipality or State may see fit to treat property and legitimate investment in public utility on the junk-value basis (Quoted in U.S. Senate, 1928, p. 384).

The political solution to a political problem would be state public utility that replaced limited-term franchises with indeterminate permits for the established firm and a requirement to obtain a "certificate of public convenience and necessity" from new entrants. While the open-ended permit was technically revocable, in practice it was not.

Cumulative Statewide Regulation

The cumulative march of regulation was also evident as state commissions reached deeper and deeper into managerial decision-making to make public utility regulation more effective. Summarized Ruggles (1937):

> There has been a steady growth in commission jurisdiction over more types of utilities, and greater authority over the managerial affairs of the utilities. This latter tendency was apparent as early as 1890 [in Massachusetts with manufactured gas], but it is doubtful if anyone at that time could have anticipated the extent to which internal operations of utilities would be made subject to actual regulation by utility commissions. . . . Increased attention was focused especially on such matters as the power to change contract rates, to issue terminable or indeterminate permits, to control depreciation rates, to approve consolidation and mergers, and to authorize the construction of electric transmission lines (p. 56).

Municipalization as Cumulative Intervention

Electric municipalization was cumulative intervention to the basis point intervention of municipal street ownership. Municipal streets were simply joined by municipal lighting for the streets. Later municipalizations were cumulative to "home rule" regulation where the government firm was inspired by the political problems of franchise regulation. Prominent economists such as Richard Ely (1883) made this argument for municipalization in books and articles politicians made the argument in their respective locales. Detroit, for example, established an electric municipality in 1895 after political corruption was uncovered with franchises (Rudolph & Ridley, 1986).

The Lure and Myth of Scientific Regulation

The Lure

A companion rationale for state regulation in place of local regulation – greater professionalism – was enunciated by Henry Spurr (1924), the editor of *Public Utilities Fortnightly:*

> Regulation by a commission ought to be better than regulation by direct action of the legislature. The legislature does not have time to ascertain facts upon which specific regulatory action should be based. It is not in session throughout the year. It could not act quickly in an emergency such as that created by the war. A commission, on the other hand, may be continuously in session. It can ascertain the facts upon which its legislative and administrative action should be based. It can conduct hearings and give both sides a chance to produce their evidence. Theoretically . . . this would see to be the best form of regulation. (p. 175)

Maryland, for example, established a state commission in 1910 to replace ad hoc regulation with "continuous control":

> The failure of the legislature to control the utilities effectively was due . . . to the increasing number of bills brought before it every session and the conduct of some of its members. . . . Under the pressure of numerous local bills, control became a matter of exchanging votes and favors. It was impossible to form any unified state program of utility control. . . . Only when the whole matter of utility control was placed in the hands of a specialized commission could a policy of continuous control be exercised (Brown, 1936, p. 107).

C. O. Ruggles, professor of Public Utility Management at Harvard University, similarly concluded, (1937) "The early public utility commissions came into existence because regulation by such means as franchises, charters, and direct legislation proved to be too rigid to cope with the complex economic and social problems of highly dynamic public utilities" (p. 1).

The Myth

A comprehensive study of power regulation published by The Twentieth Century Fund in 1944 approvingly described the evolution of power regulation from "inflexible" and "corrupt" local regulation to state-level "scientific regulation by administrators armed with authority to determine facts and issue rules and orders." Yet just pages later the study described some of the following theoretical problems encountered by rate-setting regulation as a surrogate for competition. What is the "fair value" of an asset, and what is a "fair return" on that asset? How should entrepreneurial performance be rewarded or penalized within this framework? Should the rate base be valued at depreciated original cost, reproduction cost, a combination of the two, or other factors (such as future capital attraction)? Economists know that value is not embedded cost, however calculated, but the revenue stream associated with an asset, which under regulatory rate-setting creates a circularity problem. The method of depreciation is vital to determine the level of present vs. future rates, yet it, as the Fund report continued, "can be only roughly estimated" and "has become a focus of wide controversy." What standard should determine whether costs are prudent or not? What is a "fair" rate structure between customer classes now and in the longer run given the "special costs" of each? Regulation "must also be consistent," yet different states apply different methodologies and have different authority to regulate.

Given these difficult and even intractable problems, a series of judgement calls come into play that make decision-making dependent on the involved personalities and political situation. Whatever the case for regulation, public utility regulation cannot be "scientific," duplicate a competitive market, or synthesize market entrepreneurship.

The manifestation of these theoretical problems was the empirical reality that regulation scarcely measured up to the expectations of even its proponents. Summarized Charles Morgan in 1923:

> Regulation is still in a state of flux. It has seemingly taken on an entirely new aspect of late, perhaps an aspect, which seems altogether unexpected and unwarranted to those who were its early protagonists. Originally a "people's" or a "consumers' " movement, today regulation has become by force of circumstance the champion of the rights of the utilities (p. 76).

"Regulation by Competition": The Foregone Alternative

The problems of regulation beg the question: why not the free and open market? There was another alternative to the interventionist choices of franchise regulation, public utility regulation, and municipalization. It was the "acute competition" that Insull feared but consumers, left to their own devices, did not.

"Regulation by competition" is anchored on open entry (either no franchise requirement or at least unlimited franchises) that provides actual rivalry in some cases and potential competition in all cases to the established firm(s).

This market framework allows "as-agreed" transactions in place of government edicts. Without regulation, regulatory problems would not have existed, and new regulation would not have been necessary to address the problems created by existing regulation. With regulatory costs absent, and unconstrained incentives, market entrepreneurship and its benefits would have been maximized.

Private street ownership would have facilitated the market regime. Lighting contracts could have been less political. Street usage (rental) for electric infrastructure could have been priced to better decide the question of whether duplicate wires and poles were necessary.[13] The forsaken free-market alternative would receive long overdue attention with the widely recognized "breakdown of regulation" in the 1930s, examined below. By then, however, it was too late. Following earlier precedent in the electric industry (and other industries such as natural gas), political inertia would add new regulation rather than remove existing regulation.

THE "BREAKDOWN" OF STATE REGULATION

The quid pro quo of franchise protection for rate regulation offered more upside than downside for affected firms. Franchise protection meant that rates no longer had to be restrained by potential or actual competition. The resulting inelastic demand created a bountiful managerial opportunity to increase costs, rates, and profits within the regulatory constraints. Since regulators are "incapable of forcing the utility to operate at a specified combination of output, price, and cost," (Stigler & Friedland, 1962, p. 11), the utilities had more than a fighting chance for advantage. The ability of the utilities to adjust and thrive under public utility regulation would be accomplished to a greater extent than anyone predicted – a development that directly led to federal accounting, securities, and power industry regulation in the mid-1930s.

Advantages of the Regulated Over the Regulators

The regulated had several important advantages over state regulators. One was a greater familiarity with their business. It is always difficult for "outsiders" to know as much as "insiders" whatever the regulatory constraints, and this was particularly true in the maiden years of commission regulation of electricity. Generally accepted accounting practices, in particular, were reshaped to escape regulatory constraints, a development that would lead to more cumulative regulation.

A second advantage was a disparity of resources available for regulatory disputes. While a commission had to work within its appropriated budget, a firm could pass through its regulatory expenditures to ratepayers. A single rate case could result in the firm spending more money in its defense than the commission's annual budget (Rudolph & Ridley, 1986). In 1926, it was estimated that 39 states together spent less than $5 million regulating utilities of all kinds (Behling, 1938).

The utility's ability to hire experts (called "hired imagination" by a critic) and lobbyists ("ex-judges, ex-commissioners and ex-governors are preferred") provided the balance of power in many important rate proceedings (Wilcox,

1924). Commission accounting departments were understaffed relative to the utilities they regulated. Many commissions did not determine "yardstick" costs to assess actual costs, for example (Ruggles, 1937). As Mosher (1929, p. 181) noted, "The commissions accept [the annual reports of operating companies]; they do not audit them. To do this would require a staff of experts such as no single commission can under present conditions afford." Higher salaries kept more talent on the private side than on the commission side. These advantages translated into rate case victories for the regulated unless the commission was preordained against the utilities. The evidence is that state commissions were more cordial than adversarial toward electric utilities in the early period.

The ability to capture "monopoly profits in the guise of costs" (Behling, 1938, p. 47) was a particularly subtle aspect of franchise-protected enterprises. Day-to-day decisions with operating expenses, public relations costs, regulatory proceeding budgets, and affiliate charges (discussed below) were highly subjective and very difficult for outside regulators to intelligently assess.

Creating Regulatory Gaps

Electric utilities circumvented rate and profit constraints by integrating their corporate structure. By internalizing their costs, unregulated affiliates could book profits from regulated affiliates with little constraint. Vertically integrated holding companies "organized and owned" finance, investment, engineering and service subsidiaries, and each could "run up expenses" though contracting with the parent (Gray, 1924, p. 105). While some state commissions tried to disallow certain inter-subsidiary transactions, the burden was on the regulators more than the company.

The rise of long distance electric transmission led to increasing movements of electricity across state boundaries, which by the early 1930s accounted for nearly 15% of total sales. This created a jurisdictional problem for states given the Commerce Clause of the U.S. Constitution. Federal regulation or none at all applied to interstate flows, rates, and service. The FPC first identified this regulatory gap in its 1925 annual report and considered, and rejected, a regional multi-state compact as a solution.

Holding companies created interstate jurisdictional problems for the states even when electric flows did not traverse state boundaries. If financing and engineering costs for a new power generation plant went to subsidiaries that operated in another state, for example, state regulators had to take these costs as given or risk violating the Commerce Clause. Thus the integrated, interstate holding company presented a double barrier to effective state regulation.

Overcapitalization

Another regulatory gap concerned overcapitalization. An 1898 Supreme Court decision allowed the regulated company to receive a "fair return upon the value of that which it employs for the public convenience."[14] Through consolidations, the acquiring firm often received assets with a cost value in excess of its economic value as measured by profitability. Explained John Gray (1924):

> When a holding company buys up a multitude of small plants and establishes large central generating plants a very large part of the old investment becomes useless. But . . . it is still carried on the books nominally as stand-by equipment. The public then pays . . . as if the old investment [was] in full use (pp. 104–105).

The acquiring firm could also engage in asset "write-ups" where it issued securities for a greater value than the purchase price of the acquired assets. This automatically increased the rate base upon which a regulated rate of return was applied. The larger capitalization also reduced dividends as a percent of capital – a result that could satisfy a regulatory requirement. In all, consolidations across service territories and across states had a regulatory reason in addition to any scale economies that existed.

Winter of Discontent

The above problems under public utility regulation, leaving consumers without competition and without effective rate regulation, did not go unnoticed. Summarized one prominent economist of the day:

> After a twenty-year struggle with rate regulation the public authorities today are scarcely in a better position than when they started. During these two decades they have conducted endless investigations, caused the expenditure of hundreds of millions of dollars, piled up mountains of records and opinions; and mostly have not reduced rates when fairly justified, nor advanced them when reasonably needed. They are all but helpless before the huge task of prescribing rates for the many utilities operating under greatly varying conditions, rapidly shifting prices and tremendous transitions in industrial organization – unless principles and policies of regulation are definitely established and exact methods prescribed (quoted in Bauer & Costello, 1949, p. 372).

Such criticism by state and federal officials, other academic reformers, and the press led the NELA to establish a public relations committee for the first time in 1921. Despite its efforts, criticism would mount and become a national issue by the end of the decade. The increasing concentration of the industry created an appearance problem, the problems of regulation aside. By 1932, nearly one-half of the investor-owned utilities were controlled by three holding companies: The Insull Group, Electric Bond & Share (later General Electric), and United

Corporation (controlled by J. P. Morgan). Two-thirds of all investor owned utilities were controlled by the top fifteen holding companies (Hawes, 1987).

Franklin D. Roosevelt, then governor of New York, expressed concern over utility practices under regulation during the "roaring '20s" when business criticism was not common:

> The condition of over-capitalization by the issuance of watered stock has come about under the regulation of public utilities by public service commissions, so that the policy has failed to maintain that degree of protection for the public, which was contemplated at the outset. It appears to me that the policy of public service commission regulation has broken down and proved itself ineffectual for the purposes originally intended (quoted in Prendergast, 1933, p. 267).

Pennsylvania Governor Gifford Pinchot, after reviewing a 5,181-page study of the problems of the state's Public Service Commission, forced several commissioners to resign for listening "complaisantly to their utility master's voice" (Prendergast, 1933, p. 268). On the academic front, Felix Frankfurter, a well-known law professor at Harvard University and later a U.S. Supreme Court Justice, traced the achievements of the public utility commissions prior to the First World War only to add:

> Pessimism has supplanted the earlier feeling of hope .... Informed opinion is in substantial agreement that the present system is not adequate for the old evils which brought it into being, and is incapable of coping with new problems of greater subtlety and deeper concern to society (quoted in Prendergast, 1933, p. 269).

The "breakdown" of regulation was not from a want of regulation at the state level. State regulation had become increasingly comprehensive in the elusive quest to effectively control managerial decision making.

FEDERAL RESPONSE

Investigation

Federal interest in regulating the electric power industry began with a Senate Resolution dated February 9, 1925, instructing the Federal Trade Commission (FTC) "to investigate ... and to report to the Senate the manner in which the General Electric Company has acquired and maintained such monopoly or exercises such control in restraint of trade or commerce and in violation of law."[15] The first comprehensive government study of the U.S. electric industry, released two years later as a 272-page report, examined the entire investor-owned and municipal industry to compare against General Electric. General Electric's 8% profit margin was not particularly excessive, and no major policy conclusions were reached by the report. Senate Resolution No. 83, dated February 15, 1928, instructed the FTC to undertake a thorough study of the nation's gas and electric holding companies and draw conclusions for public policy.

Seven years and 101 volumes of testimony later, the verdict was in. While some "real public benefits" of the holding company structure and ownership concentration were cited – capital attraction, territorial diversification, economies of operation (i.e. scale and scope), rapid implementation of technological improvements, and timely service extensions – the disadvantages carried the day, not only in the report but in the popular press. The negatives included "excessive construction and management fees," "intercompany profits on transfers of properties or securities," "write-up's, improperly capitalized intangibles and inflation," "manipulation of stock-market prices," and "pyramiding in holding-company groups."[16] The study concluded:

> The cumulative effect of some of these abuses undoubtedly resulted in the maintenance of higher than reasonable rates to the consumer and unfavorably affected the value of the securities in the hands of many investors. For these conditions the Commission concludes that a thoroughgoing reform is necessary in the intercorporate relations within the holding-company groups, in corporate and financial structure, in accounting practice, and in the extent and methods of public regulation.[17]

The FTC's conclusions were echoed in other parts of the federal government. In the summer of 1931, a reorganized FPC began to investigate the waterpower companies licensed by the commission and their parent holding companies. A preliminary report released in July 1932 (Splawn Report) advocated federal control of holding companies, a recommendation that was repeated in their 1932 annual report. In July 1934, FDR convened a National Power Policy Committee to "develop a plan for the closer cooperation of the several factors in our electric power supply – both public and private – whereby national policy in power matters may be unified and electricity be made more broadly available at cheaper rates to industry, to domestic, and particularly to agricultural consumers."[18] The committee, composed of representatives from the FPC, Securities and Exchange Commission, Public Works Administration, War Department, Tennessee Valley Authority, Forest Service, Bureau of Reclamation, and Mississippi Valley Committee, released its findings in March of the next year, documenting holding company practices and control and proposing legislation that would become law in the same year.

Hearings were held by the House Committee on Interstate and Foreign Commerce and the Senate Committee on Interstate Commerce between 1933 and 1935 that also made a favorable record for the holding company regulation and interstate commerce regulation that was to come. Resisting a major utility-sponsored campaign against federal holding company regulation, the two-part Federal Power Act, also called the Wheeler-Rayburn Act for its sponsors Sen. Burton Wheeler (D-Mont.) and Rep. Sam Rayburn (D-Texas), would become law.

What was the mood of the electric industry toward federal regulation? Opinion was initially against, but by 1932 it was reported (Prendergast, 1933) that there was "of late more acceptance in utility circles of the idea of regulation of holding companies, even of limited Federal regulation where states have no power to act" (p. 96). The new pragmatism was to shape regulation rather than condemn it per se.

Public Utility Holding Company Act of 1935

Title I of The Public Utility Act of 1935, better known as the Public Utility Holding Company Act of 1935 (PUHCA), was designed to rectify a "lack of effective public regulation" that created "abuses . . . injurious to investors, consumers, and the general public." The identified problems created by electric, manufactured gas, and natural gas holding companies were:

(1) Inadequate investor information because of an absence of uniform accounting standards;
(2) Security issues based on "fictitious or unsound asset values having no fair relation to the sums invested in or the earning capacity of the properties and upon the basis of paper profits from intercompany transactions;"
(3) Overcapitalization "prevent(ing) voluntary rate reductions;"
(4) Overcharges for "services, construction work, equipment, and materials," reflecting "an absence of arm's-length bargaining or from restraint of free and independent competition."

All of these practices "present problems of regulation which cannot be dealt with effectively by the States."

By December 2, 1935, all public utility holding companies in interstate commerce had to register with the Securities and Exchange Commission (SEC) and provide detailed reports and conform to various prescribed standards.[19] Intercompany loans were prohibited, and other financial transactions within holding companies such as dividends, security issuances, and asset sales were strictly regulated. Effective April 1, 1936, registered holding companies could not enter into intracompany service, sales, or construction contracts except as expressly permitted by the SEC.

The most dramatic action of the new law was to "limit the operations of the holding company system of which such company is a part to a single integrated public utility system" effective January 1, 1938. Dismemberment could not occur, however, if "the loss of substantial economies" occurred (p. 820).

"The public utility holding company, as a device of financial legerdemain," stated Arthur Dewing (1953, p. 2), "was to pass from the scene." Between 1938 and 1955, when the SEC's divestment work was mostly concluded, 214 holding companies controlling 922 electric and gas utilities and over a thousand non-utility companies were reduced to 25 holding companies with 171 electric and gas subsidiaries and 137 nonutility subsidiaries. Assets of nearly $13 billion dollars had been divested in the process. The effective result was to reduce holding companies to one integrated gas or electric system without non-functionally-related subsidiaries "to facilitate rather than supplant state regulation ... to return effective jurisdiction to the State [commissions]" (Hawes, 1987, p. 2-22)

Evaluation of PUHCA

The quest for vertical and horizontal consolidation, particularly across state boundaries, and the "financial legerdemain" within elaborate holding companies, was inspired by more than achieving pro-consumer scale economies in a market setting. These practices were managerial innovations to escape regulatory constraints to exploit inelastic demand (charge what the traffic would bear) created by legal monopoly. The same incentive to integrate and consolidate across state lines and engage in opportunistic accounting practices would not have occurred under "regulation by competition." As such, PUHCA was *a regulatory response to a regulatory problem* – cumulative federal intervention to plug regulatory gaps with state intervention.[20]

From this perspective, the verdict of Alfred Kahn (1971, p. 73) that "there seems to be little dissent from the conclusion that the job the SEC did in dismantling the jerry-built holding company structures needed doing and was well done" can be reconsidered. Not only could have the huge multi-decade regulatory effort been foregone, PUHCA's negative side effects, such as undoing economic integration along with opportunistic integration (despite the language of the law), could have been avoided. Future integration, furthermore, was also blocked by the law, leaving voluntary collaboration, which, Kahn (1971, p. 73) admits, "typically fell considerably short of achieving the full possible advantages of complete integration, and particularly the integrated planning of investment."

The irony and legacy of PUHCA is that once its job was complete, the managerial challenge for electric utilities became how to integrate and interconnect neighboring electric systems. PUHCA was a response to the Great

Depression, which itself has been directly linked to activist government monetary and fiscal policies that created the business cycle (1920s boom and 1930s bust) and kept the general economy mired in high unemployment and low output until World War II (Rothbard, 1975; Friedman & Schwartz, 1963). Interstate companies of all kind were regulated by the Securities Act of 1933 and the Securities Exchange Act of 1934, which established the SEC; PUHCA just magnified such regulation for public utility holding companies. Even with boom and bust, some conservatively managed holding companies (two being the American Gas and Electric Company and the United Gas Improvement Company) remained financially sound. In fact, "the utility operating companies suffered less than almost any industry group during the depression years" (Hawes, 1987, p. 2-22). Market forces dismembered the unsound holding companies, such as Samuel Insull's Middle West Utilities, before PUHCA came into play. The formation of new holding companies fell out of favor with investors once the Great Depression set in. Seen in this light, PUHCA's costs – private and public compliance costs and arbitrary prohibitions on corporate structures – were deadweight losses that public utility deregulation could have entirely avoided.

The FTC's summary report, which provided most of the groundwork for PUHCA, failed to interpret, or even consider even as a minority view, the diagnosed problems as the result of existing regulation rather than the absence of comprehensive (federal in addition to state) regulation. Thus a thoroughgoing free market interpretation was left out of the entire debate. The report had to tiptoe around its stated fact that "there has been a general decline . . . in electric rates, not only during the last thirty years, but also during the last decade" by arguing that rates would have been still lower under "just and reasonable" federal regulation. The report concludes that holding companies hurt both consumers and investors, yet what may have been bad for one could have been good for the other outside of some level of pure inefficiency. If rates were really inflated, investors should have gained; if investors were really hurt, captive consumers must have been spared higher rates while keeping their lights on.

Federal Power Act of 1935

The passage of Part II of the Public Utility Act of 1935 (Federal Power Act) reflected several motivations. The most important rationale was the aforementioned need to complement state regulation as well as PUHCA by closing a regulatory gap. But Federal Power Commissioner Clyde Seavey cited another reason in House debate on the bill:

> The machinery of this regulation will permit the coordination of these various sources of power in the United States. . . . The need for such coordination for national purposes, I

> think, was vividly demonstrated during the World War period. There is provided in this act for the pooling of power in a comprehensive way. This pooling will permit the leveling off of the evil effects of surplus and shortage in local communities . . . and will also stabilize investments in those territories likewise or bring about a better security back of these securities that are issued by those operating companies.[21]

The Federal Power Act (FPA) extended regulation to "the transmission of electric energy in interstate commerce and to the sale of electric energy at wholesale in interstate commerce." Jurisdiction over local distribution and intrastate transmission was left with the states.

Within six months of the FPA, all jurisdictional companies had to secure an order from the FPC to conduct business in interstate commerce. The FPC was empowered to set "just and reasonable" rates by ascertaining the "fair value" of a utility's property, setting the "proper" depreciation rate, and prescribing a system of accounts. The Commission also could order "proper, adequate, or sufficient service" so long as it did not require enlarging generating facilities or impairing service to existing customers. The FPC was also directed to "promote and encourage" interconnections between and within defined regions to "assure an abundant supply of electric energy throughout the United States with the greatest possible economy and with regard to the proper utilization and conservation of natural resources." Such action also could not impair existing service or require expanded generation. In emergencies, however, the Commission could order facilities to be built and dictate business practices, so long as it was "just and reasonable" and fairly compensated. FPC authority also extended to mergers and security issues. The importance of the FPA would grow as the FPC and, later, the Federal Energy Regulatory Commission liberally interpreted their jurisdiction under it.

Jurisdiction would be claimed over: (1) utilities that sold power to an intrastate intermediary who then sold it in interstate commerce; (2) power from its point of origin if a later sale affected interstate commerce; and (3) intrastate electricity if commingled with interstate electricity (Ferrey, 1994).

Evaluation of FPA

While PUHCA eradicated many regulatory gaps, the FPA removed another important one to make it also an exercise in cumulative intervention. Explained the Twentieth Century Fund study (Burns, 1948):

> The FPC was given jurisdiction over electricity in interstate commerce in order to close a gap in regulation. A considerable quantity of electricity is transmitted in interstate commerce and sold at wholesale to companies engaged in distribution to ultimate consumers. Since the wholesale rate is an interstate rate, a state commission does not control it, yet it has an

> important effect on the costs of a company whose rates to ultimate consumers are subject to state commission control. Obviously, regulation of the rates to ultimate consumers could not be effective or intelligent unless the state commission investigates the reasonableness of the wholesale rate, but this was beyond its control (pp. 78–79).

The cumulative march of regulation had now gone from the local level to the state level to the federal level to achieve comprehensive regulation of the power industry as depicted in Fig. 1.

SUMMARY AND CONCLUSIONS

Reexamining the origins of political electricity casts a decidedly free-market light on the current debates to restructure the electric industry along market-driven lines. The textbook "market failure" rationale for the regulatory covenant, whereby franchise protection was exchanged for cost-and rate-of-return-based regulation, is found to be theoretically and empirically lacking. Even if the natural monopoly model is held, the evidence is that the conditions for natural monopoly were not get in place in the power industry when the regulatory covenant was implemented. Competition was never "over" in the open franchise period, and falling prices, increasing quantity supplied, and service-quality improvements suggested that consumers were beneficiaries during the quasi-free market era. Either actual rivalry between two or more firms, or the mere possibility of entry where one firm predominated, created a competitive situation throughout the cycle of the changing industry makeup of individual firms.

Competition was so great that the interests of the status quo, led by "The Chief," Samuel Insull, raised the white flag by asking regulators to replace competition with legal monopoly and, in effect, bureaucratize business management. This business/political trade followed precedent from the intrastate manufactured gas industry (Act to Create a [Massachusetts] Board of Gas Commissioners, 1885) and the interstate railroad industry (Act to Regulate Commerce, 1887).[22]

Once it gained a foothold in the electric market, government involvement took on a life of its own, as basis point intervention gave way to spiraling cumulative intervention. The interventionist dynamic first played out with increasingly stringent public utility commission intrastate requirements and would spread to federal regulation of company structure (Public Utility Holding Company Act of 1935) and rates (Federal Power Act of 1935). The well-coined term, "plugging regulatory gaps," applied.

The historical record of early (pre-1935) government intervention with electricity has implications for at least three current debates with electric restructuring. The first is the utility's argument for recovering uneconomic

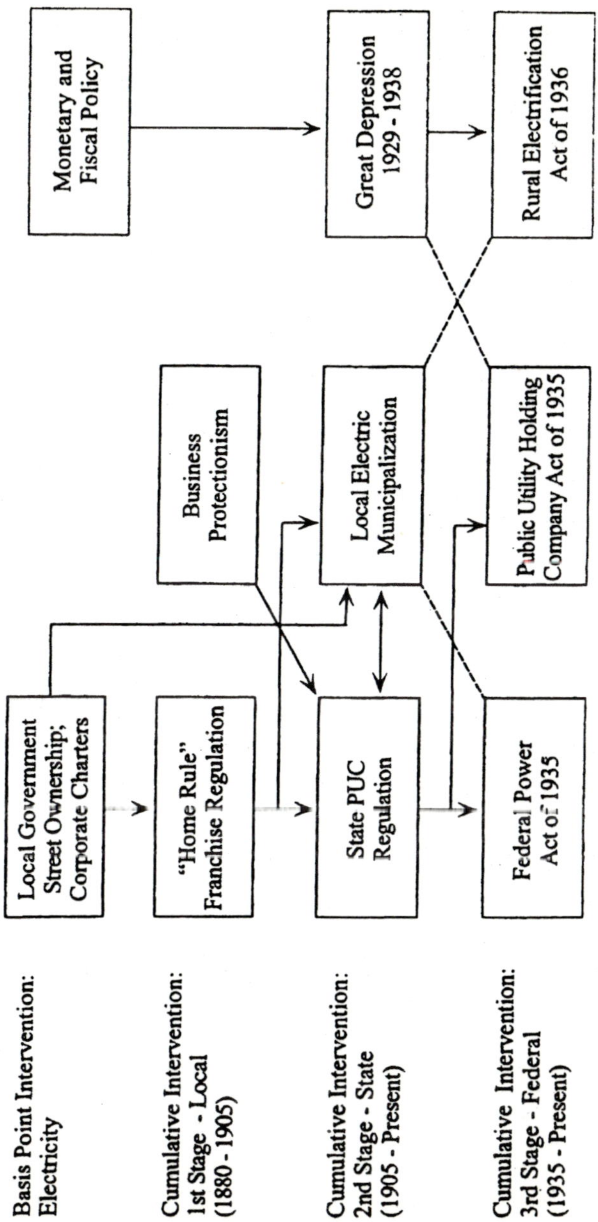

Fig. 1. The Dynamics of Public Utility Regulation in the U.S. Electric Industry.

("stranded") costs from captive ratepayers. Reliance on the regulatory covenant in the absence of explicit contractual obligations is weakened by the fact that business convenience and not market failure (consumer welfare) was responsible for the fateful turn from competition to franchise monopoly. Consumers did not receive compensation for legal monopolization in the various states earlier in this century, and franchised firms received their desired cost-plus oasis. Why later, with the advent of competition, should have consumers paid a "strandings" charge from those utilities with uneconomic assets not backed by explicit contracts?

Second, the rationale for PUHCA was never sound, resting on either non-problems or problems created by pre-existing government intervention. In a competitive world where the preferences of consumers are controlling, the rationale to dictate industry structure is not clear.

Historical revisionism casting relatively favorable light on the pre-regulatory era of the industry, finally, imparts optimism toward a less regulated and even completely unregulated era for the electricity industry. Once retail competition joins wholesale competition to complete the open-access restructuring, complete with performance-based alternatives to cost-based rate regulation, consumers and the industry will look increasingly hard at the last vestiges of political electricity. To the extent that private parties find that the benefits of self-regulation through settlement contracts outweigh the costs of even light-handed regulation (such as with transmission rates), the deregulatory dynamic could result in a regulatory bypass era (Bradley, 1996). At this point, the longstanding political era of public utility regulation of the electric industry would come to a close with the political means of government intervention in the marketplace replaced by the economic means of self-regulating and self-help market entrepreneurship.

NOTES

1. Adapted from: Bradley, R. L., Jr., (1996) The Origins of Political Electricity: Market Failure or Political Opportunism. *Energy Law Journal*, *17*(1), pp. 59–102. Reprinted by permission of the *Energy Law Journal.*

2. While primary incorporation franchises were often issued by the state, municipalities issued secondary franchises governing street lighting and the use of public thoroughfares (Jarrell, 1978).

3. For the fascinating story of the behind-the-scenes effort of Insull (and Theodore Vail on the telephone side) to sway public opinion toward regulation via "editorial boilerplate services, the dispatching of mangers to become leaders of community groups, the production of ghostwritten articles, and the alteration of school textbooks" (Olasky, 1987, Ch. 4).

4. In 1907, some 45 firms had the legal right to serve the Chicago electric market (Behling, 1938).

5. The Wisconsin law made existing franchises open-ended, required new utilities to receive a certificate of convenience and necessity, regulated service and rates, and controlled the capitalization and the issuance of securities (Jarrell, 1978).

6. Carl Jackson, Letter in Response to Senate Resolution No. 83 from the Chairman of the Federal Trade Commission, U.S. Senate, 70th Congress, 1st Session, Utility Corporations 381 (1928).

7. In 1932, 95% of all power, 91% of all customers, and 94% of all revenue was generated from the private power side (Behling, 1938).

8. Insull (1924) applied the natural monopoly argument to "gas, or electricity, local transportation, or the telegraph, or the telephone, or the steam railroads in any given territory."

9. Insull's strategy was "one part quality service, two parts hard selling, and three parts rate cuts." McDonald (1962, p. 104). Insull criticized his fellow executives for not following a low-rate strategy to avoid inflaming the public and encouraging municipalization.

10. It is worth noting that in a few cities competitive electric service persisted throughout the 20th century. There is no evidence that any of the pitfalls of competitive markets argued by natural monopoly proponents were realized in these cases (see Primeaux 1986).

11. Quoted in Hausman and Neufeld (1991, pp. 244–245).

12. Electricity was "a recognized utility from the outset because of its occupancy of streets and consequent franchise requirements" (Bauer & Gold, 1939, p. 14).

13. As Demsetz (1968, p. 62), the alleged problem of overduplication of facilities may well have been due to "the failure of the community to set a proper price on the use of these scarce resources."

14. *Smyth v. Ames*, 169 U.S. 466, 547 (1898).

15. Quoted in a letter from the Chairman of the Federal Power Commission in response to Senate Resolution 329, 69th Congress, 2nd Session (1927).

16. Summary Report of the Federal Trade Commission to the Senate of the United States Pursuant to Senate Resolution No. 88, 70th Congress, 1st Session., Economic, Financial, and Corporate Phases of Holding and Operating Companies of Electric and Gas Utilities No. 72-A, at 43 [Washington, D.C., GPO 1935].

17. Ibid. 882. The blame for the problem was placed on managers' "love of power or greed for gain" and "a disgraceful laxity in the corporate laws of many states."

18. From the Twentieth Century Fund Report (1948) *Electric Power and Government Policy*, p. 711.

19. Holding companies were defined as directly or indirectly owning 10% or more of a gas or electric public utility.

20. The Act itself makes this point, detailing the problematic holding company practices, which "are not susceptible to effective control by any State."

21. Hearing before the Committee on Interstate and Foreign Commerce, House of Representatives, 74th Congress 1st Session, Public Utility Holding Companies.

22. On the push of the major interstate railroads for the regulatory covenant, see Kolko (1965). On the bellwether Massachusetts law that served as a model for subsequent gas laws in other states, see Bradley (1996).

REFERENCES

Abrams, E. (1940). *Power in Transition.* New York: Charles Scribner's Sons.

Bauer, J., & Costello, P. (1949). *Public Organization of Electric Power.* New York: Harper.

Baker, C. (1889). *Monopolies and the People.* New York: London: G. P. Putnam's Sons.

Behling, B. (1938). *Competition and Monopoly in Public Utility Industries.* Urbana: University of Illinois Press.

Bradley, R. (1996). The Distortions and Dynamics of Gas Regulation. In: J. Ellig & J.Kalt (Eds), *New Horizons in Natural Gas Deregulation* (pp. 1–30). Westport: Praeger.

Brown. G. (1936). *The Gas Light Company of Baltimore.* Baltimore: Johns Hopkins University Press.

Burns, A. et al. (1948). *Electric Power and Government Policy.* New York: The Twentieth Century Fund.

Byatt. I. (1979). *The British Electrical Industry: 1875–1914.* Oxford: Clarendon Press.

Demsetz, H. (1968). Why Regulate Utilities. *Journal of Law and Economics, 11*, 55–65.

Dewey, R. (1934). The Municipal Plant: Is it Coming or Going. In: C. Duval (Ed.), *Government Ownership of Power and Light Utilities* (pp. 51–64). Austin: University of Texas Press.

Dewing, A. (1953). *The Financial Policy of Corporations* (5th ed.). New York: Ronald Press Co.

Dow, A. (1898). Public Lighting in Relation to Public Ownership and Operation. In: *National Electric Light Association: Twenty-first Convention.*

Ely, R. (1888). *Problems of Today.* New York: Thomas Crowell & Co.

Ferrey, S. (1994). *Law of Independent Power: Development, Cogeneration, Utility Regulation.* New York: Clark Boardman Co.

Friedman, M., & Schwartz, A. (1963). *A Monetary History of the United States, 1867–1960.* Princeton: Princeton University Press

Glaeser, M. (1927). *Outlines of Public Utility Economics.* New York: Macmillan.

Gould, J. (1946). *Output and Productivity in the Electric and Gas Utilities, 1899–1942.* New York: NBER.

Gray, J. (1924). The State Abdicates: Utilities Govern Themselves. In: C. Duval (Ed.), *Government Ownership of Power and Light Utilities* (pp. 95–106). Austin: University of Texas Press.

Hausman, W., & Neufeld, J. (1991). Property Rights v. Public Spirit: Ownership and Efficiency of U.S. Electric Utilities Prior to Rate-of-Return Regulation. *Review of Economics and Statistics, 73*, 414–423.

Hawes, D. (1987). *Utility Holding Companies.* New York: Clark Boardman Co.

High, J. (1991). Introduction: A Tale of Two Disciplines. In: J. High (Ed.), *Regulation: Economic Theory and History* (pp. 1–17). Ann Arbor: University of Michigan Press.

Insull, S. (1898). Presidential Address in *National Electric Light Association: Twenty-first Convention.*

Insull, S. (1924). *Public Utilities in Modern Life: Selected Speeches (1914–1923).* Chicago: Private Publication.

Jarrell, G. (1978). The Demand for State Regulation of the Electric Utility Industry. *Journal of Law and Economics, 21*, 269–296.

Kahn, A. (1971). *The Economics of Regulation.* New York: John Wiley & Sons, Inc.

King, C. (1914). *The Regulation of Municipal Utilities.* New York: D. Appleton and Company.

Kolko, G. (1963). *The Triumph of Conservatism: A Reinterpretation of American History.* New York: Free Press of Glencoe.

Kolko, G. (1965). *Railroads and Regulation, 1887–1916*. Princeton: Princeton University Press.

McDonald, F. (1962). *Insull*. Chicago: University of Chicago Press.

Morgan, C. (1923). *Regulation and the Management of Public Utilities*. Boston: Houghton Mifflin Co.

Mosher, W. (1929). *Electrical Utilities: The Crisis in Public Control*. New York: Harper & Brothers.

Nash, L. (1925). *The Economics of Public Utilities*. New York: McGraw-Hill Book Company.

National Civic Federation (1907). *Municipal and Private Operation of Public Utilities*.

Olasky, M. (1987). *Corporate Public Relations: A New Historical Perspective*. Hillsdale, NJ: Lawrence Erlbaum Associates.

Prendergast, W. (1933). *Public Utilities and the People*. New York: D. Appleton-Century Co.

Primeaux, W. (1986). *Direct Electric Utility Competition: The Natural Monopoly Myth*. New York: Praeger.

Rothbard, M. (1975). *America's Great Depression*. Kansas City: Sheed & Ward, Inc.

Rudolph, R., & Ridley, S. (1986). *Power Struggle: The Hundred-Year War Over Electricity*. New York: Harper & Row.

Ruggles, C. (1937). *Aspects of the Organization, Functions and Financing of State Public Utility Companies*. Boston: Harvard Business School Press.

Schap, D. (1986). *Municipal Ownership in the Electric Utility Industry: A Centennial View*. New York: Praeger.

Spurr, H. (1924). Have the State Commissions Fulfilled their Intended Functions? In: C. Duval (Ed.), *Government Ownership of Power and Light Utilities* (pp. 174–184). Austin: University of Texas Press.

Stigler, G., & Friedland, C. (1962). What Can Regulators Regulate? The Case of Electricity. *Journal of Law and Economics*, *5*, 1–16.

U.S. Senate, 70th Cong., 1st Sess., *Utility Corporations* (1928). Washington: Government Printing Office.

Wilcox, D. (1924). The Reasons for Municipal Ownership. In: C. Duval (Ed.), *Government Ownership of Power and Light Utilities* (pp. 167–173). Austin: University of Texas Press.

4. THE "REGULATORY CONTRACT"

Daniel H. Cole

INTRODUCTION

What is the nature of the relationship between state regulators and regulated electric utilities? This question is at the center of ongoing debates over utility deregulation. Some (for example, Sidak & Spulber, 1997, Ch. 4) argue that the regulatory relationship constitutes a contract. Others such as Michaels (1995, p. 21) claim that the "regulatory contract" is a myth of recent vintage. Both sides agree, however, that the issue is vital. If there is a regulatory contract between states and utilities, then deregulation would, if it substantially altered the terms of the contract, constitute a breach. If there is no regulatory contract, then the government can alter the regulatory system however it wishes (consistent with constitutional due process and property-rights protections) without regard for the costs those changes impose on electric utilities.[1]

This chapter suggests that both sides may be wrong. The existence or non-existence of a regulatory contract may be immaterial as far as deregulation is concerned. Whether or not there is a "regulatory contract," deregulation (or reregulation) may lawfully modify, terminate, or replace it with a substituted contract; in neither case should there be a compensable breach.

NOT ALL CONTRACTS ARE ALIKE

Begin by assuming that there is a regulatory contract between utilities and states, for if there is not then arguments about contract substitution and termination are irrelevant: in the absence of a contract, the state could change its relation

The End of a Natural Monopoly: Deregulation and Competition in the Electric Power Industry, Volume 7, pages 77–88.

ISBN: 0-7623-0995-4

to electric utilities at will. State and federal courts have long characterized relations between utilities and states as contractual. But what is the precise nature of those contractual relations? This question is important because different types of contractual relations entail different rights, obligations, and remedies.

Leases, licenses, mortgages, and bailments all constitute contractual relations, but they entail significantly different sets of rights, obligations, and remedies at law. Unlike parties to simple contracts, landlords have no common-law duty to mitigate damages in the event of a tenant's breach of a lease.[2] If the landlord breaches, the tenant typically will have a different set of remedies to choose from than parties to ordinary contracts. Leases and ordinary contracts, meanwhile, both convey greater security than licenses or bailments, which are contractual (or quasi-contractual) relations that, at common law, the licensor or bailor could terminate at any time.

Consequently, the conclusion that a regulatory contract exists between electric utilities and state regulators does not take us very far toward determining the legal implications of deregulation. We must assess the nature of that regulatory contract. Is it an ordinary bilateral contract between parties dealing at arms' length in the open market? Or is there something special about the nature of the regulatory contract and the rights and duties it entails (perhaps based on the status of the parties)? Even if we conclude that the regulatory contract is an ordinary contract, subject to ordinary contract duties, obligations, and remedies, we still must attend to the precise terms of that contract. One or both of the parties might have reserved the right to terminate it or to amend its terms (in exchange for valuable consideration and upon reasonable notice of termination or amendment). Even if no one expressly reserved the right to terminate, the courts may imply that both parties have the right unilaterally to terminate in certain circumstances.[3] Moreover, the history of relations between the parties after the contract is created might reveal that the original regulatory contract has been superceded by a "substituted contract" (see Farnsworth, 1982, pp. 284–285). Only after assessing the nature and precise terms of the (presumed) regulatory contract will we be in a position to determine whether deregulation (or reregulation) constitutes a breach.

THE CIRCUMSTANCES OF THE ORIGINAL REGULATORY CONTRACT

What were the historical circumstances under which the (presumed) regulatory contract was created? Contrary to the conventional wisdom, the utilities, rather than the states, initiated regulation (Reutter, 1997, p. 101).[4] It was "[a]t the urging of several utility managers [that] states agreed that electricity supply constituted an industry similar to the telephone and public works industries and should, therefore, be considered a natural monopoly" (Hirsh, 1991, p. 147). When the regulatory contract was negotiated, the electricity market was open and highly competitive. As Barnes (1942, p. 168) noted, "[c]ompetition was the earliest form of regulation." In Chicago in 1907, for example, 45 electric power companies competed for customers (Behling, 1938, p. 20, *citing* National Civic Federation Report, 1907, Vol. I, Pt. II, p. 719).[5] That was before one of those utilities, the Chicago Edison Company (later Commonwealth Edison), led by Thomas Edison's former administrative secretary Samuel Insull, successfully lobbied for a regulated monopoly from the state.

Insull claimed that there was too much competition in the open electricity market, causing diseconomies of scale and wasting resources (Bonbright, 1961, p. 100; McCraw, 1984, pp. 9–10; Hirsh, 1991, pp. 150–151). Analysts at the time and later agreed:

> Competition which was relied upon to insure for the public reasonable rates and satisfactory service proved to be elusive and non-enduring and failed to measure up to expectations. It continually was disappearing as a result of bankruptcies, consolidations, and formal or informal agreements, leaving in its wake torn-up streets, 'dead' wires and useless poles and pipes, enormous overcapitalization, and paralyzed service. Whereupon, the public paid for the competitive folly in high rates to cover dividends on unused, unnecessary investment, and watered stock (Behling, 1938, p. 20).

Insull's primary concern, however, was not the public's interest in minimizing rates, preserving social resources, or maximizing economies of scale. Like other utility managers, he championed the public interest only to the extent that (he thought) it coincided with his utility's private interest. Insull supported regulation that would maximize his utility's profits by destroying "inconvenient" competition and averting public take-overs (see Demsetz, 1968, p. 61).[6] State regulation first arose in states where competition was strongest (see Jarrell, 1978); and often, as Milwaukee Mayor Daniel Hoan lamented in 1907, that regulation was not "'for the people'" but "'for the power oligarchy'," (quoted in Rudolph & Ridley, 1986, p. 40). It was also a source of enrichment for corrupt politicians (see Glaeser, 1957, p. 72).

When the State of Illinois granted Samuel Insull his regulatory monopoly in 1914, it effectively reduced the number of power providers in Chicago from 45 to 1 (Hirsh, 1991, pp. 148, 152). Thereafter, Insull branched out utilizing a holding-company structure. "By 1916, he controlled 118 power systems operating in nine states, as well as steadily rising layers of power companies, subregional and regional holding companies with Middle West Utilities at the top" (Rudolph & Ridley, 1986, p. 42).

What does this history tell us about the nature of the regulatory contract between the State of Illinois and Chicago Edison? It suggests (among other things) that the regulatory bargain implicated the interests of many utilities that were not nominally parties to the "contract" between Chicago Edison and the State of Illinois. Those other utilities had made investments in reliance on the free and competitive market, facilitated by a State policy of noninterference that was obliterated by the grant of a regulatory monopoly to Chicago Edison. Did those other utilities, after they were forced from the market, have a claim against the state for breach of (an implied) contract or an unconstitutional taking of property without just compensation? If they did not, it is worth wondering whether Commonwealth Edison or any other utility should have such a claim now, when the States are returning (more or less) to the *status quo ante.* To compensate the losers now would perpetuate the competitive advantage they gained when they were made winners through the regulatory process.

Moreover, the winners when the electric-power industry was originally regulated may well have benefited from the failure of the states to compensate losers. Had the states been forced to compensate losers for their stranded investments (that is, for investments made before open-market competition was replaced by regulated monopolies), they might have declined to enter into the regulatory contract in the first place, or been forced to raise state tax rates (possibly including taxes on utilities). Simply put, the utilities that received franchises were subsidized by those that did not, beyond the monopoly entitlements they received.

Still, a deal is a deal. And since the states promised a return on (approved) investments in exchange for the utilities' promise to serve, it arguably would be legally and morally wrong to allow them to avoid their responsibility by deregulation (see Sidak & Spulber, 1997, p. 106). This assumes, once again, that the original regulatory contract did not authorize the States unilaterally to alter the terms of the of the contract. To determine whether or not that assumption is accurate, we must must inquire further into the terms of the regulatory contract.

THE TERMS OF THE REGULATORY CONTRACT

The Regulatory Contract as a Franchise Agreement

"The regulatory contract is a bundle of public utility statutes, utility commission precedents, adjudicatory decisions, rulemakings, hearings on the record, formal notices of proposed rulemaking, and public commentary" (Sidak & Spulber, 1997, p. 109). This definition, in itself, suggests that the regulatory contract is not like an ordinary contract (if it is a contract at all), leaving one to wonder what relevance the rules of ordinary contract law might have in this context. But at the center of the regulatory contract, it has been argued (for example, by Sidak & Spulber, 1997, p. 110), is a rather ordinary-seeming franchise agreement. That franchise agreement is not the sum and substance of the contract, but it is at the heart of contract-based claims for compensation in deregulation. Indeed, courts have often characterized relations between states and utilities as franchises (see, for example, *General Motors Corp. v. Tracy,* 519 U.S. 278, 117 S.Ct. 811, 819 (1997)).

Unilateral Termination or Modification of Franchise Agreements

If the regulatory contract is, in essence, a franchise agreement, then it is not at all clear that the states cannot unilterally terminate it without constituting a breach. Relying on Barnes (1942, p. 219), Sidak and Spulber (1997, pp. 130–131) assert that the lack of any specified duration in the (presumed) regulatory (franchise) contract between states/municipalities and utilities created either a perpetual contract or one terminable by the states/municipalities only upon payment of compensation. But this is an inaccurate account of franchise law, as the law existed at the time the regulatory contract was consummated.

According to Farnsworth (1982, p. 533), "courts have often applied the rule of termination at will to exclusive agency and distribution agreements."[7] Gellhorn (1967, p. 473) notes that "when the contract was for an indefinite duration, either party had the right to terminate at will. Cause was not required." And this rule governed even though "substantial sums invested in the franchise business may be difficult or impossible to recover."

Because of the perceived unfairness to franchisees (stemming in particular from a perceived inequality in bargaining position between the parties), the general rule of termination at will for franchise contracts has been substantially modified in most states (see Glickman, 1969–1999). Today, some states allow franchisors to terminate franchise contracts, including those of indefinite duration, only for "good cause" (*Carl A. Haas Auto. Imports, Inc. v. Lola Cars, Ltd.*, 933 F.Supp. 1381 (N. D.Ill. 1996)). Others require the franchisor to give the franchisee reasonable notice of termination. Still others, operating under the so-called "Missouri doctrine" of agency law, permit the franchise to be terminated only after the franchisee has a reasonable time to recoup their *initial* investment (Farnsworth, 1982, pp. 533–534; Gellhorn, 1967, pp. 479–480).[8] Some even more recent enactments require terminating franchisors to compensate for *recent* investments. But such buy-back provisions typically apply only to specified industries; and no state's list of protected franchisees includes electric utilities (Glickman, 1969–99, § 4.03[7][d]).

These modifications in the law of frachising, it is worth noting, came long after the states and electric utilities entered into their regulatory contract. At the time their contract was consummated, the general rule was that franchises of unlimited duration could be terminated at will. If some court chooses to apply one of the more recent rules prohibiting termination at will of franchises, that in itself would constitute a substantial modification of the original regulatory contract to the detriment of the states.

The history of utility regulation suggests, moreover, that the usual reasons for protecting franchisees from at-will termination by franchisors do not apply in the case of regulated electric utilities. In the first place, there seems to have been little, if any, disparity in bargaining position between electric utilities and state regulators at the time the regulatory contract was framed. As we have seen, it was the utilities that initiated the regulatory contract and pushed for exclusive franchise agreements for their own benefit. And after more than eight decades (a far longer term than most franchises survive[9]), utilities have had more than enough time to recoup their "initial" investments and the vast majority of their subsequent expenditures. Indeed, courts have ruled that the "Missouri doctrine seemingly [is] not applicable where the relationship has already endured for some time" (*Bushwick-Decatur Motors, Inc. v. Ford Motor Co.*, 116 F.2d 675, 676 (2d Cir., 1940)). "[N]o court," according to Gellhorn (1967, pp. 482–483), "appears to have extended the doctrine of reasonableness to give the dealer an opportunity to recoup any new investment, regardless of when made. Thus, the minimum duration requirement has had no apparent effect on dealers who have been terminated suddenly some time after the franchise relationship was adopted."

Meanwhile, the legislative and administrative processes leading up to deregulation surely provide more than reasonable notice to the regulated utilities; it is simply beyond belief that some utility might not be aware of the changes in the air. Therefore, termination of the regulatory contract should not give rise to the policy concerns that have led most states to impose restrictions on franchisors' rights to terminate other types of franchise agreements. In their absence, the state or municipality, as regulatory franchisor, should be able to unilaterally terminate without breaching the regulatory contract.[10] This was, after all, the common law in existence at the time the regulatory contract was consummated. At the very least, the onus should be placed on those who would prevent the states from terminating at will to explain why well-heeled electric utilities require special legal protection against unilateral termination by the state.

One argument they might make is that the Constitution prohibits the states from passing laws "impairing the Obligation of Contracts" (U.S. Const., Art. 1, sec. 10, cl. 2). In 1923, the U.S. Supreme Court ruled that, under the Contract

Clause, the State of Wisconsin could not substantially amend the terms of a public-utility contract, even though it had expressly reserved the right to alter or repeal the franchise in its state constitution (*Superior Water, Light, and Power Co. v. City of Superior*, 263 U.S. 125 (1923)). That case, however, concerned a contract of specific duration, which franchisors typically may not terminate at will. It is unclear whether the Court would have prevented the State from unilaterally terminating or modifying the contract, had it not specified a duration. Indeed, termination technically should not constitute an "impairment" where the contract, by its lack of any specified duration, permits termination-at-will according to the common law at the time the contract was created.

There is reason, in any case, to doubt the currency of *Superior*, which was a creature of the long-gone *Lochner* era, during which the U.S. Supreme Court struck down all manner of state economic regulation under the Contract and Due Process Clauses.[11] Since the late 1930s, the Supreme Court has been far more tolerant of state regulation of economic activities, including electric-power production and distribution. This is clear from the recent history of utility regulation.

Sidak and Spulber (1997, p. 188) note (surprisingly without disapproval[12]) that "[e]ven before 1996 some state legislatures modified the regulatory contract by repealing statutes that prohibited competitive entry into regulatory structures such as local exchange telephony." These recent legislative modifications have not been struck down, although they undoubtably introduced significant changes in the regulatory contract's terms, to the detriment of franchisees. If this kind of contract modification does not (today) constitute a breach, then why would other modifications that impose costs on regulated utilities?

A "Just and Reasonable" Return on Investment

Whether the regulatory contract is a franchise or some other type of compact, its terms – as interpreted by the courts – clearly do not require full recovery, and may not require any recovery, of investments stranded as a result of deregulation. This reflects another way in which states and muncipalities have unilaterally modified the regulatory contract (without breaching it) over the decades. As one court recently explained,

> "[t]he basis for agency ratemaking authority has traveled a path from 'fair value' of 'used and useful assets' (see *Smyth v. Ames*, 169 U.S. 466 (1898)), this language giving way to 'prudent investment' language, to specific valuation methods based on an 'end-result test', which enables agencies to use any rate-making method of their choosing provided that the 'end result' of the process is 'just and reasonable' rates (see *Power Commn. V. Hope Gas Co.*, 320 U.S. 591 (1944))" (*In re Matter of Energy Association of New York v. Public Service Commission*, 653 N.Y.S.2d 502 (1996)).

The regulatory contract, thus, does not guarantee utilities any certain rate of return on their investments. As the New York Court of Appeals explained in *Matter of Abrams v. Public Service Commission* (67 N.Y.2d 205, 214–5 (1986)), "if the end result is a just and reasonable balancing of consumer and investor interests, the PSC may employ the 'prudent investment' test or any other formula or combination of formulae without offending the Federal Constitution or decisional law." From this statement of law, the court in *In re Matter of Energy Association of New York v. Public Service Commission* (653 N. Y. S. 2d 502, 515 (1996)) concluded that

> the one immutable rule of ratemaking comes down to this: Is the 'end result' 'just and reasonable' – and fair as between the utilities' customers and their stockholders. That is a determination of the regulatory body, subject only to the prohibition against arbitrary and capricious decision making. The courts must otherwise defer to the expertise of the regulatory body!

So, the question becomes whether it is "just and reasonable" or "fair" to impose any or all of the costs arising from deregulation on utilities' shareholders? To attempt to answer this question with simplistic assertions about the sanctity of contract is unhelpful: the regulatory contract itself, as interpreted by the courts, provides regulators with substantial latitude in allocating costs between utilities' shareholders and customers.

Still, we might argue that because utility investments had to be approved by state regulators to be included in the rate-base in the first place, it would be unfair and a breach of the regulatory contract *not* to compensate them fully for those investments. But this argument, again, does not reflect what the law actually requires. A "just and reasonable" rate of return is not based on a "backward-looking" review of what seemed "prudent" at the time an investment was made; rather, it is based on a "forward-looking" determination of whether some past investment "currently is being used to provide service to the public" (Baumol & Merrill, 1997, p. 1044, discussing *Dusquesne Light Co. v. Barasch*, 488 U.S. 299 (1989)). A capital investment that is not currently useful for public service need not be included in the rate base – i.e. need not be compensated for – even if it seemed "prudent" at the time it was made. Thus, the regulatory contract does not (indeed, has never) guaranteed utilities risk-free investing. It is no breach of the contract, therefore, for states and municipalities to deny compensation for non-useful investments, however prudent they seemed at the time they were made.

"DEREGULATION" AS A SUBSTITUTED REGULATORY CONTRACT

"Deregulation" need not terminate or modify the regulatory contract. Instead it may constitute a "substituted contract," negotiated between the utility industry and the states/municipalities. As Farnsworth (1982, pp. 284–285) notes, "[t]he effect of a substituted contract is to discharge the original duty and to replace it with a new duty based on the substituted contract." Thus, where the original regulatory contract required utilities to provide service to all customers in the specified region of their monopoly entitlement in exchange for a guaranteed rate of return on investments, the substituted regulatory contract might absolve the state or muncipality of its guarantee in exchange for releasing the utility from its obligation to serve all comers.

Does "deregulation" actually constitute a substituted regulatory contract? In theory, both parties to the original contract must agree to the substituted contract. And there is little chance that utilities with unrecouped investments would agree to a substituted contract that would strand those investments – unless, of course, they perceived that deregulation would provide compensating (or reciprocal) benefits. But remember, the original regulatory contract affected the interests of many parties, creating "winners" – utilities that received franchises – and losers – utilities that were excluded and, for all practical purposes, put out of business by the regulatory contract. The original regulatory contract was not agreed to by every utility whose interests it affected. So why should the new, substituted regulatory contract have to by agreed to by each affected utility? Perhaps the best way to view the regulatory contract is as an agreement between state regulators and the electric-utility industry as a whole, rather than individual companies.

The new, substituted (deregulatory) contract is being negotiated in circumstances not unlike those that attended the creation of the original. On neither occasion was there arms-length bargaining between players in a free and open market. The original regulatory contract was a highly politicized bargain between governments and a minority of companies in the utility industry that sought to structure electricity markets to their advantage. The substituted "deregulatory" contract is a highly politicized bargain between governments and a (probably larger) group of utilities that are seeking to re-structure electricity markets to their advantage. To portray either arrangement in strictly market-contractarian terms is misleading.

CONCLUSION: WHAT IS REALLY AT STAKE IN DEBATES OVER THE REGULATORY CONTRACT

Beneath legalistic disputes about the existence and implications of the regulatory contract lies a fairly straightforward question of cost (re)distribution. If the regulatory contract is upheld and states/municipalities are required to compensate for the stranded investments of their former franchisees, consumers will bear the costs in the form of higher electric rates and/or reduced competition. If states and municipalities are permitted to terminate the regulatory contract without compensating for the stranded investments of their former franchisees, the stockholders of those utility companies will bear a substantial one-time hit, reducing (marginally) the market-value of those companies in the short term.[13] Competitors, meanwhile, will be marginally advantaged, resulting (in theory) in lower electricity rates for consumers.

It is easy to understand why state and municipal governments would prefer to impose the costs of deregulation on individual utilities rather than on consumers/voters (just as they would prefer to impose the costs of land-use regulations on discrete landowners rather than taxpayers/voters). And it is just as easy to understand why regulated utilities would prefer to impose those costs on their consumers rather than on their shareholders. The ultimate distribution, however, cannot be premised on the existence of a regulatory contract between those utilities and the states. For even if such a contract exists, it may not be breached by the state's (lawful) unilateral termination, modification, or bilateral substitution. Consequently, the utilities would have no contract-based claim to compensation. The allocation of the costs of deregulation ultimately is not a legal decision for the courts but a political one for the legislatures.[14]

NOTES

1. Sidak and Spulber (1997, p. 450) concede that "[t]he existence of a regulatory contract is a necessary condition for the recovery of stranded investment. There must have been a clear understanding of the terms and conditions of regulation with respect to entry controls, rate regulation, and service obligations. If any of those three essential components is absent, a regulatory contract has not been formed, and a deregulatory taking could not have occurred."

2. Courts or legislatures in many states have, in recent decades, reformed the common law rule to impose mitigation requirements on landlords; but a sizeable minority of states, supported by the Restatement (Second) of Property, continue to follow the old common-law rule (see Dukeminier & Krier, 2002, pp. 516–517).

3. In *Stonaker v. P. G. Publishing Co.*, 338 Pa. 292 (1940), for example, the court noted the "general rule is that when a contract provides that one party shall render service to another, or shall act as his agent, or shall have exclusive sales rights within certain territory, but does not specify a definite time or prescribe conditions which shall determine the duration of the relation, the contract may be terminated by either party at will.".

4. This is consistent with general economic theories of regulation (see Stigler, 1971; and Peltzman, 1976).

5. Part of the reason for such a large number of utility servers was technological: Then-existing technology made it "impossible" to distribute electric power over areas in excess of one mile (Behling, 1938, p. 19). But, of course, another part of the reason was the openness of the market.

6. At the 1898 convention of the National Electric Light Association (of which he was president), Insull advised members to seek a regulated monopoly as the best means of maximizing profits and averting public take-overs of electricity production and distribution (Rudolph & Ridley, 1986, pp. 38–39). And he took the same position a quarter-century later, in a speech to the Engineers Club of Dayton, Ohio in October 1914 (Insull, 1924, p. 4, quoted in Reutter, 1997, p. 59).

7. Farnsworth cites *Stonaker v. P. G. Publishing*, 338 Pa. 292 (1940); *Bushwick-Decatur Motors v. Ford Motor Co.*, 166 F.2d 675 (2d Cir. 1940); *E. I. DuPont de Nemours & Co. v. Claiborne Reno Co.*, 64 F.2d 224 (8th Cir.), *cert. denied* 290 U.S. 646 (1933). *Also see Warrick Beverage Corp. v. Miller Brewing Co.*, 170 Ind. App. 114, 352 N.E.2d 496, 500 (1976) (holding that either party to a distributorship agreement of indefinite length "could have terminated their duties of performance at will without cause"); *State v. Ohio Public Service Co.*, 2 Ohio L. Abs. 680 (Oh. Apps. 1924) (holding that a public utility franchise contract which is silent as to duration is terminable at the will of either party).

8. For cases requiring reasonable notice for unilateral termination, see, e.g. *Millett Co. v. Park & Tilford Distillers Corp.*, 123 F.Supp. 484 (N. D.Cal. 1954) (holding three months notice to be reasonable). For cases requiring reasonable time to recoup original investments prior to termination, see, e.g. *Lockewill, Inc. v. United States Shoe Corp.*, 434 A.2d 1222 (Pa. 1981) (providing agent "a reasonable opportunity to avail himself of [his] primary expenditures and efforts.").

9. Most franchise agreements last from 10 to 20 years (see Emerson, 1998, p. 565).

10. It is important to distinguish this argument from Sidak and Spulber's (1997, p. 131) argument (following Barnes, 1942) about "terminable franchises." They argue that some franchises might be terminable upon payment of compensation. (In fact, all regulatory franchises are effectively terminable by the state upon payment of compensation, whatever the franchise agreement stipulates, under the state's eminent domain power.) My argument, by contrast, is that franchises of unlimited duration may be terminable at will without compensation.

11. On the *Lochner* era and its demise, see, for example, Siegel (1984, 1991).

12. Indeed, Sidak and Spulber (1997, p. 117) assert that "the government's introduction of competition into the regulated market in itself would not breach the regulatory contract." This is hard to square with their other arguments about breach of regulatory contracts. After all, if those contracts posited exclusive service regions, then the unilateral opening of those regions to competition would (technically) constitute a breach, unless the regulator had some authority under or aside from the contract to unilaterally change its terms.

13. For some utilities, the financial burden would be substantial, indeed. Pacific Gas & Electric Co. has the highest estimated stranded costs – amounting to almost $12.3 billion (Maloney, McCormick & Sauer, 1997, p. 118, Table 5). The average utility's total estimated stranded cost is just over $477 million (derived from Table 5). It is important to note, however, that these stranded cost estimates are not offset by estimates of stranded benefits, defined as the earning of market returns on assets that were already fully depreciated under regulation (see Chapter 8; Cearley & McKinzie, 1995, pp. 16, 19, 21). Moreover, 65 of the 88 utilities that comprise the industry (according to Maloney, McCormick & Sauer, 1997, Table 5) have no stranded costs at all.

14. Questions related to stranded investments generally and cost-distribution in particular are addressed in Chapter 8 of this book.

REFERENCES

Barnes, I. (1942). *The Economics of Public Utility Regulation*. New York: F. S. Crofts & Co.

Behling, B. (1938). *Competition and Monopoly in Public Utility Industries*. Urbana: University of Illinois Press.

Bonbright, J. (1961). *Principles of Public Utility Rates*. New York: Columbia University Press.

Cearley, R., & McKinzie, L. (1995). The Economics of Stranded Investment – A Two-Way Street. *Electricity Journal, 8*, 16–23.

Dukeminier, J., & Krier, J. E. (2002). *Property*. New York: Aspen.

Emerson, R. (1998). Franchise Terminations: Legal Rights and Practical Effects When Francisees Claim the Franchisor Discriminates. *American Business Law Journal, 35*, 559–645.

Farnsworth, E. (1982). *Contracts*. Boston: Little, Brown.

Glaeser, M. (1957). *Public Utilities in American Capitalism*. New York: Macmillan.

Glickman, G. (1969–1999). *Franchising*. New York: Lexis Publishing.

Jarrell, G. (1978). The Demand for State Regulation of the Electric Utility Industry. *Journal of Law and Economics, 21*, 269–296.

Hadfield, G. (1999). Of Sovereignty and Contract: Damages for Breach of Contract by Government. *Southern California Interdisciplinary Law Journal, 8*, 467–537.

Hirsh, R. (1991). Regulation and Technology in the Electric Utility Industry: A Historical Analysis of Interdependence and Change. In: J. High (Ed.), *Regulation: Economic Theory and History* (pp 147–177). Ann Arbor: University of Michigan Press.

Insull, S. (1924). *Public Utilities in Modern Life*. Chicago: privately published.

Maloney, M., McCormick, R., & Sauer, R. (1997). On Stranded Cost Recovery in the Deregulation of the U.S. Electric Power Industry. *Natural Resources Journal, 37*, 59–123.

McArthur, J. (1998). Cost Responsibility or Regulatory Indulgence for Electricity's Stranded Costs? *American University Law Review, 47*, 775–857.

McCraw, T. (1984). *Prophets of Regulation*. Cambridge, MA: Belknap Press.

Michaels, R (1995). Stranded Investment Surcharges: Inequitable and Inefficient. *Public Utilities Fortnightly*, (May 15), 21.

National Civic Federation Report (1907). *Municipal and Private Operation of Public Utilities* (Vol. I, Pt. II).

Peltzman, S. (1976). Toward a More General Theory of Regulation. *Journal of Law and Economics, 19*, 211–240.

Reutter, K. (1997). From Franchise to State Commission: Regulation of the Electric Utility Industry, 1907 to 1932. Ph.D (Econ.) Dissertation, Auburn University.

Rudolph, R., & Ridley S. (1986). *Power Struggle: The Hundred-Year War over Electricity*. New York: Harper & Row.

Sidak, J., & Spulber, D. (1997). *Deregulatory Takings and the Regulatory Contract: The Competitive Transformation of Network Industries in the United States*. Cambridge: Cambridge University Press.

Siegel, S. (1991). Lochner Era Jurisprudence and the American Constitutional Tradition. *North Carolina Law Review, 70*, 1–111.

Siegel, S. (1984). Understanding the Lochner Era: Lessons From the Controversy Over Railroad and Utility Rate Regulation. *Virginia Law Review, 70*, 187–263.

Stigler, G. (1971). The Theory of Economic Regulation, *Bell Journal of Economics and Management Science, 2*, 3–21.

5. THE ZENITH OF THE NATURAL MONOPOLY SYSTEM

Peter Z. Grossman

INTRODUCTION

Chapter 2 questions the validity of the natural monopoly model as applied to electric power, and Chapters 3 and 4 suggest that the electric industry was not in need of a vast system of state and federal regulation because of a market failure problem. The question then is not why there is a national effort today for deregulation (or at least regulatory reform), but why it didn't happen earlier. Indeed, from the end of World War II through the 1960s, the system went largely unchallenged. According to the prevailing wisdom of the time, electric power was the paradigm natural monopoly and government regulation was needed to curb it. But if that premise was dubious (as it likely was), why did the system remain unquestioned for decades?

The simple answer to this question is that this system worked – well enough anyway. But more specifically, there were four reasons for the preservation and acceptance of the natural monopoly system. First, the regulated natural monopoly system functioned adequately under the particular circumstances of the post-war period; the lights generally stayed on and consumers could take affordable electric energy for granted. Second, it would have been costly to change; transition costs might well have led to net costs to social welfare. Third, path dependence made it difficult to see any alternative; few wanted to change because it had "always" been done this way. And finally, the real price of electricity was falling so no one felt especially disadvantaged and few would

The End of a Natural Monopoly: Deregulation and Competition in the Electric Power Industry, Volume 7, pages 89–106.

ISBN: 0-7623-0995-4

have seen any great benefit to change. But as circumstances changed the weaknesses of the system would inevitably become apparent.

This Chapter focuses on the 20-year period after World War II when the regulated natural monopoly system enjoyed general support, and explores the special circumstances that allowed that support to endure as long as it did.

THE NATURAL MONOPOLY SYSTEM

The natural monopoly system was of course both a regulatory regime and an industry composed of multi-product electric utility firms. The nature of these components, the way they evolved in the 1940s and 1950s illustrate both the reasons for the system's endurance and its eventual failure.

It should be emphasized at the outset that the natural monopoly argument was at root an argument about efficiency. According to theory, as noted in Chapter 2, natural monopoly creates a market failure, which means that an inefficient quantity is produced because it is sold at the "wrong" (too high of a) price. Thus government regulation is needed to force down prices to the efficient level, increasing consumption and enhancing social welfare. With the help of regulators all electric power that could be supplied profitably would be, or, put another way, the provision of electric power would be allocatively efficient.

But if the economic argument is an efficiency argument, then we must address the question: did the natural monopoly regulatory regime in fact enhance efficiency over any alternative and so raise social welfare?

THE ELECTRIC REGULATORY SYSTEM

As Chapter 3 showed, electric power faced various regulatory statutes and procedures at local, state and federal levels. Under the Federal Power Act of 1935, the Federal Energy Regulatory Commission was given authority over electric power interconnections, pooling activities and wholesale power trades, while PUHCA, passed the same year, gave the SEC regulatory authority over corporate structure and governance of investor-owned electric utilities.

Still, most of the regulatory work of the natural monopoly system remained at the state level. State public utility commissions (PUCs) were (and largely remain) politically appointed bodies[1] designed to oversee the industry. They were charged with setting rates, monitoring the provision of service, and even approving the construction and safety of new electric generating and transmission facilities (Hammond 1986). The theory of what the PUCs *should* have been doing to benefit social welfare has differed markedly with the reality. But for reasons that will be explored below, for a time, it did not matter.

Theory

In theory, regulation of the electric power system would allow society to gain the benefits of natural monopoly, while forcing firms to charge competitive prices to customers. The theory of natural monopoly leads, naturally as it were, to regulated monopoly. This would be, according to theory, the most efficient outcome.

Assume, first, for the sake of argument, that in fact electric power production is a natural monopoly because of pervasive economies of scale and falling average costs across the entire range of output. Therefore the single firm is by definition going to be the lowest cost producer, and so the inevitable form of industrial organization. However, allowed to operate as unregulated monopolies, these profit maximizing firms will price at the point where marginal revenue equals marginal cost (see Chapter 2). This will always mean that the price actually charged will be significantly higher than a competitive price, and the output consequently will be too low (as higher prices mean that the quantity demanded will decline). This would mean that resources are not allocated optimally; there would be so-called deadweight losses to social welfare as electric companies scooped up excess profits from their dominant market position.

Under these circumstances, in theory, regulators should set prices for electricity so that the price (and profits) for the firms would be approximately that which would result in a perfectly competitive market. In a competitive market, price should equal marginal cost. That is, the firm should recoup from each sale the cost including the opportunity cost (the value of the next best alternative use of the capital) of making that next additional unit. In fact price-equals-marginal-cost is the condition of competitive market pricing and profit maximization. In theory, then, to correct the presumed market failure, government should establish a regulatory regime for natural monopolies that would permit the single monopoly franchise to capture the available economies of scale. But then the firm would be required to set prices at marginal cost so that no excess profits are earned and no deadweight social losses accrue (see Fig. 1).

Actually, the process can be a bit more complicated depending on the nature of the average and marginal costs of production. Average costs, as noted in Chapter 2, are also the unit costs. If a firm does not recoup its average costs, it will lose money on each sale and will be forced out of business. In the case of a falling average cost curve, it is possible that it will intersect the demand curve at a point above the marginal cost curve (see Fig. 2). For example, the marginal cost of a telephone call may be extremely low, less than a cent but average costs may be somewhat higher if the total number of calls is not so

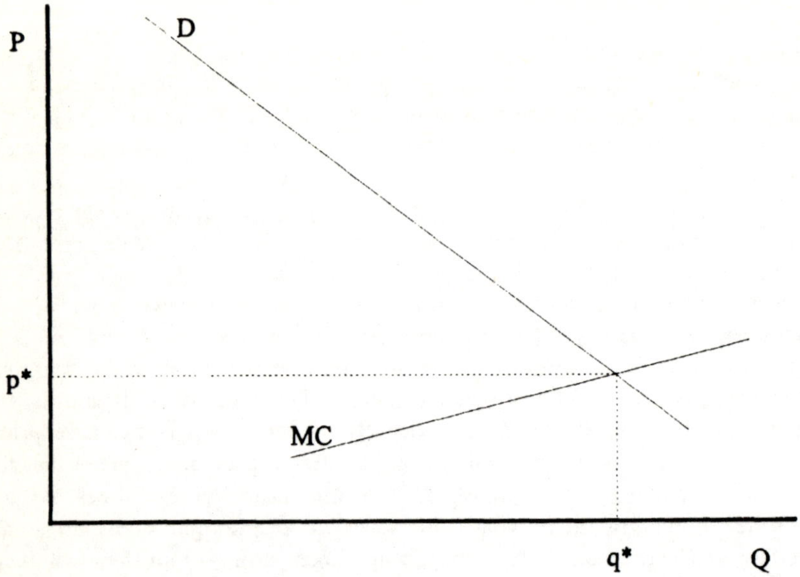

Fig. 1.

Note: If the marginal and average costs of production are known for the monopoly firm, then assuming MC ≥ AC, regulators will choose a price equal to marginal cost, eliminating deadweight losses and optimizing social welfare.

great relative to the average cost of labor and capital for the firm. Forced to charge marginal costs (as shown on Fig. 2) the telephone provider (or any firm that faced such a condition) could face bankruptcy.

There is also a second problem with marginal cost pricing: the marginal cost of electric power changes, not just day to day, but frequently during a day. On an average day, there are typically very different "loads." At midnight, there may be very little demand, certainly not more than can usually be supplied by a single "base load" generator. Base load facilities are generally the largest units, the ones that are able to capture the greatest economies of scale, the ones that produce most of a company's power during a day and over a year. Marginal costs of this power are low. On most days, the demand will pick up during daylight hours as businesses draw on electric power. If the base load plant can handle this added demand, then marginal costs may not rise appreciably. But at five p.m. on a hot summer day when residential air conditioners are running at full blast, when power providers face "peak load," more power is going to be needed than a base load generator is likely to be able to supply.

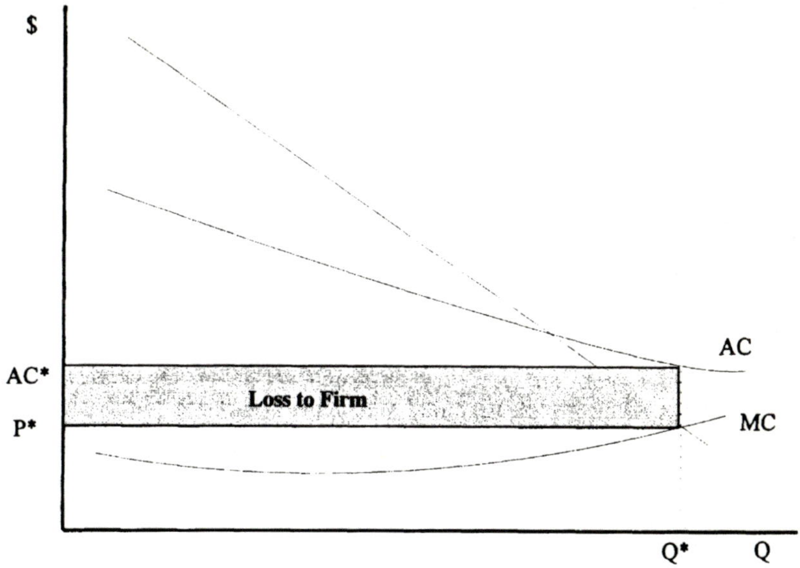

Fig. 2.

Note: A firm loses money at first-best price, [P* = marginal cost], when average costs exceed marginal costs. Adapted from Train (1991).

There are two reasons for this: a generator cannot run at one-quarter speed. It either runs or it doesn't. So the base load output will be more or less the same at midnight as it is at five in the afternoon. To use the base load plant to meet all demand would mean that a firm would need a very large generator indeed – one far greater than it would need for most of any given day. Even though there may be economies of scale from so large a generator the output would mainly be wasted and the purchase of such a generator would be inefficient.

To understand why, consider the following: let's say a fisherman can sell 10 fish a day and it costs $100 to catch them, but with more capital and labor, only $180 to catch 20 because of some economies of scale. Though there are economies in catching 20 it is wasteful and pointless to catch all of them if the market is only 10. Apply the same idea to electric power: At midnight a generator that can produce 1000 kilowatts of power runs full blast but only one-quarter of the output (250KW) is consumed over the next hour; the company can sell all 1000 only between 5 and 6p.m. Now say the cost of producing 1000 kilowatts per hour (or 1000 kilowatt-hours or KW-h) is $100, while the cost of producing 250 KW-h from a smaller generator is \$50. Average cost of the bigger generator is 10¢/KW-h; while it is 20¢/KW-h for the smaller one. But it is clear that through most of the day the bigger unit wastes \$50 since most of its output isn't consumed. Never mind that average cost of the power is lower than that produced by a smaller generator. The fact remains the cost per unit actually consumed and paid for is much higher with the larger unit, which is clearly an inefficient utilization of resources.

This would not necessarily be true but for another aspect of electric power: it cannot be easily or cheaply stored. If it could be cheaply stored, the generating company could capture extra power generated at midnight and hold it aside for use at 5 p.m. But since this is not cost effective, power is usually produced and consumed at approximately the same time, and firms do not produce power for peak load until that time approaches.

But to do that efficiently means firms must carry additional generating units that are used for relatively brief periods during a given day. Peak load units are typically, smaller, more quickly brought on line and more costly per unit of output than base-load plants. Thus for a marginal cost pricing scheme to work, consumers would have to face a different price at almost every hour of the day – given the fact that consumption of some electric power goes on all the time. If in fact there was accurate marginal cost pricing, it would create useful incentives for conservation at peak-load hours.

Though purely competitive pricing has been problematic for regulated industries designated natural monopolies, economists have proposed ways to get closer to competitive market pricing. One alternative could be average cost pricing – an average that could include the variation in demand. As long as average cost exceeds marginal cost, this would in fact be the efficient pricing scheme, but if marginal cost begins to exceed average cost, then under an average cost-pricing schedule, a firm will produce at a level where it loses money on each additional sale.

Another problem is that average costs are often difficult to determine for separate products where there is a vertically integrated multi-product firm – as electric utilities (as discussed in Chapter 2) are in fact. When there is generation, transmission and distribution of electric power handled from the same facility, what is the average cost of each output? As Braeutigam (1989, p. 1321) explains, "[I]f there are shared costs of production . . . then there is no unambiguous way to allocate common costs. Thus there is no clear way to determine an economically meaningful measure of the average cost associated with each service."

Economists have proposed other schemes. Assuming marginal cost less than average costs, so-called "Ramsey" pricing[2] would allow a "markup" over marginal cost depending on the relative elasticity of demand for the good. "Peak load" pricing, on the other hand, would vary prices during a day specifically to account for peak load. In general, the idea would be for off-peak users (such as those using power at midnight) to pay the variable costs of generating power, while peak load users would pay the variable costs plus the cost of capital needed for peak power output (Braeutigam, 1989).

For all of theories of optimal (or second-best) pricing, however, economists assume that regulators would be able to estimate the average and marginal costs and understand the demand curve for electric power since costs, both average and marginal, will depend on output and output will depend on demand. Moreover to get this right, the regulators have to be able to understand the costs and demand *in the future*. Historical numbers may be useful as a guide, but the prices are set by the regulators for the future, not the past. It would do a utility little good to charge a price that meets *last* year's average costs if this year's differ substantially, which is entirely possible given simple chages in weather patterns for example.

Practice

While efficient pricing has some theoretical problems, economic pricing models give plausible illustrations of how in theory regulators could approximate socially efficient prices for industries deemed natural monopolies. Indeed, it is fair to say, albeit trivial, that if regulators had a nearly complete information on electric demand and production cost, now and in the near future, a scheme could be devised whereby the "right" amount of power (i.e. socially efficient allocation) would be produced and would be sold at the right price.[3] The regulator would do as well as a decentralized market in terms of allocative efficiency.

Of course, the reality of regulation has been quite different from the theory. During the period 1945–1970 especially, public utility commissions did not use marginal-cost pricing, average-cost pricing, Ramsey pricing or peak-load pricing. Regulators used what is called "rate-of-return" regulation. Essentially, electric utilities were promised a "fair" rate of return on capital, and the rate structure was intended to support this. The system so far from achieving the most efficient outcome, "obviously violate[d] allocational criteria" (Shepherd & Geis, 1966, p. 277). Indeed, one of the key problems with the natural monopoly regulatory system has been that the economic rationale for it (efficiency) has seldom been the actual motivation for the various rules under which it operates or the rate structures it imposes. As Hammond (1986, p. 55) has put it, "Efficiency has not . . . been the primary pricing goal of electric utility regulators."

Instead of marginal costs as benchmark for pricing, PUC regulators followed a pricing regime based on the basic idea that electric power rates for consumers should provide the required revenues to cover operating costs, plus taxes and depreciation, and provide a "fair" return on investment. The latter is entered into the rate structure by allowing utilities a designated rate of return on the so-called "rate-base" which is essentially a company's capital stock.[4] Since the 1944 case *FPC v. Hope Natural Gas Company*,[5] regulatory commissions have utilized the basic formula that the rate of return should be "commensurate with returns on investments in other industries having corresponding risks . . . [a return that also] should be sufficient to assure confidence in the financial integrity of the enterprise so as to maintain its credit and attract capital" (p. 603).

In fairness, this formulation if it could be determined with some exactness could lead to a rate structure that approximates marginal-cost pricing and hence efficiency. That is, if marginal costs are precisely known they will include the opportunity cost of capital and the cost of production and so the practice would come close to theory.

But the rate-of-return formulation has a number of problems that result in pricing structures that "have historically borne little resemblance to patterns of marginal costs" (Hammond, 1986, p. 55). First, consider the fair rate of return as spelled out in the *Hope* case. Since electric companies were presumed to be natural monopolies with legally guaranteed monopoly franchises, exactly to what industries could they be compared in order to determine "corresponding risks?" Indeed it was often presumed that such investments had virtually no risks since the regulators would always allow the investment to be recouped. Allowed rates of return have not simply been plucked randomly out of the air, but there is no specific number that can objectively define the "fair" rate of return for a natural monopoly.

Second, what exactly constitutes the rate base of a utility and how should it be calculated? Should it be on the basis of replacement costs of capital or depreciated book value of capital? In fact, there have often been cases where capital has been undervalued by PUC formulae. But more important, if rates were to be determined on the size of the capital stock, the utilities had a decided incentive to expand capital regardless of whether it was needed or not. In other words, the formula so far from producing an efficient market-comparable outcome, merely would encourage inefficient over-building (Averach & Johnson, 1962).[6]

Third, even the measure of operating costs is unlikely to represent something comparable to market-determined marginal cost. In a competitive market, firms are forced by other producers to operate as efficiently as possible or, if not, as high-cost producers they may well be driven from the market by more efficient firms. But the rate-of-return system guaranteed that the firm would cover its costs regardless of whether or not it operated efficiently (Hammond, 1986). It has been suggested that this system also gave utilities incentives to find accounting methods that made costs seem as large as possible – implying that the biggest reward came from making a plausible case that a firm was a high-cost producer not an efficient one (Shepherd & Wilcox, 1979).

Finally, the greatest problem with the rate-of-return regulatory system as it was practiced was that the utilities themselves created the rate structure. Commissions had to approve rates but as Anderson (1981, p. 65) notes during the post-war period until the 1970s, PUCs lacked the "expertise, time and access to data" that were needed to evaluate the proposed rates. While utilities produced volumes of data and utilized expert testimony from accountants and economists, the commissions often had few experts available with small budgets and few resources.[7] In any case, in the post-war period, most PUC commissioners saw their role as making sure that rates would meet the required revenues of the utilities, were mostly non-discriminatory, and were not likely to produce exceptionally high profits. No consideration was given to marginal-cost pricing of electric power or the efficiency of the outcome that the schedule of rates produced (Anderson, 1981; Hammond, 1986).

Once rates were approved they remained in place unless challenged. Since they were based on projections, if they failed to meet revenue requirements, the utilities would return and request a rate increase, which was typically granted. If rates provided more than the revenue requirement, unless there was a specific complaint and a demand for hearings for rate reductions, the excess was simply pocketed by the power companies (Anderson, 1981). There was no provision for automatic rebates.

The rates that utilities implemented in the post-war period were not designed for efficiency either. Given that marginal costs change through the day, an efficient rate structure would have to be *time* sensitive, with higher prices charged at peak times, lower at off-peak times. But post-war electric rates were *use* sensitive with *lower* rates for those that used the *most* electric power. This system was called "declining block tariffs" and intended to encourage users to be as profligate as possible with electricity consumption. Consumers were charged a base monthly fee for electricity and then increasingly lower rates as more electric power was consumed. But since these prices were not sensitive to time of use, the block tariffs did not provide incentives for efficient consumption and could not have truly reflected the marginal cost of production. In fact, it is quite likely that in some of the "all-electric" homes of the 1950s and 1960s the greatest quantity of electricity was used specifically at times of peak load.

Thus at that time power was essentially cheapest – implying that the rate schedule promoted inefficiency in electric use.[8]

In any case, the block rate system was intended to encourage as much consumption as possible, not efficiency. Utilities marketed electricity use strenuously, advocating electric homes, electric home heating and other intensive uses of electric power (Hirsh, 1989). And these efforts had a great deal of success, as electricity consumption in the U.S. increased by 7–9%, per year, for more than two decades in the post-war era. The implications of this steady expansion will be discussed later in this chapter, but if nothing else, the expanded demand for electric power increased the need for more capital, which in turn increased the rate base, allowing utilities to go back to a PUC and ask for a rate hike.

In all, regulatory practice, in theory intended to correct a supposed economic inefficiency, had nothing to do with efficiency at all. Yet this system of rate-making and regulatory oversight stayed pretty much unchanged until the 1970s.[9] And it meant that regulation by PUCs of the natural monopoly system was in reality, to quote one commissioner, "non-existent." Utilities were regulated monopolies in name only. They were by fiat monopolies to sure but barely regulated at all.

THE TECHNOLOGY: GIANT GENERATORS AND INTERCONNECTIONS

In general the electric power companies had an interest in efficiency but it was technical efficiency, not economic. Throughout the period, there was a continuing effort to engineer increasingly larger generating units that would push the limits of efficient conversion of heat energy into electricity.[10] The drive for higher thermal efficiencies and larger sizes dominated the planning process of the electric industry. As Hirsh (1989, p. 80) argues, there was an industry culture that emphasized "engineering values over 'normal' management" practices.

Actually, there was an implicit economic component to the drive for technical efficiency. The more efficient ever-larger generators were capable of producing more output at proportionally lower quantities of inputs. In other words, they would achieve maximal economies of scale and so should have represented a cost savings. But this savings was largely assumed. True, the larger units could generate more power with proportionally less capital and raw materials, but little consideration was given to other costs such as long-term maintenance or reliability. In fact, there appears to have been little real concern as to whether these larger, more elegantly engineered units were in fact cheaper to build and operate than any alternatives. A study in the 1970s strongly suggested that there were no appreciable economic scale benefits in terms of capital cost for any generator size above 200 megawatts (MW), a magnitude that had been reached before war and less than one-fifth the size of the largest units of the 1970s (Lee et al., 1990). It also proved to be the case that at very large sizes steam generators were more susceptible to breakdowns and their long-term overall efficiency seemed increasingly problematic (Berlin et al., 1974). But the only issue that seemed to matter to utility managers was whether a new unit could be constructed that appeared to be more economical by dint of the engineering virtues of a larger output rating and a higher thermal efficiency.

In fairness, on those terms, that is, measured from the goal of greater thermal efficiency and size, the electric industry was successful. Efficiency of new units climbed by about 8% for the "best" units, and the largest units were more than triple the size of the biggest pre-war generators (Hirsh, 1989).

Utilities also began to construct what some thought would provide the ultimate technological and economic electric production unit: the nuclear-fueled generator. Nuclear power, which is really just the creation of heat energy through nuclear fission, was, proponents claimed, going to provide the U.S. with abundant quantities of cheap electricity. Indeed, power would be so abundant it would be produced at close to zero marginal cost, in fact "so cheap that [its] cost can hardly be reckoned" (cited in Ford, 1982, p. 30).[11] The prediction of a very low cost for nuclear power, which history would prove one of the worst forecasts ever, was based in part on the belief that nuclear plants could be constructed cheaply. But it was also based on the fact that the government in its effort after 1953 to promote "Atoms for Peace" limited industry liability for nuclear accidents and subsidized the fabrication of nuclear fuel (Ford, 1982).[12] In any case, throughout the country, utilities, with high expectations for the future of nuclear power, began to plan and build nuclear power generating stations. They did this despite unfamiliarity with nuclear technology; worse, they actually believed that the technology was not something for them to worry about. Nuclear power was just an exotic way to boil water to turn a steam turbine and drive an electric generator – something they knew very well.

Moreover, just as other steam plants were growing larger and larger – especially for base load power provision – so it made sense for nuclear generators to be as large a possible, too. This was, of course, presupposed to mean that they would gain maximal economies of scale from nuclear technology. But nuclear technology turned out to be more costly and difficult to operate at larger outputs. In fact, it became increasingly *dangerous* to operate at large outputs especially for companies without experience in nuclear operation.

But the utilities built nuclear plants on a customized basis without much regard to the perils or the costs, both of which they ignored. Massive cost overruns in nuclear plant construction seemed to be of little moment since the firms assumed they could recoup their costs regardless of how high they were. The cost problems and the electric industry's insouciance about them were to a great extent the result of a regulatory system that allowed all capital costs, usually without question, to be built into the rate base. In other words, the post-war electric regulatory system convinced utility managers that they did not need to think about capital costs, that building plants whether nuclear or fossil-fuel fired was riskless (Hirsh, 1989).

The electric system expanded in another important way as well. Throughout the nation most electric utilities formed power "pools" and interconnected their systems. Actually, the movement toward pooling and interconnection began in the 1920s and continued through the 1930s.[13] The Public Utilities Holding Company Act (PUHCA) specifically noted that the federal government should "promote and encourage" interconnections of systems throughout the country. Interconnection increased during the war in part for national defense needs, and afterwards, because of shortages that developed in response to rapidly growing consumer demand. By the 1960s, most of the nation was interconnected in vast power grids. East of the Rocky Mountains, for example, 120 different electric providers were connected more or less formally in a huge grid system (Grossman, 1981).

The main justification for this system was reliability. A grid allowed any utility to buy power from another electric company to make up any temporary or even long-term shortfall in supply to meet demand. But interconnection offered an efficiency prospect as well. Two utilities (or groups of utilities) with different times or seasons of peak load would have a smaller capital requirement since peak power could be shifted from one to the other, and the peak capital requirement for both companies would be reduced. This in theory would lead to a more efficient allocation of capital and lower electric rates for consumers.

The national grid engendered a considerable amount of hubris on the part of the industry and federal regulators. In 1964, in a report to Congress, the Federal Power Commission claimed that the American electric system was so reliable that even a nuclear attack would not put it off line (Grossman, 1981). The country saw the next year just how wrong this claim was, when the entire northeastern portion of the U.S. and parts of Canada were blacked out simultaneously. The grid itself had spread the power failure through a flaw in the system called the *cascade effect* (Grossman, 1981). In any case, the great blackout notwithstanding, it remained an article of faith among both regulators and utilities that the technology would prevent or solve any electric problems within the context of the vast network of interconnected monopoly power producers. There was no noticeable challenge to the regulated natural monopoly paradigm.

WHY THE NATURAL MONOPOLY SYSTEM ENDURED

Because neither the technology nor the regulatory process addressed the very heart of the natural monopoly paradigm – allocative efficiency – it may seem strange that few challenged the premise of the natural monopoly model or the basic regulatory system it justified. But it should be kept in mind that it is different to establish a regulatory system than it is to change it. A regulatory regime is a formal institutional arrangement that inevitably provides benefits to certain groups in a society (North, 1990). Such winners from existing institutions would obviously seek to preserve them. Indeed to the extent they would seek institutional change it would be to increase their advantages. Presumably, power companies and government regulators were the winners from the existing regulatory structure. For others to demand change that actually alters the incentive system to benefit new groups (say consumers), these organizations must believe that the costs of organizing to affect and institute change will be less than the benefits of change.

It does not appear to be the case that the benefits of changing or eliminating the natural monopoly system outweighed the costs in the period between 1945 and 1965 for the following reasons: predictability, the direction of electricity prices, path dependence, and transition costs.

Predictability

In general, decentralized decision making (i.e. markets) about production and consumption of inputs as well as outputs will be more efficient than any alternative since market participants get the correct signals through the price mechanism on relative scarcity. But as has long been recognized, non-market decision making with respect to production would be at least as efficient as markets if information about demand and scarcity were completely known.[14] Put more generally, central planning should work as efficiently as markets in the event that the planner is omniscient and has complete information about market demand. Of course the insolvable problem for central planning on a macroeconomic level is that such understanding has simply never been, and cannot be, achieved.

But in post-war America for more than two decades, there was a remarkably consistent growth of electric power demand that allowed for almost infallible forecasts of the future needs for capital. Electricity demand rose at the rate of approximately 7–9% each year, doubling about every decade. The very predictability of demand growth made the planning process very straightforward. It did not require substantial expertise on the part of commissions (or utilities for that matter) to evaluate capital expansion plans and decide whether or not to add that capital cost to the rate base. It is doubtful that capital development of the electric industry in the U.S. during the 1940s and 1950s would have differed substantially under pure competition than it did under natural monopoly regulation. It is difficult to argue in fact that there was grossly inefficient development during that time. More importantly, since efficiency arguments were mainly academic and seldom entered into the policy debate at all, there was little reason for consumers to protest against a system that could continue successfully to keep up with their demand.

The real question for such a system was how it would operate when demand became less predictable as it did in the 1970s. As one might expect, the natural monopoly system performed badly. Indeed, as Hirsh (1989) documents, one of the main problems for the electric system in the 1970s was the unshakable assumption that demand growth *would* continue at 7–9% per year because it *always* had grown at that rate. When demand was changing, the natural monopoly system, like the central planner, could no longer provide an efficient outcome and one of the major weaknesses of the system was clearly revealed. Until that time, it is difficult to see how a different system would have produced great efficiency gains in capital development. Surely the gains would not have led many, aside from some disinterested economists, to demand institutional change.

Electricity Prices

There was little impetus for change because consumers also benefited from falling energy costs. From 1960 through the early 1970s, for example, prices per kilowatt-hour for residential customers fell by about 35% in real (that is inflation adjusted) terms.[15] This may have been due in part to some scale economies and benefits the grid system was assumed to provide.[16] But it was also true that average rates fell because of the addition of large supplies from government hydroelectric facilities (especially in the Pacific Northwest) which provided very large quantities of power with low maintenance and no fuel costs. Steam plants that burned coal and oil also gained from lower fuel prices. Oil prices, for example, were 27% lower (in real terms) in 1970 than they had been in 1950.

With real prices falling, there is unlikely to be demand for change. Indeed, low prices might even be construed as a signal that the natural monopoly paradigm is an accurate reflection of reality. Anyone demanding change would have to demonstrate that prices would be even lower with market competition. While that might have been possible, the argument would largely have been conjectural with little if any empirical evidence to support it.

Moreover, since the block tariff system obscured the real cost of power, it would have been difficult to find that evidence. How could, in fact, consumers lower their prices for power? With the perverse incentives of the system, individuals could accomplish this (on average) simply by consuming more. Whatever the long-run efficiency arguments of the declining block tariff, it did seem to imply to consumers that they were doing well under the existing system. It is not surprising that there was little consumer demand for changes in regulation. Indeed, there were few consumer complaints about excessive rates or excessive electric utility profits (Anderson, 1981).

Of course there is a connection between electricity prices and the predictability of energy demand. Since new capital construction in the electric industry fit demand growth forecasts very well, there was little need for the utilities to raise rates excessively to pay for too many unneeded additions to the rate base.

Path Dependence

As North (1990, p. 99) explains, "Once a development path is set on a particular course, the network externalities, the learning processes of organizations, and historically derived subjective modeling of the issues reinforce the course."

From this perspective consider the electric industry and the natural monopoly regulatory system. For whatever reason, the system was put in place beginning in the early part of the twentieth century. A great deal of time, effort and money was invested in developing and improving this system. As Chapter 3 shows, the industry sought from the outset to take advantage of the state regulatory process and developed within their organizations a particular expertise in dealing with regulators (the learning process noted in the quote from North 1990 above). Even when the federal government became involved in the 1930s, legislation was cast with the eye of removing imperfections and omissions from the state regulatory process but not superceding it. By 1945, the government (state and federal) as well as industry had operated as if the natural monopoly paradigm and its attendant regulatory structure were real. It was the only model that most in both organizations believed appropriate to electricity provision. The argument was largely circular: Electric utilities were in need of a specific form of regulation because they were natural monopolies. How did we know they were natural monopolies? Because government regulators had declared them to be.

But as simplistic and circular as the arguments may have been, as long as there was no obvious example of gross inefficiency, there were simply far more people invested in the existing system than in any possible alternative. Thus predictability and low prices only reinforced the general belief that the natural monopoly model had to be true, and the regulatory structure containing it was the best we could do.

Transition Costs

An existing institutional structure, especially one so entrenched as the natural monopoly regulatory system is costly to create and it is also costly to change. We are learning this now. It has not been easy to go from the old regulatory system to the new. As the California debacle has demonstrated (see Chapter 10), regulatory reform can have very high costs especially if it is managed badly. In fact, there is often temptation to tinker with a failing system on the margins to preserve it rather than to abandon it completely.[17] This is due partly to the fact that entrenched interests who benefit from an existing system will put obstacles in the path of change. But it is also true that it entails costs to make a regime change and uncertainty about the value of benefits that might be received once the change is made.[18] This may lead to reluctance to undertake significant change. Given – once again – the relative success of capital forecasting and the moderate prices for consumers, a costly effort at regulatory transition would not have been economically rational.

CONCLUSION

The two decades immediately after the Second World War represented the zenith of the natural monopoly regulatory system. Even though it was based on unsound and even contradictory premises, even though it involved a distinctly inefficient rate-making system, it worked well enough. There was no particular reason to challenge it or the natural monopoly premise.

But the weaknesses of the system and the underlying model would be revealed in the years that followed. The energy crisis of the 1970s, forced up costs for fuel, and unsound nuclear power development forced up capital costs, and together they forced rates upward by enough so that the expected benefits of change no longer seemed too slight. Moreover, higher prices dampened demand growth, but expansion of the electric system proceeded as if higher prices would have no impact on consumer demand (Hirsh, 1989). Thus there were higher prices for inputs, requests by the utilities for rate hikes, overbuilding, requests for more rate hikes, and finally, consumer protests.

This state of affairs led to some conflict between regulators and industry, and finally a demand for institutional change. The process of change is explored in subsequent chapters, and is a process still ongoing into the twenty-first century.

NOTES

1. In a few cases, PUC commissioners have been elected; most have been appointed.

2.Named for economist Frank Ramsey. The model applied to public utility pricing comes from Boiteux (1971).

3. Or to go even further: an omniscient regulator would always produce a socially efficient outcome.

4. The formula that commissions used was essentially: RR = OC + D + T + r(RB), where RR = the "revenue requirement; OC = operating costs; D = depreciation; T = taxes; r = the rate of return; and RB is the rate base (Anderson, 1981, pp. 64–65).

5. 320 U.S. 591.

6. For another analysis of the incentives for excess capital accumulation among public utilities see Baumol and Klevorick (1970).

7. According to Anderson (1981) rather than try to innovate in the rate-making process many commissions mainly followed the examples of the largest commissions, particularly those in New York and California.

8. It is worth noting that peak load pricing was implemented as early as the 1950s in Europe (Hammond, 1986).

9. In the mid-1970s, New York State took the lead in trying to bring the rate structure more closely in line with marginal cost pricing and allocative efficiency (Anderson, 1981). By this time, however, it was becoming clear to many people that the regulated natural monopoly model no longer applied.

10. The efficiency of any engine has theoretical limitations. The steam engine's is based on the idealized Rankine cycle (Cassedy & Grossman, 1998, Ch. 3).

11. The statement, made in 1946, is from Robert Hutchins, Chancellor of the University of Chicago. In later years, there was the ubiquitous comment that nuclear power would be "too cheap to meter."

12. The landmark Atomic Energy Act was passed the following year.

13. The first pool, the Pennsylvania-New Jersey-Maryland Interconnection (P-J-M), was formed in 1926.

14. Some economists, notably Oskar Lange and Fred Taylor (1938) believed that a planner or planning board, with something less than omniscience using a trial-and-error process could still reach efficient market-like outcomes.

15. Historical information on electricity prices is from the Department of Energy, Energy Information Administration.

16. It should be noted that there is no inherent reason why the same scale economies could not also have been obtained by firms within a more competitive industry. The fact that technology may improve to lower costs does not presuppose that an industry must therefore be a single firm natural monopoly.

17. Ironically, this kind of tinkering can sometimes create greater costs in the long-run than wholesale change.

18. The cost must be considered in terms of expected costs and benefits. These entail consideration of the probability of different outcomes.

REFERENCES

Anderson, D. (1981). *Regulatory Politics and Electric Utilities.* Boston: Auburn House Publishing.

Averech, H., & Johnson, L. (1962). Behavior of the Firm Under Regulatory Constraint.*American Economic Review, 52*, 1053–1069.

Baumol, W., & Klevorick, A. (1970). Input Choices and Rate-of-Return Regulation. *Bell Journal of Economics and Management Science, 1*, 162–190.

Berlin, E., Cicchetti, C., & Gillen, W. (1974). *Perspectives on Power.* Cambridge, MA: Ballinger Publishing.

Boiteux, M. (1971). On the Management of Public Monopolies Subject to Budget Constraints. *Journal of Economic Theory, 3*, 219–240.

Braeutigam, R. (1989). Optimal Policies for Natural Monopolies. In: R. Schmalensee & R. Willig (Eds), *Handbook of Industrial Organization* (Vol. II, pp. 1289–1346). Amsterdam: North Holland.

Cassedy, E., & Grossman, P. (1998). *Introduction to Energy* (2nd ed.). Cambridge: Cambridge University Press.

Ford, D. (1982). *The Cult of the Atom.* New York: Simon and Schuster.

Grossman, P. (1981). *In Came the Darkness.* New York: Four Winds.

Hammond, C. (1986). An Overview of Electricity Regulation. In: J. Moorhouse (Ed.), *Electric Power: Deregulation and the Public Interest* (pp. 31–61). San Francisco: Pacific Research Institute for Public Policy.

Hirsh, R. (1989). *Technology and Transformation in the American Electric Utility Industry.* Cambridge: Cambridge University Press.

Lange, O., & Taylor, F. (1937). *On the Economic Theory of Socialism.* Minneapolis: University of Minnesota Press.

Lee, T., Ball, B., & Tabors, R. (1990). *Energy Aftermath.* Boston: Harvard Business School Press.

North, D. (1990). *Institutions, Institutional Change and Economic Performance.* Cambridge: Cambridge University Press.

Shepherd, W., & Gies, T. (1966). *Utility Regulation: New Directions in Theory and Practice.* New York: Random House.

Shepherd, W., & Wilcox, C. (1979). *Public Policies Toward Business* (6th ed.). Homewood, IL: Irwin Press.

EDITORS' FOREWORD TO CHAPTER 6

Chapters 2 through 5 cast doubt on the claims that the electric power industry is or ever was a natural monopoly. Indeed, in those chapters, concept itself is challenged. It is doubtful, too, that the electric industry, for technical or efficiency reason, ever had to be a collection of vertically and horizontally integrated monopoly firms. This cannot be very credibly argued from a theoretical standpoint, and it has never been demonstrated empirically. In fact, as an empirical matter, it is very difficult to call any industry intrinsically a monopoly.

But Chapter 2 did not rule out the possibility that *some* industry could be most efficiently organized as a single firm for a period of time. Moreover. Chapter 5 has noted that the very fact of an established form of industry organization may create its own rationale to continue that form of organization (path dependence). That in turn may make it more costly to change an industry. Given path dependence the transition costs of change may outweigh any benefits that accrue from change.

Thus at some times in history, in some places, it could it have been the case that the electric power industry, or more likely, one or more products of the industry such as transmission and distribution would have been most efficiently organized in a single firm. And this raises another question: might it still be true that some part of the electric power production and distribution would best be organized in single firm monopolies?

Many economists and electric industry analysts would say yes to this question. They would claim that transmission, and possibly also distribution, is, was, and will be for the foreseeable future a "natural" monopoly and should remain a government owned or regulated entity. The following chapter by Joseph Tomain, which largely recounts the legal and structural changes that affected the electric industry from the 1960s forward to the 1990s, also adopts the view that transmission should remain a monopoly.

The main argument in favor of a single monopoly transmission firm concerns the set up costs of a transmission system. There are large, and largely sunk, costs in putting down an electricity grid, and the economic incentive for multiple systems would appear small since such a transmission network will only make money if the network of users is large. That is, because fixed costs are large, they are most efficiently spread over a large number of users. By contrast, the marginal cost of serving additional customers is low. If the fixed costs are indeed large enough, there might only be room for one provider in most markets.

And if there is only likely to be one transmission provider, government regulation would seem necessary because a transmission system operator has the opportunity for strategic behavior. An electric grid presents what some refer to as a bottleneck problem. To get to the final users, all generator output has to squeeze into the same transmission system. This gives an operator the chance, simply by throwing a switch, to make access more difficult for anyone. Generating companies will either be forced to surrender most of their profits to the grid operator – in other words, the grid will earn monopoly profits – or the generators will be forced to sell giving the transmission operator a classic "natural" monopoly, vertically-integrated monopoly firm.

This argument, though widely accepted, has always been a bit more problematic that it first seems. First, as Chapters 2 and 3 noted some localities have had competitive firms with competitive transmission and distribution systems, and despite the theory, the competitors remained both independent and profitable. The point here is that it is not clear just what scale or how large these network benefits are. The network benefits are clearer with something like a telephone system. If one person has the only telephone receiver, that hook up is useless, but it gains increasing value the more people who join in the network. With electric power one person can get the same benefit from an electrical hook up whether he is the only person connected or there are a million people plugged in. There is also the question raised by Demsetz (1968) and discussed in Chapter 2: even if there is only one firm is a regulated monopoly the only alternative?

But there is also increasing doubt about the premises of the monopoly argument for transmission. There are more reason than ever to believe that transmission can be competitive as well, certainly in the near future. Künneke (1999) points out that technological change in the last few decades has made competition possible in three different ways. First of course is inter-network competition where consumers would have choices of which transmitter's, as well as which generator's, services they wish to use. If the network benefits of a transmission system are not great, then most localities could have competing transmission systems.

Künneke (1999) points out that there could be intra-network competition as well. Here a single grid would remain but it would function as a public highway and any transporter might use it to route power to its customers while competitors use the same system to transmit power to theirs. With the increasing power of information services, the ability to monitor, measure and control power along the highway can be accomplished at lower and lower costs. This kind of competition, once thought improbable, appears more likely.

A third option might be distributed generation where general transmission services compete with the alternative of local generation. In some cases, large, energy intensive industries are already able to switch from a transmission system to their own sources of power. The ability of any customer to withdraw from the transmission system at once reduces the market power of transmission operators, even if there is only one.

Still, it is generally believed that transmission will remain a monopoly for the foreseeable future. If nothing else, the transition problems in the marketization of power generation (see Chapter 10 especially) make it probable that the process will go slow. For the time being, the uncertainty about the transition costs of competitive transmission, if nothing else, will keep it from moving forward.

REFERENCES

Demsetz, H. (1968). Why Regulate Utilities. *Journal of Law & Economics, 11*, 55–65.

Künneke, R. W. (1999). Electricity Networks: How 'Natural' is the Monopoly? *Utilities Policy, 8*, 99–108.

6. WHITHER NATURAL MONOPOLY? THE CASE OF ELECTRICITY*

Joseph P. Tomain

INTRODUCTION

The electric industry in the U.S. presents an excellent case study of government regulation. Like other network industries such as natural gas, telephone, and railroad, electricity regulation was based on the central political-economic idea that certain industries had natural monopoly characteristics *and* that the goods they provided were in the public interest (Tomain, 2000). Further, like all government regulation, the regulation of the electricity industry has embedded within it a deep tension between a preference for government and a preference for markets as the favored tool for social ordering. This tension is present today as the industry experiences a significant restructuring.

As a fundamental matter of political economy, markets and the property exchanged and valued in them exist only because of government protection. In short, markets do not exist without government. Still, the degree of protection

* Author's note: Chapter 6 was written before we understood much about the California electricity crisis of 2000. The chapter was also written before the events of 9/11 and before the Enron debacle. In another article, the author takes the position that California, Enron, and 9/11 have no impact on the wisdom of electricity deregulation as an energy policy. The revelations of market manipulation in the spring of 2002 by Dynergy, Reliant, Enron, and other actors, however, raise serious questions about the difficulty of designing a deregulatory policy for the electricity industry. At the same time, the widespread charges of market manipulation indicate the persistence of natural monopoly problems in transmission.

The End of a Natural Monopoly: Deregulation and Competition in the Electric Power Industry, Volume 7, pages 111–139.

ISBN: 0-7623-0995-4

distinguishes government treatment of some industries from the treatment of others. The degree of government intervention into markets also distinguishes different historical periods in the development of industries.

In its beginning at the end of the nineteenth century, electricity was an unregulated competitive industry. Later, as the industry consolidated, government regulation was justified as a way to stem the abuses of market power. The particular market imperfection in the electric industry was said to be natural monopoly and government responded with command and control regulations setting the prices that could be charged by utilities and limiting the profits that utilities could earn.[1] Price and profit controls are a form of heavy-handed economic regulation that comes with costs of its own. Starting in the mid-1960s, traditional utility regulation appeared to have run its course as market distortions arose and as policymakers began to look at regulatory reform and deregulation (Tomain, 1998). Today, we are in the thick of electric industry "restructuring" which will be explained in this chapter.

"Restructuring" is used advisedly. It would be wrong to say that the electricity industry is being deregulated with the idea that electricity will be bought and sold like gasoline at the pump. While it is true that the heavy hand of command-and-control price regulation is being lifted in favor of market-based price mechanisms, still government regulators have a large and continuing role to play in regulating the electricity industry. It is currently the case that restructuring entails a significant amount of regulation, and this will likely continue to be true in the future.

THEORIES OF REGULATION

Theories of, or justifications for, government regulation can be characterized two basic ways. The first characterization is called the public interest theory in which natural monopoly, or other market imperfection, is controlled for the delivery of a reliable service or a good in the public interest. The second characterization of government regulation is private interest group or public choice theory, which holds that government regulates at the behest of and for the benefit of the regulated industry rather than for the public. In the case of electricity, public choice theory holds that government regulation enabled industry expansion and growth for the direct economic benefit of privately owned utilities.

Academics like to set these concepts in opposition, but this is unrealistic. Neither theory alone explains the government regulation of the electricity industry.[2] Clearly many adherents of natural monopoly theory were motivated by a desire to serve the public interest. They felt that regulation was needed to stem actual or potential abuses in the industry. Such abuses certainly existed in the case of other large industries, notably railroads and gas companies (Troesken 1996). There also were clear examples of abuse within the electric power industry (abuses of shareholders in the 1920s for instance, Hirsh (1989)), and regulation did offer a long-term solution to such problems. Chapter 3 of this volume, on the other hand, presents arguments and evidence that the electric industry specifically sought state regulation and won, among other benefits, freedom from competition and guaranteed return on investments.

The weaknesses of the natural monopoly argument have already been explored in preceding chapters, but the public choice theory has weaknesses as well. First, both producers and consumers gained from traditional utility regulation. Even arguing that the utilities benefited from traditional rate regulation does not undermine the argument that the public also benefited, for example, from the increasing availability of electricity. Second, the political critique is largely irrelevant because it is in the nature of mixed economies to regulate industry in varying degrees by the very definition of political economy (Lindblom, 1977). In other words, the public choice model – the capture thesis[3] – is easily reduced to a preference for market over government; it does not contradict the fact that mixed market economies are about degrees of government involvement, not about the presence or absence of government in markets. The current policy debates concerning utility industry restructuring are about the *extent* of public utility regulation; they are not about the presence or absence of government regulation.

Rarely are things so clear as either theory would have it. Regulation, rather, is often comprised of mixed political and economic motives. Traditional utility rate regulation, for example, can be seen as consumer protection against monopoly power because prices are set at near-competitive rather than monopolistic levels. Rate regulation can also be seen as a reward to the regulated, privately owned utility through nearly guaranteed rates of return for its capital investments. Traditional utility regulation also establishes guaranteed service areas which both benefit utilities by protecting them from competition and benefit consumers by providing universal service. Thus, while it is a great academic fun to generate a theory of the regulatory state that either emphasizes a preference for government or market, or for public or private interest, the evidence is strong that the regulatory state is mixed and always has been (Croley, 1998; Mashaw, 1997; Priest, 1993; Tomain & Shapiro, 1997).

Currently, the regulation of the electric industry is undergoing a significant transition (Kearney & Merrill, 1998). Specifically, federal and state regulators and industry actors are experiencing a dramatic restructuring. Among other developments, command-and-control price and profit regulation is being lessened;

electricity generation is being deregulated; consumer choice is being promoted; and, competition is strongly encouraged. The restructuring means that the underlying assumption of natural monopoly is being re-examined. The theme of this chapter is that the regulatory state has abandoned the idea that the *entire* electricity industry is a natural monopoly while retaining the idea that the transmission segment has natural monopoly characteristics requiring continued regulation. Neither public interest theory nor private interest theory alone is robust enough to explain this restructuring. There will be winners and losers among industry incumbents and new entrants as well as among large and small consumers even as the heavy hand of government regulation lightens with a shift toward a more competitive market.

PRECURSORS TO ELECTRIC INDUSTRY RESTRUCTURING

As noted in Chapter 5, the traditional regulatory system based on natural monopoly assumptions worked well enough in the immediate years after World War II. But predictably, traditional utility regulation could not last forever. There are natural business cycles for industry and government and their interaction. (Bernstein, 1955; Goldin & Libecap, 1994; Shapiro & Tomain, 1998). A business, for example may start competitively then seek consolidation with the intent to reduce competition thus resulting in competitive market failure. In such a case, government regulation can attempt to correct that failure until regulation experiences failure itself (Rabin, 1986; Hovenkamp, 1991; McCraw, 1984; Schlesinger, 1986). The regulation of the electric industry has gone through that cycle from an unregulated competitive market, to perceived market failure, to regulation, then to regulatory failure (Tomain, 1998). Now politicians, regulators, and other interested actors are responding to the regulatory failure in the electric industry. What ultimately stimulates changes in the regulatory life cycle is anyone's guess. Nevertheless, the key driving variables are politics and the economy. Relative to the electric industry, political and economic variables contributed to the significant regulatory restructuring which we have been experiencing over the last two decades.

Economic and Political Variables

Starting in roughly 1965 the industry reached technological and financial plateaus at which industry expansion slowed considerably; generation was overbuilt; economies of scale were not being realized; costs were increasing;

and alternative providers were coming into the market. Economic indicators were such that utilities could no longer rely on the annual 7% growth rate that they enjoyed since the end of World War II (see Chapter 5). The traditional rate formula which encouraged capital expansion put utilities in the position of continuing to dump money into rate base thus increasing costs. Inflation and other economic indicators caused marginal costs to exceed average costs; utilities ran into trouble with cost overruns, cancellations, and the like. In short, competition was peeking from behind regulatory blankets (Tomain, 1998; Hyman, 1997).

Politically, things also changed dramatically in the mid-1960s. Production costs began to increase and rates began to rise for a number of reasons: General economic inflation; increased concern about the environment and an attendant increase in regulatory costs; Vietnam War expenditures; an unstable world economy; the 1965 Northeast blackout; and the failure of nuclear power all contributed to unsettling the electric industry (Tomain, 1997). OPEC added to this state of affairs by flexing its cartel muscles and closing the oil spigot which pushed inflation to double digits and raised energy prices generally. It was also the case that the demand for electricity was more price elastic than anticipated and consumers both reduced their electricity consumption and sought energy from alternative sources thus reducing their dependence on traditional utilities. Large consumers, for example, became self-generators and small consumers installed solar panels. The reduction in consumption also caused rates to increase for remaining customers. All of these events made the formerly staid public utility commissions politically charged agencies as critics attacked the basis of traditional rate regulation from both sides. Producers wanted rates to be more market sensitive and ratepayers wanted to avoid rate shock.

It is one of the curiosities of our political system that in the popular mind Democrats are perceived as pro-government and Republicans are seen as pro-market. The reality is that no president in the twentieth century failed to criticize and try to reform "big government." It is also the case that the deregulation policy of the so-called Reagan Revolution began with the Carter Administration most notably in the airline, trucking, rail, and energy industries. Thus, throughout the 1970s, the movement to deregulate the electric industry gained momentum. The deregulation movement, however, can be evaluated either as a failure because regulation continues; or, the movement can be seen as a success because the energy infrastructure has been built and the industry is responding to changing times, if not precisely at the speed of an electron. Ironically, the need to restructure the electric industry was uncovered by regulation aimed at something entirely different.

PURPA's Surprise and the Role of Competition[4]

The combined effects of the political and economic events in the late 1960s and early 1970s raised general public concern about the country's energy future and raised particular concern in the Carter White House that saw the Energy Crisis as the "moral equivalent of war."[5] Jimmy Carter gambled his presidency on solving the Energy Crisis through two major legislative initiatives. The first legislative package was the massive and ambitious National Energy Act[6] which addressed conventional fuels. The National Energy Act had several purposes, including moving the country away from a dependence on foreign oil, promoting the use of coal, increasing energy efficiency, modernizing utility ratemaking, stimulating conservation, encouraging the creation of a new market in electricity, and restructuring a distorted market in natural gas. Carter's second initiative, the Energy Security Act of 1980,[7] addressed conservation and alternative fuels from biomass, wind and solar to tar sands and oil shale. The surprising part of the National Energy Act was the Public Utility Regulatory Policies Act (PURPA) which was a piece of the whole aimed at securing reasonably priced energy for the nation through conservation, increased use of alternative sources, and a slight movement toward market-based rates.

PURPA encouraged states to move away from declining block rate-making because it promoted consumption; toward marginal-cost pricing because it was more efficient; and, encouraged independent power production through cogeneration and small power generation as alternative energy sources. What surprised everyone was how much new electricity was available and how eager independent power producers (IPPs) were to enter the market. In hindsight, the success of PURPA revealed that traditional regulation had run its course. Generating units, with then existing technologies, could not continue to get bigger and commercial nuclear power was not "too cheap to meter." In other words, unregulated producers existed that were willing to supply the market with electricity priced lower than the electricity being supplied by incumbent regulated utilities and the new entrants profited by doing so with a little help from government.

Congress passed PURPA in small part to encourage the growth of generation not owned by utility companies as a conservation measure. PURPA required local electric utilities to buy the power produced by two types of non-utility generators (NUGs), which PURPA calls "qualifying facilities"[8] (QFs) – small electric generators (80 megawatts or less) and cogenerators. A cogenerator is an electric generator that also produces another form of energy such as steam which is put to use either to generate electricity or for another use such as heat. QFs were authorized to sell their power to the local utility at that utility's "avoided cost," that is, the price the utility would have paid for that power had it generated or bought the power itself. And, most importantly, the local utilities were required to buy electricity at that avoided cost.

It is at this point in the regulatory story that transmission becomes important and that regulators begin to rethink its regulation. While QFs could sell their power to the local utility, they did not have access to the utility's transmission lines to "wheel"[9] their power to any other utility or end user. Consequently, the creation of QFs had two dramatic consequences. First, their existence marked the formal introduction of competition into generation. Second, the purchase requirement began to force open the door of access. The program was notably successful. From 1989 through 1993, both the number of QFs and installed QF capacity doubled.

PURPA not only changed the market, it stimulated a deeper rethinking of the concept of natural monopoly. Under the traditional regulatory schemes, the industry of private vertically integrated utilities owning and operating generation, transmission, and distribution was perceived as a natural monopoly. And, according to the theory, the natural monopoly was the most efficient provider of electricity. However, cheaper electricity was available from sources other than vertically integrated IOUs because the generation segment of IOUs was simply too big and costly to maintain. In microeconomic terms, marginal cost exceeded average cost signaling the regulatory failure of traditional rate regulation because the traditional formula set rates on average, historic costs. In other words, traditional utilities were losing money both because they could not charge market rates and they had overbuilt, thus making it difficult to recover costs. As a result, smaller units and newer technologies became increasingly attractive.

PURPA thus caused a rethinking of regulation at both ends of the fuel cycle. At the generation end, the existence of NUGs indicated that the generation end of the market was competitive. Not surprisingly at the buyers' end, consumers wanted to purchase the cheaper electricity. While all consumers, of course, would like cheaper electricity, all consumers are not similarly situated. First, large consumers have more bargaining power because they buy larger quantities of electricity and they can switch fuels more easily. Second, often small users were cross-subsidized so that market prices might not be favorable to them.

New generators needed access to transmission lines owned and controlled by utilities to expand their market and to compete effectively. However, FERC did not have explicit authority under the Federal Power Act to order utilities to wheel power for IPPs and, therefore, sought to get the utilities to provide transmission access "voluntarily." In rate and merger cases, FERC approval was conditioned on the utility's agreement to open transmission under its control to all generators on a nondiscriminatory basis. These "open access" conditions initiated FERC's role in the new market.

PURPA then had two effects on regulatory theory. First, the entire electric industry was perceived as not being a natural monopoly because the generation sector was competitive and there were competitive elements for the distribution sector as well.[10] Second, questions were raised about the continued wisdom of treating the transmission segment as a natural monopoly.

THE CURRENT STATUS OF GOVERNMENT REGULATION

The Energy Policy Act of 1992

By the early 1990s, PURPA made two things clear. First, alternative power producers wanted to get into the market. Second, the wholesale market in electricity was not as robust as it could be because transmission access was not open because of two limiting factors. Non-utility generators, other than QFs, found it difficult to enter the market because they had no exemption from the requirements of the PUHCA. These generators seemed particularly desirable because they could provide new generation capacity which promised to supply electricity at a lower cost. The second constraint on market expansion was FERC's lack of authority to mandate wheeling over transmission lines. In 1992, Congress passed the Energy Policy Act (EPAct)[11] and partially eliminated both these constraints.

EPAct advanced the restructuring of the electricity industry first by authorizing firms exclusively in the business of selling electric energy at wholesale, called exempt wholesale generators (EWGs), to be exempt from PUHCA's ownership restrictions.[12] This exemption set the stage for a more competitive, and unregulated, wholesale market to materialize.

Second, EPAct authorized FERC to order utilities that owned transmission facilities to transmit wholesale power over their systems. The Act gave FERC broad authority subject to a public interest standard to order "virtually any transmission owning entity in the U.S. to wheel power for wholesale transactions at the request of a broad range of potential applicants involved in wholesale power transactions" (Lock & Stein, 1999, p. 81). However, EPAct prohibited FERC from ordering access to transmission for retail power sales, thus FERC's wheeling authority did not reach retail. To be a legitimate reseller of electricity, the entity must buy power wholesale and use transmission or distribution facilities that it owns or controls to deliver all the power to the ultimate electric consumers.[13] This requirement is designed to prohibit retail customers from gaining access to cheaper wholesale electric power by owning less than all of the distribution or transmission facilities. As general legislation, EPAct advanced the restructuring ball by promoting EWGs and by beginning to open transmission access. It remained for FERC to implement the Act.

To best understand the importance and the current status of transmission regulation, it is appropriate to understand a little physics. First, as noted in Chapter 2, electrons travel through the network virtually instantaneously – essentially at the speed of light. Second, electricity cannot be stored efficiently.

The first principle of physics is a good thing for consumers, but a headache for regulators. As long as the network is open, consumers can draw down electricity. The regulatory headache is that no one knows the point of origin of any electricity. They simply know how much is in the system and how much generators are willing to charge. Nor do they know the direction in which electricity is flowing. In other words, unlike every other product, buyers and sellers are not purchasing a specified product from each other. Instead, the industry has created the myth of the "contract path" (Koch, 2000).

The second principle of physics is good for producers and a headache for consumers and regulators. Producers have a steady demand and a need for their supply. Consumers and regulators must worry about reliability.

What all this means for transmission can be summarized in one word – bottleneck. Consumers want the product, producers want to supply it, and the owners of the transmission facilities want to make a profit by controlling access. However, because the transmission segment has both monopolistic and monopsonistic attributes, profits can become super-competitive.

The transmission segment is pivotal for the operation of the electric industry. In the simplest terms, the transmission segment moves electricity from producers to consumers. Transmission must also maintain an adequate and reliable flow of electricity through the system. Consequently, the transmission segment must have adequate *capacity*, maintain *reliability*, avoid *congestion*, and do so at *reasonable* prices with *no discrimination*. Neither monopolists, nor monopsonists think this way – they would rather just maximize profits.

FERC Initiatives

FERC used its wholesale wheeling authority under EPAct aggressively and effectively ended case-by-case wholesale transmission orders. FERC's major open-access regulation was Order No. 888[14] implementing EPAct (Norton & Richardson, 2000). By promulgating Order No. 888, FERC required all public utilities that own, control, or operate facilities used for transmitting electric energy in interstate commerce to file open-access transmission tariffs that contain minimum terms and conditions for non-discriminatory service. Order 888 also requires utilities to "functionally unbundle" their transmission service from their generation and power marketing functions, and to provide unbundled ancillary transmission services. The unbundling was intended to reduce or eliminate opportunities for self-dealing by utilities owning both generation and transmission assets. Functional unbundling means that the activities are functionally separated within the corporation; they need not be put into separate corporate entities. FERC did not require divestiture or the formation of independent transmission organizations in that order.

Order No. 888 mandated open-access transmission of wholesale electric power on a non-discriminatory basis to create a more robust competitive market in wholesale power by allowing generation access to more customers. FERC estimated that open-access transmission would save U.S. electric consumers between $3.8 and $5.4 billion a year, and encourage more technical innovation in the industry.[15] To protect the nation's power supply reliability, the order provided utilities with a fair opportunity to recover prudently incurred regulatory costs as well as the costs of making the transition to a competitive wholesale market.

Traditionally, public utilities provided electricity and the transmission of that electricity as a bundled product at a single price. Order 888 requires that electricity and transmission be unbundled and sold as separate products as a way to achieve non-discriminatory open-access transmission. Specifically, utilities must file separate tariffs with separate rates, terms, and conditions for wholesale generation service, transmission service, and any ancillary services. Ancillary services range from actions taken to effect the transmission, such as scheduling and dispatching, to services that are necessary to maintain the integrity of the transmission system during a transaction. To ensure that a utility does not favor itself with its own transmission facilities, the order requires that a utility must take transmission service and ancillary services for all of its new wholesale sales and purchases of electricity under the same tariff that applies to outside users of its transmission.

Order No. 889 established an electronic information system to aid the competitiveness of the wholesale market made possible by open access to transmission. This system, called OASIS (open access same-time information system), provides existing and potential transmission users the same access to transmission information that the transmission owner enjoys. Order No. 889 also requires public utilities to comply with standards of conduct intended to preclude anticompetitive behavior by transmission owners, such as favoring affiliated generators or power marketers with transmission services.

At the wholesale level, Orders 888 and 889 had a dramatic impact on the industry. Since their inception in 1996, the industry has experienced significant changes including the development of retail competition in the states; the divestiture of generating units by traditional utilities; an increase in energy company mergers; a notable increase in the number of power marketers and independent generators; and the establishment of independent system operators to manage transmission.[16] Those orders, however, did not address the entire industry. Specifically, retail wheeling was untouched. So too, was the appropriate form for a transmission facility.

Orders 888 and 889 opened the access door and established the key parameter – non-discriminatory rates. The difficult question was how to structure the proper relationship between the transmission and generation portions of a utility's business. How far should FERC go in either ordering divestiture or proposing other structural rules? Clearly, some sort of regional transmission organization (RTO) was needed but the exact form it should take was and is unsettled. RTOs are entities that are independent of the owners of generation facilities, and manage the transmission systems either as owners or as operators. FERC required utilities to "functionally unbundle" the transmission function of the utility from its generation and power marketing functions rather than mandate divestiture.

FERC promulgated standards of conduct to reinforce its principle of separation of competitive and monopoly functions. Under these standards, a utility must take transmission services under the same tariff of general applicability as do others; state separate rates for wholesale generation, transmission, and ancillary services; and rely on the same electronic information network that its transmission customers rely on to obtain information about its transmission system when buying or selling power. FERC did not require utilities to develop independent system operators in Orders 888 and 889, but FERC strongly encouraged utilities and power pools to form them voluntarily. Later FERC did move in this direction with Order No. 2000 discussed below.

Retail Competition and the States

As of December, 2000, only seven states have no active electricity restructuring activities ongoing.[17] All of the other states have either passed restructuring legislation, issued comprehensive regulatory orders, commenced commission or legislative investigations, or have legislation or orders pending.[18] Given recent events in California, however, we can expect caution as explained in more detail below. California's retail market has been open to competition since 1997 and all consumers are scheduled to participate by 2003. Connecticut's market opened in 1998, as did New Hampshire's. Many states are phasing in competition. For example, Pennsylvania has opened one-third of the peak load in each customer class to competition; Arizona has opened 20% of its IOUs' load to competition; and Montana allows competition for the retail load of large customers (greater than one megawatt). Yet the states' experiences have been uneven.

For electric restructuring, the summer of 2000 will long live in the memory of the industry and regulators as a time for testing the bold California experiment to bring deregulation to the retail level.

While a megawatt of electricity generally sells for approximately $20 to $25, Californians saw price spikes as high as $1400 per megawatt hour while in some areas of the country spot prices were reported at nearly $10,000.[19] As a result of the power crunch, consumers experienced a doubling of electricity bills, rolling blackouts in northern California, and several Stage 1 and Stage 2 power alerts. Various regulatory reforms, both at the state and federal level, are required to address this situation (Edison Electric Institute, 2000).[20]

Clearly such an experience has shaken the faith in the deregulation project and analysts have sought various reasons for the price spikes including structural problems with the California deregulatory scheme; limitations on utilities' ability to contract with end users; and, restrictions on where market participants can buy and sell electricity. In addition, because of the uncertainty, investment in generation has declined and there has been an unexpected high growth in demand, thus contributing to the shortage. At the same time, natural gas prices have increased, reserve margins have declined, and there has been limited construction of transmission facilities (Edison Electric Institute, 2000). Because of the California experience, federal and state regulators have sought to set new trading rules in the California market, impose price caps on the cost of electricity to consumers, and to otherwise loosen the market while protecting consumers from price shocks while also stabilizing the investment climate.[21] We may very well find it to be the case that the electric spikes of the summer of 2000 are limited to California. However, nationally, problems with under-investment in generation and transmission, as well as declining reserve margins, indicate that in those areas of the country that do not have a surplus of electricity, that price spikes are not unlikely to occur until adequate capacity comes on line.

Pennsylvania has developed an electricity restructuring plan that is more moderate than California's. The heart of the plan is a competitive transition charge through which utilities are allowed to recover their stranded costs (see Chapter 8) and charge customers a fee for the period it takes them to recoup that investment. In return, utilities have agreed to freeze rates in order to protect consumers. After the stranded costs are incurred, the rate freeze is lifted and market rules will operate. The hope, of course, is that new generation will be developed as demand increases.

Pennsylvania has high hopes for their electricity restructuring including:

- $1.9 billion increase in gross state product
- Employment increase of 36,400 full and part-time jobs
- Personal income increase by $1.4 billion
- Price index decrease by 0.47%
- Population increase by 51,400 persons as a result of a more robust economy. (Pennsylvania Department of Revenue, 2000).

Pennsylvania is also an active participant in the Pennsylvania-New Jersey-Maryland Interconnection (PJM) which operates as an independent system operator and power exchange, assuming control of transmission systems within its borders. The PJM is the exact type of RTO that FERC envisioned. Over the last year PJM has developed issues that deserve attention, such as high prices and volatility, thin market, poor liquidity, and high emissions of hydrocarbons (Hanger, 2000).

As the electric industry moves from one regulatory regime to another, whether in wholesale or retail, transition costs will be incurred. New forms of accounting and doing business and associated administrative costs are involved. However, the most significant transition costs involved past investments in previous regulatory requirements also known as stranded costs. To date, most states have allowed their utilities the opportunity to collect their stranded costs. Typically, stranded costs are recovered through a temporary surcharge levied on the distribution of kilowatt hours of electricity to all consumers in the jurisdiction. A few states allow some customers to bypass this surcharge if they generate their own electricity. Several states have conditioned stranded cost recovery on divestiture of some or all of the utility's generation.

One of the primary political forces behind the passage of legislation in the states to open electricity to retail competition is the belief that it will result in lower electric rates. Some states are reluctant to rely on a competitive market to achieve this and have enacted programs and temporary regulatory controls designed to assure it such as mandating a rate decrease for a period of time. Price caps, however, can have the negative effect of reducing supply when market prices exceed the price caps and price caps discourage investment.

To finance the transition, some states, such as California, Connecticut and Illinois have made state bonds available to the incumbent utilities owning generation assets to allow them to refinance at a lower interest rate. The states require this cost savings to be passed on to the utilities' traditional retail customers in the form of a rate decrease. Initially in California, the rate decrease had the effect of lowering the price for retail electricity for residential customers below the point where new entrants can effectively compete for a share of the market. Then the market changed as demand grew and generation could not meet demand. In other states, the incumbent utilities have been prohibited form recovering any stranded costs if to do so would require them to raise their retail electric rates. At least one state has authorized its political subdivisions to aggregate load, in competition with private load aggregators, for purposes of contracting with competitive generators.

About half of the states that have introduced retail electric competition have set up programs to enable them to continue to have jurisdiction over the externalities associated with the generation and distribution of electricity. Most of these states have imposed a surcharge on the distribution of electricity, usually called a competition transition charge to fund programs designed to promote electricity efficiency, demand side management programs, research and development of renewable fuels, environmental improvement, universal electricity service, low income assistance, and utility employee health, retirement, and retraining programs. Some states have a renewable resource portfolio requirement that must be met by electricity providers seeking to be licensed to do business in their jurisdictions. At least one state has required all power marketers doing business in its jurisdiction to follow a standard format for all their disclosures, explanations, and sales information in order to enable consumers to better compare prices and offerings. With the state initiatives to make the retail end competitive, access is the last link in a much more competitive electricity environment. The tough question, and a question that is unanswered as of yet, is how to open transmission access to competition.

FERC ORDER 2000[22] *– Regional Transmission Organizations*

As a result of information learned from PURPA by regulators and the market, natural monopoly attention was drawn to transmission. Also, because the electricity industry was dually regulated, restructuring had to proceed at both federal and state levels.

While a regulatory bright line could be drawn between interstate wholesale sales of electricity and retail sales, that bright line is one of political convenience only, not physical reality. Historically, the federal government limited its reach to interstate wholesale sales and left retail regulation to the states. Regulatory restructuring has continued to follow this neat division between state and federal regulation. This continued allegiance to dual regulation may make political sense. It does not make good economic sense.

The restructuring movement prefers competition to heavier-handed price controls believing that the market can generate lower prices, increase consumer choice, and produce reliably. However, the restructuring movement also recognizes that transmission poses the potential for the abuse of market power. Still, attention to the transmission segment is necessary and the form of organization must be addressed.

To further industry restructuring, FERC proposed and adopted a rule designed to formalize the formation of independent transmission organizations under the name Regional Transmission Organizations (RTOs). Even with the advances made by Orders 888 and 889, FERC found that the market was still insufficiently competitive because of engineering and economic inefficiencies and because of continued opportunities for undue discrimination.

Regarding engineering and economic inefficiencies, FERC found that:

(1) the reliability of the bulk power system was being stressed;
(2) there were increasing difficulties in computing transmission capacity;
(3) regional coordination was desirable for congestion management;
(4) there was increased uncertainty with transmission planning and expansion; and
(5) pancaked rates hindered market development.[23]

Regarding undue discrimination, FERC was concerned both with self-dealing and the appearance of self-dealing[24] because both retarded the development of competitive markets. Overt self-dealing occurs when a utility owning transmission and generation charges itself a transmission charge lower than that charged to other customers, giving them a competitive edge. The appearance of self-dealing raises the transaction costs of doing business because the market is not seen as reliable, thus reducing efficiency gains from competition.

The restructuring of the electric industry has been underway for over two decades even though the basic idea is simple. The old system has run its course; the infrastructure has been developed; there is competition in generation; and, consumers want cheaper electricity. All they need is access. Unfortunately, while transmission is an essential facility, historically it has not had common carrier status.[25] Transmission owners have not had to serve all customers. The challenge is to move from a privately owned and controlled transmission system that was integrated with generation to one that is more open and non-discriminatory. The key impediment is that for the most part the transmission segment is privately owned and private owners have a fiduciary duty to their shareholders to maximize value. In other words, private owners will raise prices to what the market can bear. Given the short-run relative price inelasticity of electricity, prices can have a severe impact on consumers. There is little incentive to give up either ownership or operation. The consensus is that some form of independent operation is necessary because the transmission segment must attain competitiveness.

To this point, interregional coordination has proceeded on a voluntary basis. Historically, the transmission network developed as one might expect. At first there was a direct link between Edison's Pearl Street generator and its consumers at low voltage direct current. Alternating current allowed for longer distance transmission and encouraged consolidation among generators and then voluntary interconnections occurred. The first major power pool was the Pennsylvania, New Jersey, Maryland Interconnection (PJM) in order to balance load, realize operating economies, save capital investment and enhance system reliability (Lock & Stein, 1996). These interconnections have extended throughout the country to form three power pools east and west of the Rocky Mountains and in Texas. These three pools together with the Hydro-Quebec System form the North American Electric Reliability Council (NERC), another voluntary organization, to coordinate operations, planning, and transmission.

Given the move to a more competitive environment, FERC found that the voluntary coordination that previously existed was no longer effective because the volunteer groups were "not vested with the broad decision-making authority needed to address larger issues that affect an entire region, including managing congestion, planning and investing in new transmission facilities, pancaking transmission access charges, the absence of secondary markets in transmission services, and the possible disincentives created by the level and structure of transmission rates."[26]

While policymakers might readily agree on the necessary goals for the competitive performance of the transmission segment, there is little consensus on the means of getting there. Into this fray steps FERC with Order 2000 which set the parameters for establishing RTOs. Proposed in June, 1999, the final rules were issued in December, 1999 and the industry is in the process of tea leaf reading relative to what form an RTO can and should take. Order 2000 describes two fundamental approaches to satisfying the order. Those approaches include the non-profit independent system operator (ISO) and the for-profit independent transmission company (Transco). While hybrids are possible, questions about their legality arise. The ironic beauty of a choice between an ISO and a Transco as a qualifying RTO is that it reproduces the debate between government regulation and market control. Although both forms of organization would have independent boards, the ISO is a non-profit organization committed to non-discriminatory service and the Transco is driven by profit. Both forms present complications and there are arguments pro and con as will be described below.

Is Transmission a Natural Monopoly?

Regardless of the natural monopoly skeptics, electric utilities were regulated under the political-economic concept of natural monopoly with the not unreasonable belief that one utility in a given area could provide cheaper service than multiple providers. At the end of the twentieth century, policymakers have witnessed the erosion of the natural monopoly idea as the electricity infrastructure was built and as the traditional rate formula began to have perverse economic effects. As a consequence, industry and regulators noted competition at the generation end and are now focusing on transmission. The question is fairly raised whether the transmission segment is a natural monopoly or whether it is subject to competitive forces. The simple answer is that for the foreseeable future transmission is likely to remain a natural monopoly.

Certainly, transmission looks like a typical bottleneck in a network industry. But there are two complementary ways to test whether it functions as a natural monopoly. First, does the transmission firm exercise market power? In other words, can it set super-competitive prices? Second, is the transmission market competitive or contestable?

Recently, critics have argued that transmission is not a natural monopoly because these firms do not exercise market power and are increasingly subject to competition (Awerbach, Hyman & Vesey, 1999). Regarding market power the authors argue that the transmission line owner does not necessarily have the monopoly power "to charge whatever it wants."

Maybe. But this argument over-describes monopoly power and under assesses the role of the price of the transmission charge. First, monopoly power is not "whatever" anyone wants to charge. Instead, and the literature is clear, it is a super-competitive price. Monopoly power increases prices, reduces output, and constitutes a deadweight loss in consumer surplus (Shapiro & Tomain, 1998; see also Chapter 2). Clearly a firm can set a price significantly higher than a competitive price and lower than "whatever" they might like and still be exercising market power. Also, the cost of transmission represents roughly 7% of a utility bill (Awerbach et al., 1999, p. 2). Consequently, at the margin it may very well be the case that the transmission rate can be a deal breaker. But this is not a frequent occurrence. In this regard, the transmission charge functions much like a real estate broker's commission. In some instances, that commission is bargained down or shared, but rarely.

Natural monopoly opponents also argue that the transmission market itself is competitive or contestable due to new technologies, which would enable generators who are dissatisfied with transmission charges to move closer to their end users through "distributed generation" (as noted in the Introduction to this chapter). Or end users themselves would become self-generators. Thus, they argue, the transmission market is contestable. There are two responses to this argument. First, such moves simply have not happened in significant numbers because the transaction costs are high. Second, contestable market theory has proven to be less powerful than promised particularly in the industry in which it started, the airline industry. (Compare Bailey & Baumol, 1984 with Havel, 1997; Carstensen, 1989.) The general consensus is that for now and for the foreseeable future, transmission is a bottleneck and operates as a natural monopoly, a position acknowledged even by some of natural monopoly critics (Awerbach et al., 1999, p. 19).

Organizational Form: ISO v. Transco

FERC Order 2000 establishes the parameters for any RTO which may take the form of the non-profit ISO or the for-profit Transco. The rule requires transmission owning utilities to file a RTO proposal with FERC by October 15, 2000 or file an explanation as to why they cannot. The order further requires that the RTO must commence operations by December 15, 2001 (Hyman, 2000).

FERC sets four minimum standards for any RTO. An RTO must have:

(1) Independence.
(2) Scope and Regional Configuration.
(3) Operational Authority.
(4) Short-Term Reliability.

The order also sets out the minimum functions that an RTO must perform including:

(1) Tariff administration and design.
(2) Congestion management.
(3) OASIS participation.
(4) Market monitoring.
(5) Planning and expansion.
(6) Interregional coordination.

Each of these characteristics and functions is explained in great detail in the order. For our purposes, the listing is sufficient to raise the question about the form of organization that the RTO should take. To date, Orders 2000 and 2000-A have been interpreted that the RTO can be an ISO or a Transco. There is a degree of the surreal surrounding choosing between ISOs and Transcos. First, FERC has authorized only a few ISOs and has denied at least one Transco.

Thus, the track record is limited to ISOs. Second, the arguments in favor and against each form are simply arguments with little or no data and limited rhetorical power. Third, FERC Order 2000 explicitly says that no simple form is preferred and, complicating matters a bit, the order has been interpreted by commentators as "preferring" each method over the other.[27]

ISO

The central force behind the ISO is that it is a non-profit operator of the transmission system. As such, the ISO owns no facilities. Rather, it operates transmission facilities that are made available to it by generating units. The ISO exists to serve the public interest in having available for consumers reasonably priced, reliable electricity.

The situation of a non-profit as a non-owner operator of transmission units presents certain complications. The first complication is its relationship with the generators. The ISO is to be "independent" of a generator, specifically to avoid self-dealing. Consequently, its Board of Directors must have no conflicts of interest with the generators. How far can this go? At what point does an independent board have adequate understanding of the industry and sufficient incentive relative to the generators such that it can exercise influence over the generators or the owners of the transmission company to invest in maintenance and expansion of those facilities?

These questions present the hardest problem for the ISO. The Board of Directors of the ISO will have a fiduciary duty running either to the state or to the federal government, whoever gives the ISO their charter. Consequently, they have some motivation to act independently and they have some motivation to keep the ISO in business, which is to say to keep electricity running through the system. Although at least two commentators argue that FERC's principles for the ISO apply equally to Transcos, most commentators make assertions over which form is the superior form of organization (Angle & Cannon, 1998). Not surprisingly, most industry arguments are made in favor of the for-profit Transco. The arguments against the ISO generally focus on insufficient incentives. The insufficient incentives come from hypotheses about profit motivation. Critics argue, for example, that while an ISO may have an incentive to maintain the short-term reliability of the system, that its distance from ownership of generation gives it little incentive or control over long-term reliability. Following this analysis, critics argue that the ISO has little ability or incentive to make capital investments in plant, innovate through the use of new technologies, or engage in cost-setting for management efficiencies (Awerbach et al., 1999; Angle & Cannon, 1998; Michaels, 1999).

Transco

To some small extent, the arguments critical of ISOs are the mirror image of the arguments in favor of Transcos. Again, the central variable for the Transco is that it is a for-profit company which both owns and operates transmission assets. Its for-profit motivation is designed to maximize the value of the company and to return income and value to shareholders. Shareholders, of course, elect the Board of Directors and, presumably, conflict of interest rules will prevent unfair advantages going to generators. Similarly, the incentives for the Transco mirror the disincentives for the ISO. Because the Transco is profit-motivated, it must necessarily invest in plant maintenance and innovation. It must also maintain short-term and long-term reliability. The arguments in favor of the Transco, given its profit motivation, however, should not be taken too far. It is also the case that a profit-driven Transco may pay more attention to short-term gains; may cut costs in a way that affects reliability; and, may price discriminate where it is economically wise to do so.

At a fairly deep level, then, the non-profit nature of the ISO presents problems as does the for-profit nature of the Transco. There are, however, alternatives available. One alternative is to engage in a transitional movement starting with an ISO moving to the Transco. The other alternative is to create an ISO or a Transco and regulate the rates with performance-based ratemaking which allows a sharing of profits between ratepayers and shareholders (Awerbach et al., 1999, Ch. 6; Hebert, 1998; Angle & Cannon, 1998, pp. 249–263).

The difficult question for state and federal regulators and for industry actors is which form of RTO to choose. Not surprisingly, industry actors form Transcos. Regardless of form, however, Transcos and ISOs must achieve five goals. Every RTO must have sufficient capacity, provide reliable service, manage congestion, not discriminate, and offer reasonable prices. The chart below compares ISO and Transcos by first listing their characteristics and then listing the incentives driving each form of organization. To be sure, at this early date, the checkmarks in each column are guesses. The guesses are based upon arguments made in the literature. It may very well be the case that either form performs well or poorly because of the strange nature of the organization.

One can argue vociferously, as many have, that the Transco be better situated to build transmission lines because of its for-profit motive. It is not obviously the case that Trancsco has sufficient assets or economic leverage to do so. Similarly, while one might argue that the ISO should be in the position to offer a reliable service at reasonable prices because its stated mission under government charter, it is equally not clear that it has the economic leverage to force generators to sell to it in sufficient quantities to keep prices low as well as reliable.

We may very well have worked ourselves into a situation in this country in which there is a significant lag between the construction of new generation and transmission and the full and reliable operation of an RTO. This lag is due in part to the problem of stranded costs. Stranded costs, privately owned utilities argue, must be recouped before they can participate as full market actors largely because they are saddled with costs as incumbents with which new entrants are not burdened. This argument means that unless stranded costs are incurred, the playing field is leveled between incumbents and new entrants, there will be a lag between investment in new generation and construction of new transmission. The experience in California in 2000 demonstrates that this problem can become dramatic as demand surges ahead of supply and as price spikes ensue. Consequently, caution must be used when comparing ISOs to Transcos this early on in the restructuring of the electric industry (Koch, 2000).

ISO v. Transco		
CHARACTERISTICS	ISO	Transco
	non-profit non-owner operator independent "stakeholder" board fiduciary duty to charter	for-profit owner operator independent "shareholder" board fiduciary duty to shareholder
INCENTIVES		
Short-term reliability	✓	
Long-term reliability		✓
Capital investment		✓
Innovation		✓
Planning		✓
Reasonable prices	✓	
Maintenance		✓

Recapitulating arguments in the literature, it would seem that the ISO may have an edge on short-term reliability given the mandate of its charter and the ISO may have more of an incentive to keep prices reasonable. Likewise, because of its for-profit status, the Transco, assuming that it has some economic leverage over investments may promise long-term reliability and innovation and planning as well as have an incentive to maintain the system as would anyone owning plant and equipment, unlike the ISO.

Nevertheless, two points should be emphasized regarding the corporate form of the transmission company. First, it is extremely unlikely that this part of the industry will become competitive or even contestable within the short or mid-terms. Neither new technologies nor distributed generation threaten the monopoly position of electric transmission. Second, the corporate forms alone are largely irrelevant to achieving the goals of reliability, reasonable pricing, congestion management, and non-discrimination. Rules and incentives can be fashioned to achieve each of these goals. In short, the real fight is political and the fight is on two fronts.

The first front involves federalism. What is the politically appropriate sharing of power between the federal and state governments? Does the old "bright line" hold? Even though we are in an era of devolution, it is odd that state PUCs should exercise controlling authority over transmission when regional grids are necessary. Unfortunately, FERC Order 2000 does not mandate RTOs and has no real enforcement teeth. The allocation of political authority is an open issue.

The second political front involves corporate form and is between industry and regulators as they negotiate both the acceptable corporate form for the Transco and the governing rules. Central to either choice of governance form is economic leverage. Which form has sufficient economic leverage to encourage investment, innovation, and maintenance in facilities? Also, which form can insure capacity and "regulate" prices?

CONCLUSION

Over the last century, government regulation of the electricity industry has fulfilled its mission of expanding its infrastructure. Now competition promises benefits in terms of products and prices, services, and innovation. The next regulatory generation will be charged with managing the transition and monitoring the newly emerging markets (Tomain, 2000).

The movement to restructure the electric industry was driven by a desire to allow consumers to reach cheaper electricity; reduce the high cost of regulation; eliminate or reduce heavy-handed price setting regulations; increase economic efficiency; and, promote competitive markets. There is no question that these reforms are large and dramatic. Their success can be evaluated by two standards both of which bear on efficiency. First, is the market more competitive? Second, are the benefits of competition greater than the transaction costs of restructuring? The regulatory apparatus needed to monitor the competitiveness of electricity markets to guard against the concentration of market power are formidable and may be more costly than the current regulation. From an economic standpoint, efficiency and transaction costs are sufficient measures. There are, however, distributional issues. The question is fairly raised – who are the winners and losers in the restructuring? More specifically, while it appears that large consumers should see lower electricity bills, it is not clear that small consumers will as well. Indeed, many issues remain to be addressed during this transitional period.

During this immediate period there are three large remaining regulatory issues that must be resolved for the electric industry in general. The first is determining how stranded costs are valued and how they are to be paid. Though most policy makers have acknowledged the need to compensate stranded costs, there are a growing number of critics of the idea who note among other objections that there is little constitutional support for the claim (see Chapter 8). Moreover, there is considerable disagreement over the valuations of stranded investments. The controversy over nuclear plant cancellations addressed exactly this issue with no clear guidance as to how courts and regulators should assess whether compensation is due (Hovenkamp, 1984, p. 808).[28] Stranded costs present the same difficulty involving estimates ranging from a low of $10 to $20 billion to a high of $500 billion.[29] The range of estimates indicates part of the problem. Utilities, naturally, want to identify as many recoverable stranded costs as possible to protect investors. Regulators are less inclined to do so in order to protect consumers. Assuming that assets can be properly attributed, then a valuation must be assessed and valuation methodology, as we have learned from trying to evaluate rate base, is not scientifically precise. There is simply no consensus on which costs should be recovered or which valuation methodology should be used. These choices are fundamentally political rather than economic.

Again assuming that an amount of stranded costs can be established: who pays? Should exiting customers pay through an exit fee? Should current customers pay through a surcharge? Should bondholders pay through securitization? Should shareholders absorb some losses? Legislatures and regulators have and will continue to assess each strategy.

The resolution of the stranded costs issue implicates another problem brought about by increased competition. As regulated firms are invited (or forced) to compete, they will be competing with new entrants. New entrants exist because entry costs are low enough to enter a market and they believe that they can price their product below the price of the incumbent. In other words, new entrants believe they have a competitive advantage and incumbents believe they have a competitive disadvantage because of regulatory burdens. The transition to a more competitive environment must at least attempt to level the playing field for incumbents and new entrants alike. Competition requires multiple producers, but incumbent producers should not be disadvantaged.[30]

The third large issue involves moving competition from the wholesale to the retail levels and this move entails opening access so that consumer choice for electricity is maximized. The rub here is that private transportation network owners are not anxious to give up their competitive (monopolistic) advantage and government is not likely to nationalize (Economides 2000). The trick is to design a form of transportation that opens access; compensates owners fairly; and, does not allow operators to discriminate among providers, especially between affiliated and non-affiliated providers. This trick will only be solved once the two political problems of federalism and corporate form are adequately addressed.

Regulators will be called upon to monitor and manage the restructured electricity market. Staffs will monitor access to and operation of the transmission networks, monitor various markets for signs of competition or concentration, and will monitor markets for service quality, price, and reliability. More ambitiously, staff may also monitor futures markets and auctions as an adjunct of service issues. Regulatory staffs could well grow larger with an attendant increase in costs. They will also require more sophisticated economic expertise so much so that deregulation, more accurately, restructuring may bring about full employment for economists. Too bad for we lawyers. The curious paradox of a market-based regulatory reform is that we may end up with more rather than less regulation.

The ideas driving the restructuring of the electric industry include allowing consumers to reach cheaper electricity; reducing the high cost of regulation; reducing or elimination of heavy-handed price setting; and increasing economic efficiency. To evaluate the success of restructuring, there are two consequences of regulatory reform: Industry restructuring may not be efficient and the transaction costs may be significant. Further, the regulatory apparatus needed to monitor the competitiveness or concentration of the market may be more costly than the current regulation.

While it is too early for answers, it is not too early to formulate interesting questions: Is the industry restructuring efficient? What does the regulatory apparatus look like and what does it cost?

NOTES

1. *Munn v. Illinois*, 94 U.S. 113 (1876). In *Munn*, the Illinois state legislature set grain elevator prices. The United States Supreme Court upheld the statute on the basis that the regulation of "virtual" or natural monopolies of goods, affected with the public interest, was constitutional.

2. The evidence for either theory is mixed with respect to government regulation generally. So for example, the Telecommunications Act of 1996, (47 U.S.C. §151 et seq.), which was enacted purportedly in the public interest, but in reality is a classic set of private industry interest group deals. A good example of regulation for the benefit of a private interest group is trucking regulation and a counter-example of public interest group regulation is airline deregulation and the list goes on.

3. Essentially the capture thesis argues that the regulatory process becomes captured by the industries it seeks to regulate (Mueller, 1989; Stigler, 1971; Posner, 1974; Priest, 1993).

4. See Energy Law Group, *Energy Law and Policy for the 21st Century* (2000, Ch. 12).

5. President's Address to the Nation, Pub. Papers 656 (April 11, 1977).

6. The National Energy Act consists of five pieces of major legislation: the National Energy Conservation Policy Act, Pub. L. No. 95–619, 29 Stat. 3206 (codified as amended in scattered sections of 12, 15, 26, 31, and 42 U.S.C. (1982)); the Powerplant and Industrial Fuel Use Act of 1978, Pub. L. No. 95–620, 92 Stat. 3289 (codified as amended in scattered sections of 15 and 42 U.S.C. (1982)); the Natural Gas Policy Act of 1978, Pub. L. No. 95–621, 92 Stat. 3350 (codified at 15 U.S.C. §§ 3301–3432 & 42 U.S.C. § 7255 (1982)); the Public Utilities Regulatory Policies Act of 1978, Pub. L. No. 95–617, 92 Stat. 3117 (codified as amended in scattered sections of 15, 16, 26, 42, and 43 U.S.C. (1982)); and, the Energy Tax Act of 1978, Pub. L. No. 95–618, 92 Stat. 3174 (codified as amended in scattered sections of 26 and 42 U.S.C. (1982)).

7. The Energy Security Act, Pub. L. No. 96–294, 94 Stat. 611 (1980), also consists of several pieces of legislation including: the Defense Production Act Amendments of 1980, 94 Stat. 617 (codified in 50 U.S.C. §§ 2061–2166 (1982)); the United States Synthetic Fuels Corporation Act of 1980, Pub. L. No. 96–294, 94 Stat. 633 (codified as amended in scattered sections of 42 U.S.C. (1982)); the Biomass Energy and Alcohol Fuels Act of 1980, Pub. L. No. 96–294, 94 Stat. 683 (codified as amended in scattered sections of 7, 15, 16, and 42 U.S.C. (1982)); the Renewable Energy Resources Act of 1980, Pub. L. No. 96–294, 94 Stat. 715 (codified as amended in scattered sections of 16 and 42 U.S. (1982)); the Solar Energy and Energy Conservation Act of 1980, Pub. L. No. 96–294, 94 Stat. 719 (codified as amended in scattered sections of 12 and 42 U.S.C. (1982)); the Geothermal Energy Act of 1980, Pub. L. No. 96–294, 94 Stat. 763 (codified in scattered sections of 16 U.S.C. (1982)); and the Acid Precipitation Act of 1980, Pub. L. NO. 96–294, 94 Stat. 770 (codified in 42 U.S.C. §§ 8901–8905, 8911–8912 (1982)).

8. 16 U.S.C. § 796 (1988).

9. "Wheeling: The delivery of electric power generated by one utility over the transmission lines of a second utility to a purchaser located in the territory served by the second utility (or a third utility) (Muchow & Mogel, 2001, p. GL-154).

10. Specifically, small distribution systems called "distributed generation," placed closer to end user has the potential of making distribution and transmission competitive. See, for example, Stavros, R. (1999). Distributed Generation: Last Big Battle for State Regulators? *Public Utilities Fornightly*, (October 15).

11. Pub. L. No. 102–486, 100 Stat. 2776 (1992).

12. 15 U.S.C. § 79z-5a (1994).

13. Section 212 of the Federal Power Act, 16 U.S.C. § 824k(h) (1994).

14. Federal Energy Regulatory Commission (FERC) Final Rule Promoting Wholesale Competition Through Open Access Non-Discriminatory Transmission Services by Public Utilities, Order. No. 888, 61 Fed. Reg. 21,540, 21,544 (1996) (codified at 18 C.F.R. pts. 35 and 385) [hereinafter FERC Order No. 888].

15. Preamble to FERC Order No. 888, *id.* at ¶ 31,652.

16. 65 Fed. Reg. 810, 813–15 (January 6, 2000).

17. Idaho, South Dakota, Nebraska, Kansas, Tennessee, Alabama, and Georgia.

18. http://www-eia.doe.gov/cneaf/electricity/chg_str/regmap.html (site visited December 20, 2000).

19. Laura M. Holson, Government Acts to Calm California's Energy Market. *New York Times*, December 16, 2000; Neela Banerjee, A Dwindling Faith in Deregulation. *New York Times*, September 15, 2000; Gregory Palast, States Deregulate Energy at their Peril. *New York Times*, August 25, 2000.

20. For further discussion of the California case, see Chapter 10.

21. Federal Energy Regulatory Commission, Market Border Proposing Remedies for California Wholesale Electrics (November 1, 2000); Federal Energy Regulatory Commission, Order Directing Remedies for California Wholesale Electric Markets, 93 F.E. R. C. ¶ 61, 294 (December 15, 2000).

22. See note 22 above; see also Order No. 2000-A (February 25, 2000), 18 CFR Part 35 (2000).

23. Transmission rates are "pancaked" when an access charge is made for transmission in every jurisdiction the transmission crosses.

24. 65 Fed. Reg. 817-18 (January 6, 2000).

25. *Common carrier* is defined as the situation in which the government has the authority to order a firm to submit to entry and exit regulation. In other words, common carriers must serve all customers without price discrimination. See Daniel L. Brenner (1992).

26. Regional Transmission Organization 1999 FERC Lexis 2692 at p. 34 (December 20, 1999).

27. Compare Lambert, J. D. (2000). *Order 200: A Subtle But Clear Preference for ISOs*, 138 *Public Utilities Fornightly*, *36*(March 1) with Hebert, C. L. Jr., & Rokach, J. Z. (2000). Order 2000: Exposing Myths on What FERC Really Wants. *Public Utilities Fornightly*, (March 1).

28. See also *Duquesne Light Co. v. Barasch*, 488 U.S. 299 (1989); *see also* Susan Rose-Ackerman and Jim Rossi, *Disentangling Deregulatory Takings* 34–35 (2000) ("... United States takings jurisprudence has not found that regulatory actions in infrastructure industries demand compensation.") (Draft manuscript on file with author). Tomain (1997); Pierce (1984).

29. See U.S. Department of Energy, at Ch. 8; www.eia.doe.gov/cneaf/electricity/chg-str/chapter8.html

30. *AT&T Corp. v. Iowa Utilities*, 525 U.S. 366 (1999); also, Babineau, A. S., Taylor, W. E., & Weissman, M. M. (1999). The Baby and the Bathwater: What the Supreme Court Thinks About Handicapping the Incumbent to Level the Field for New Players. *Public Utilities Fornightly*, (November 15).

REFERENCES

Angle, S., & Cannon, G. (1998). Independent Transmission Companies: The For-Profit Alternative in Competitive Electric Markets. *Energy Law Journal, 19*, 229, 239–240.

Awerbuch, S., Hyman, L., & Vesey, A. (1999). *Unlocking the Benefits of Restructuring: A Blueprint for Transmission* (pp. 11–55). Vienna, VA: Public Utilities Reports.

Babineau, A., Taylor, W., & Weissman, M. (1999). The Baby and the Bathwater: What the Supreme Court Thinks About Handicapping the Incumbent to Level the Field for New Players. *Public Utilities Fortnightly*, (November 15), p. 48.

Bailey, E., & Baumol, W. (1984). Deregulation and the Theory of Contestable Markets. *Yale Journal on Regulation, 1*, 111–137.

Berg, S., & Tschirhart, J. (1988). *Natural Monopoly Regulation: Principles and Practice*. New York: Cambridge University Press.

Bernstein, M. (1955). *Regulating Business By Independent Commission*. Princeton, NJ: Princeton University Press.

Brenner, D. (1992). *Law and Regulation of Common Carriers in the Communications Industry*. Boulder: Westview Press.

Carstensen, P. (1989). Evaluating 'Deregulation' of Commercial Air Travel: False Dichotomization, Untenable Theories and Unimplemented Premises. *Washington and Lee Law Review, 46*, 109–150.

Clark, J. (1987). *Energy and the Federal Government: Fossil Fuel Policies, 1900–1946*. Urbana: University of Illinois Press

Croley, S. (1998). Theories of Regulation: Incorporating the Administrative Process. *Columbia Law Review, 98*, 1–86.

Economides, N. (2000). *The Telecommunications Act of 1996 and Its Impact* (http://papers.ssrn.com/paper.tap?abstract_id=81289).

Edison Electric Institute (2000). *The Electric Summer: Symptoms – Options – Solutions.*

The Energy Law Group (2000). *Energy Law and Policy for the 21st Century*. Denver: Rocky Mountain Mineral Law Foundation.

Fukuyama, F. (1992). *The End of History and the Last Man*. New York: Free Press.

Goldin, C., & Libecap, G. (1994). *The Regulated Economy: A Historical Approach to Political Economy*. Chicago: University of Chicago Press.

Havel, B. (1997). *In Search of Open Skies: Law and Policy for a New Era of International Aviation.* The Hague: Kluwer Law International.

Hebert, C., & Rokach, J. (2000). Order 2000: Exposing Myths on What FERC Really Wants. *Public Utilities Fortnightly*, (March 1), 42.

Hirsh, R. (1989). *Technology and Transformation in the American Electric Utility Industry*. Cambridge: Cambridge University Press.

Hirsh, R. (1999). *Power Loss: The Origins of Deregulation and Restructuring in the American Electric Utility System*. Cambridge, MA: MIT Press.

Hovenkamp, H. (1991). *Enterprise and American Law 1836–1937*. Cambridge, MA: Harvard University Press.

Hovenkamp, H. (1984). Technology, Politics, and Regulated Monopoly: An American Historical Perspective. *Texas Law Review, 62*, 1263–1312.

Hyman, L. (1997). *America's Electric Utilities: Past, Present and Future* (6th ed.). Arlington, VA: Public Utilities Reports.

Kearney, J., & Merrill, T. (1998). The Great Transformation of Regulated Industries Law. *Columbia Law Review, 98*, 1323–1409.

Koch, C. (2000). Control and Governance of Transmission Organizations in the Restructured Electricity Industry. *Florida State University Law Review, 27*, 569–613.

Lambert, J. (2000). Order 200: A Subtle But Clear Preference for ISOs. *Public Utilities Fortnightly*, (March 1), 36.

Lindblom, C. (1977). *Politics and Markets: The World's Political Economic Systems*. New York: Basic Books.

Lock, R., & Stein, M. (1996). Electricity Transmission. In: D. Muchow & W. Mogul (Eds), *Energy Law and Transactions* (§ 81.01). New York: M. Bender.

Mashaw, J. (1997). *Greed, Chaos & Government: Using Public Choice to Improve Public Law*. New Haven: Yale University Press.

McGraw, T. (1984). *Prophets of Regulation*. Cambridge, MA: Belknap Press

Michaels, R. (1999). The Governance of Transmission Operators. *Energy Law Journal, 20*, 233–262.

Mueller, D. (1989). *Public Choice II*. Cambridge: Cambridge University Press.

Muchow, D., & Mogel, W. (2001). *6 Energy Law and Transactions*. Newark, NJ: LexisNexis.

Munn v. Illinois, 94 U.S. 126 (1877).

Norton F., & Richardson, B. (2000). Electricity: Open Access, Transmission and Comparability. In: D. J. Muchow & W. A. Mogel (Eds), *Energy Law and Transactions* (Chapter 82). New York: M. Bender.

Pennsylvania Department of Revenue (2000). *Electric Generation Customer Choice and Competition.*

Pierce, R. (1984). The Regulatory Treatment of Mistakes in Retrospect: Cancelled Plants and Excess Capacity. *University of Pennsylvania Law Review, 132*, 497.

Posner, R. A. (1974). Theories of Regulation. *Bell Journal of Economics and Management Science, 5*, 335–358.

Priest, G. L. (1993). The Origins of Utility Regulation and the 'Theories of Regulation Debate.' *Journal of Law and Economics, 36*, 289–323.

Rabin, R. L. (1986). Federal Regulation in Historical Perspective. *Stanford Law Review, 38*, 1189–1253.

Schlesinger, A. (1986). *The Cycles of American History*. Boston: Houghton Mifflin.

Shapiro, S., & Tomain, J. (1998). *Regulatory Law and Policy* (2nd ed.). Charlottesville,VA: Michie Co.

Sidak, J., & Spulber, D. (1997). *Deregulatory Takings and the Regulatory Contract: The Competitive Transformation of Network Industries in the United States*. Cambridge, U.K.: Cambridge University Press.

Stigler, G. (1971). The Theory of Economic Regulation. *Bell Journal of Economics and Management Science, 2*, 3–21.

Tomain, J., & Shapiro, S. (1997). Analyzing Government Regulation. *Admininstrative Law Review, 49*, 377–414.

Tomain, J. (1998). Electricity Restructuring: A Case Study in Government Regulation. *Tulsa Law Journal, 33*, 827–845.

Tomain, J. (2000). networkindustries.gov.reg, *Kansas Law Review, 48*, 829–859.

Tomain, J. (1987). *Nuclear Power Transformation*. Bloomington, IN: Indiana University Press.

Tomain, J. (2000). Toward a Sustainable Energy-Environmental Policy. In: Energy Law Group, *Energy Law and Policy for the 21st Century* (Chapter 6). Denver: Rocky Mountain Mineral Law Foundation.

Tomain, J. (1990). The Dominant Model of United States Energy Policy. *University of Colorado Law Review*, *61*, 355–392.

Troesken, W. (1996). *Why Regulate Utilities? The New Institutional Economics and the Chicago Gas Industry, 1849–1924*. Ann Arbor: University of Michigan Press.

Watkiss, J., & Smith, D. (1993). The Energy Policy Act of 1992 – A Watershed for Competition in the Wholesale Power Market. *The Yale Journal on Regulation*, *10*, 369–492.

7. UNIVERSAL SERVICE IN COMPETITIVE RETAIL ELECTRIC MARKETS: REFIN(ANC)ING THE DUTY TO SERVE FOR A POST-NATURAL MONOPOLY ERA

Jim Rossi

INTRODUCTION

During the twentieth century, the privately-owned electric utility was regulated as a natural monopoly. According to the natural monopoly paradigm, a vertically-integrated electric utility provided generation, transmission, and distribution service to all customers within a geographic service territory. While the firm was allowed to operate as a monopolist, it also had certain responsibilities: it submitted to price regulation and assumed obligations to extend service to all customers within its geographic service territory and to continue providing service, once service had commenced (Haar & Fessler, 1986).

With the advent of deregulation, it is assumed that markets will largely displace price regulation, but little discussion focuses on the implications of deregulation for utility service obligations in the electricity industry. Today, electric utilities' extraordinary service obligations – often collectively referred to as the "duty to serve" – face their largest challenge ever. The potential conflict between universal service and retail competition in electricity bears

The End of a Natural Monopoly: Deregulation and Competition in the Electric Power Industry, Volume 7, pages 141–167.

ISBN: 0-7623-0995-4

analogy to a tension in other industries, such as natural gas and telecommunications. In the natural gas industry, deregulated by the Federal Energy Regulatory Commission (FERC) in 1992,[1] local gas distribution companies have begun to offer many customers retail choice in many states (Hall & Pierce, 1997, pp. 22–24; Costello & Lemon, 1996). Yet, in New York, the natural gas industry's recent introduction of retail competition is alleged to adversely affect the quality of gas service essential to many New Yorkers for heating, leading to a legal challenge against the state by consumer advocates (Norlander, 1998, p. 8).[2] Although competitive reforms to the electricity industry lag behind the natural gas and telecommunication industries,[3] as electricity is deregulated, particularly at the retail level, similar problems can be expected to arise.

Can vigorous retail competition of the type public utility deregulation envisions coexist with extraordinary obligations to serve customers? If so, at what costs? Who will bear these costs? These questions are central to an emerging law and economic analysis known as the "jurisprudence of networks," (Sidak & Spulber, 1997) of paramount importance as regulators and courts implement competition in traditional public utility industries, including electricity, where the natural monopoly model is being abandoned or reformed.

After summarizing how the duty to serve was implemented in the electricity industry under natural monopoly regulation, this chapter addresses whether traditional service obligations can coexist with retail competition. A rationale often given for universal service obligations in the telecommunications industry is that universal service, by promoting interconnectivity, enhances network system benefits for all customers. While the network economies argument may have worked to sustain universal service in the face of telecommunications deregulation, it is tenuous when applied to the natural gas and electricity industries. Many reformers look askance at the duty to serve in competitive retail utility service markets (Pace, 1987; Bouknight & Raskin, 1987; Norton & Spivak, 1985), often pointing to conflict between retail competition in electricity and the duty to serve.[4] This chapter argues, however, that application of extraordinary service obligations to distribution companies in a competitive retail framework can coexist with improved efficiency in retail power markets. At the same time, the abandonment of the natural monopoly framework challenges regulators to articulate new rationales for service obligations and to devise new ways of paying for them.

THE PUBLIC UTILITY'S "DUTY TO SERVE" IN THE ERA OF NATURAL MONOPOLY REGULATION

Twentieth century U.S. regulators built on an ancient common law duty that applied to public utilities such as ferries, flour mills and railroads, imposing on electric utilities a "duty to serve" – an obligation to provide extraordinary levels of service to customers, especially small residential customers. As applied by courts and regulators in most states, the public utility duty to serve entailed several obligations, among them duties to interconnect and extend service if requested, to provide continuing reliable service, to provide advanced notice of service disconnection, and to continue service even though a customer could not make full payment. Unlike other obligations that applied to private firms, including those such as inns and restaurants representing or holding themselves out as serving the public,[5] in the public utility context the duty to serve required service where it was not ordinarily considered profitable.

The link between the public utility concept and the duty to serve survived many different regulatory eras and institutional arrangements, garnering a variety of intellectual explanations (Robinson, 1928; Arteburn, 1927; Burdick, 1911; Wyman, 1903). There are strong fairness or distributional arguments supporting a duty to serve; many of these overlap with the goals of the civil rights movement, without which many customers would not have had equal access to quality utility service. However, in the classic era of public utility regulation (beginning with the Gilded Age and lasting through the last decade of the twentieth century) the economics of natural monopoly regulation provided the predominant intellectual framework supporting extraordinary obligations for providers of utility services. Not all economists agreed with the economics of natural monopoly – today its rationales are considered contingent on transaction costs and technology (see Chapter 2) – but its intellectual account allowed the duty to serve to continue uninterrupted for most of the twentieth century.

The Law and Economics of Horizontal and Vertical Integration

Among regulatory lawyers, natural monopoly regulation is often understood by reference to a "regulatory compact," a fictional contract between the utility and the state (see Chapter 4). Under this compact, the utility consents to certain obligations, such as the duty to serve, in return for its geographic franchise and expected recovery of its costs of service through regulated rates. The relationship between a utility and government, after all, is perhaps best understood within a long-term contract framework, given the large amounts of capital required for network infrastructure and the complexity of the underlying environment, leading to poor specification of contractual terms (Williamson, 1979; Goldberg, 1976). Some have gone so far as to suggest that this contract, though fictional, must be honored by the state as any other legal contract (Sidak & Spulber, 1997), but the regulatory compact rationale is perhaps best understood not as a legal obligation but as an account of the historical development of utility regulation (Priest, 1992).[6]

In his famous article *The Nature of the Firm*, Ronald Coase observed that all transactions in an economy are not necessarily most efficiently realized through explicit exchange in the market (Coase, 1937).[7] Oliver Williamson generalized Coase's observation to present a framework for analyzing the costs of market contracting and the optimal degree of vertical and horizontal integration. Williamson observed that the costs of market contracting vary with uncertainty, the frequency of transactions, asset specificity (the extent to which durable assets are tailored to specific transactions), and problems caused by opportunism. Transactions exhibiting these characteristics require complex contracts and tend to favor integration within organizations. As the need for contractual complexity rises, so does the cost of bilateral contracting, making internal control more attractive (Williamson, 1996).

The Williamsonian framework provides one explanation for the high degrees of horizontal and vertical integration in the twentieth century electric utility industry, central to the traditional framework of natural monopoly regulation. Ownership of multiple generators within the same horizontally-integrated firm structure could result in greater efficiency if there were significant coordination economies. In the early years of the electric power industry, technological innovations permitted the integration of large central power stations and adjacent electric generators into a single horizontally-integrated transmission system.[8] Though other chapters in this book have argued that the economic rationale for a single system was at best ambiguous, the technology that allowed such a high level of horizontal integration appeared to offer some scale economies. Companies (beginning with Samuel Insull's Chicago Edison, see Chapter 3) relied on the scale economies claim but, in return for an exclusive franchise, (precluding others from providing service within its franchise area) and rate regulation (guaranteeing recovery of capital costs), agreed to an important condition: the extension and continued provision of service to all customers. Universal service was thus a key part of the natural monopoly franchise bargain (Platt, 1991).

In addition, vertical integration of generation, transmission, and distribution functions within the same firm was thought to create significant operational economies. The economic arguments for vertical integration were bolstered by electricity's technical characteristics (noted in Chapter 2), including the physics of transmission, the high costs of storage, the high degree of coordination necessary to sustain reliable service. The vertical integration of generation and transmission was the market's recognition of two technical phenomena that made de-integration potentially costly: (1) "electrical equilibrium," the transmission stasis necessary to avoid blackout, requires that the sum of power demanded must equal the sum of power supplied at generation buses minus the amount of power lost in transmission; and (2) individual generators cannot physically direct their output to any particular customer or demand point. A vertically integrated generation and transmission utility was able to economize on these technical complexities by engaging in "economic dispatch" (utilizing the least expensive generator to meet its customer demands), monitoring generation to maintain internal electrical equilibrium, and diversifying its contracts to allow an operationally flexible combination of generation capacity to meet its customer load. These reasons were thought to demand the natural monopoly system, which by the middle of the twentieth century was virtually universal in the industry.[9] This high degree of vertical integration in the industry, it was argued, minimized the costs of contracting by internalizing costs, many of which are informational (Casson, 1997), within a single firm.

Efficiency of the Duty to Serve Within the Natural Monopoly Franework

Under the natural monopoly regulatory framework, the duty to extend service, even where it is not immediately profitable, can be economically efficient. As Richard Epstein has suggested, "the obligation of universal service to all comers is the obvious and effective way to overcome the holdout advantage that common carriers would otherwise possess against their customers" (Epstein, 1997). Put another way, utilities subject to a duty to extend service are not given an ordinary property right to exclude. Instead, the utility is protected by a liability rule, which allows customers to take service on demand in return for compensation, as determined through an elaborate ratemaking system. Effectively, service extension obligations are imposed on the utility, rather than assumed by the consumer, because the utility is better positioned to spread the costs of extension among multiple customers, thus minimizing the wealth impact on poorer customers.

Cost spreading is a primary rationale behind the extension obligation applicable to utilities, but "service continuation" obligations are understood by analogizing to long-term bilateral contracts between a supplier and a buyer and the identification of the superior risk bearer (Williamson, 1976). In industries with large up-front capital investments, long-term contracts are necessary to entice suppliers to make investments. Without long-term contracts, guaranteeing a reliable pool of buyers of a good, many suppliers would not make the necessary capital investments to produce or distribute the good. For example, in the natural gas industry, long-term contracts between pipelines and local distributions companies were essential to financing the national pipeline infrastructure (Pierce, 1988).

As is ordinary in practice, long-term contracts in private industries are often negotiated so as to allow flexibility in either price or quantity. The extended durations of such contracts pose problems for planning risk management, and "gaps" in such contracts will always exist. For sales of goods, once service under such a contract commences, a supplier has an obligation to continue to meet reasonable demands for services and not renege on this obligation if a more profitable alternative comes along (U.C.C., § 2-306). For example, assume that a seller has agreed to supply all of a buyer's coal requirements for a twenty-year period. The parties base their price-per-ton figure on a Department of Labor price index. However, over time incidents such as oil embargoes and inflation cause the supplier's production costs to exceed the agreed index, so that if the seller continues to perform it will suffer substantial losses. Nevertheless, the approach of some courts in reviewing such contracts has been to hold the seller completely responsible and to grant specific performance.[10] Thus, in the long-term contract context, some courts have in effect enforced a service continuation obligation, even in the face of substantial economic losses to the seller (Joskow, 1977).[11]

This approach to enforcing contracts has some efficiency basis in the long-term contract context where the seller is the superior risk bearer (Speidel, 1981; Posner & Rosenfield, 1977). In the electric utility context, the long-term agreement was endorsed by an understanding between a utility and its customers, which regulatory lawyers refer to as the regulatory compact. One of the parties to this hypothetical agreement, the utility, is a rate-regulated monopolist. Vis-à-vis the end use customer, the utility is the superior risk bearer with respect to changes in the supply of electricity and the technological aspects of transmission and distribution. The customer, though, may be the better risk bearer with respect to its unforeseeable uses of the utility's service. At the same time, as between the utility and customers, the utility is in a better position to spread any loses associated with service cut-off among multiple customers, especially where those losses might have an impact on low-income ratepayers or small businesses. A general utility obligation to continue service, and to pay for foreseeable damages in the event of service discontinuation, places the risk of shut-off on the superior risk bearer and cost spreader.[12] The utility, then, can attempt to seek compensation for these risks and costs through regulated rates, while also providing customers adequate opportunities to contest service curtailment or to seek an alternative supplier.

Although under traditional franchise and price regulation a general duty to serve has some economic efficiency grounds, one of the economic problems created by a service extension and continuation obligation is cross-subsidization. Customers who do not benefit from service extension may be allocated a portion of the fixed costs of extension, which are built into the fixed cost component of their rates. Contribution requirements, however, imposed by many regulators, limited the degree to which utilities could subsidize service extension by increasing rates for all customers. The traditional ratemaking process, in which the impacts and cost-effectiveness of intra- and inter-class cross-subsidization are litigated, also worked to minimize the degree of cross-subsidization resulting from the service extension obligation.

In addition, the service continuation obligation facilitated intra-class cross-subsidization by building into all customers' rates the costs of customers who could not afford to pay the full costs of their bills. Although this likely led to mismatches between any one customer's costs and rates, it allowed utilities to spread these costs among all customers. When a utility removed a customer who could not afford full payment from its system by disconnecting service two things occurred: first the utility avoided the variable costs of producing energy, typically the price of the fuel required to deliver the units of energy to the customer; second, since service continuation gave the utility leverage in collection, the utility forewent any revenue that it might have been able to collect from the household if service were continued. So, assuming excess capacity, there may have been a general economic advantage to all ratepayers in keeping as many customers as possible on the system. Service continuation obligations allowed the utility to spread fixed costs (for existing capacity) over a larger number of customers and to reduce the portion of each customer's bill allocated to fixed costs (Colton 1991, p. 31). Thus, even in the event of under-payment, it may have been cost-effective for a utility with excess capacity to continue service to a customer and to accommodate the customer who could not afford service at cost by working out a partial payment plan, so long as it was reasonably expected that the customer could pay at least the variable cost of service.

Cross-subsidization was a necessary result of the duty to serve, but the impacts of cross-subsidization were minimized by contribution requirements, the ratemaking process, and cost-effectiveness considerations. Although there were inevitable cross-subsidization costs associated with the duty to serve, regulators had to strike a balance to ensure that the benefits of universal access to utility service offset these costs. The duty to serve thus led a relatively peaceful coexistence with franchise and price regulation under the natural monopoly paradigm – even, as many economists believe, if this paradigm was contingent on technology and plagued by intellectual flaws (see Chapter 2).

RETAIL WHEELING AND UNIVERSAL SERVICE IN ELECTRICITY: REFIN(ANC)ING THE DUTY TO SERVE FOR A POST-PUBLIC UTILITY ERA IN ELECTRICITY

The dawn of competition in electricity raises a tension for the common law duty to serve, historically protected by natural monopoly regulation. In competitive retail power and natural gas markets, the traditional economic efficiency arguments in favor of imposing extraordinary service obligations must be reassessed in light of structural modifications to the industry. As regulators move away from the natural monopoly paradigm, the duty to serve is facing a disruption that was largely foreign to its twentieth century existence.

It is tempting for regulators addressing the obligations of firms in electricity markets to look to other markets in which they have experience, such as telecommunications, in which universal service is often regarded as coexisting with retail competition. However, one of the primary network efficiency rationales for universal service in telecommunications is inapplicable to physical energy network markets, such as electricity and natural gas. To the extent extraordinary service obligations are continued for electricity and natural gas in the same manner that they have been for the past hundred years, regulators need to articulate alternative economic efficiency justifications or will need to explicitly embrace goals outside of economic efficiency, such as fairness or distributive justice.

The Tension Posed by the Duty to Serve in Retail Markets

Wholesale transmission access and competition among wholesale suppliers has not posed any immediate threat to the public utility duty to serve,[13] but the introduction of retail competition requires some reassessment of the intellectual foundations for, and practical application of, the traditional duty to serve. The California Public Utility Commission's first order leading to the adoption of retail choice legislation acknowledged the need for consideration of this issue as customers begin to shop for power:

> To allow eligible customers to choose without restriction between the regulated price for a bundled utility service and the price offered by the generation services market may severely reduce the utility's ability to plan for, and reliably serve, its remaining customers. Absent modifications to the compact's traditional duty to service, consumers may make choices about electric services which they find economically attractive, but which are undesirable with respect to the broader goal of allocating society's resources efficiently.[14]

The possibility of such uneconomic bypass – bypass that might work to lower costs for a single shopping customer while raising average costs for other customers[15] – necessitates consideration of the costs of the traditional duty to serve. Moreover, a system that allows power suppliers and customers to choose to deal with each other, especially if left unregulated, may allow suppliers or distributors to elect never to serve certain classes of customers, such as low-income residents, or to cease service however they wish consistent with retail power sales agreements.

Of course, perceived conflicts between vigorous retail competition and customer access can be avoided to the extent that one of these seemingly incompatible goals is simply abandoned. Since it is not likely that the movement towards competition in traditional public utility industries will cease, one option in the face of the tension between retail competition and common law service obligations is to abandon the duty to serve for competitive markets, treating traditional utility services as any other service in a competitive market. After all, as retail markets open up it will be increasingly possible for suppliers and distributors to provide a variety of service qualities to end users. Without a duty to serve, utility markets might operate much like other deregulated markets, such as trucking and banking, which rely on contractual obligations and general consumer protection laws to ensure service delivery. For example, if an electricity supplier refuses service to a customer, the customer must find alternative suppliers and competition in power generation will likely provide customers a range of power supply qualities.[16] Should a power distributor (known as a "DisCo") refuse to extend or discontinue service to a customer because it is not profitable, the customer may also attempt to find alternatives. For example, for large, heavy load customers of electricity alternatives such as self-generation or wheeling around the DisCo may be cost feasible. Markets flourish with bilateral relationships, while the duty to serve imposes a unilateral obligation on the incumbent utility. Customers already have a variety of safegaurds, including credit financing and consumer protection statutes, such as the Uniform Commercial Code.[17]

Though a challenge, it is not an impossible task for regulators to establish extraordinary service obligations in competitive retail industries. Many insurance industries provide for universal service through various sorts of assigned risk pools. For example, the property insurance industry has developed Fair Access to Insurance Requirements (FAIR) plans.[18] In the hospital industry, the obligation of hospitals to serve the indigent is explicitly made a condition in the awarding of federal construction grants.[19] Nonprofit health care providers take on an obligation to provide indigent health care, in part as a condition to the grant of certain governmental benefits, such as federal, state or local tax benefits (Simpson & Strum, 1991). It is questionable how successful these approaches to promoting universal service have been, but their existence suggests that the duty to serve can coexist with retail competition.

The Efficiency of Universal Service in Telecommunications Networks

In the telecommunications industry the extraordinary obligations applicable to service providers have come to be known as "universal service," endorsed by the U.S. Congress in the Telecommunications Act of 1996.[20] The leading rationale for universal service in telecommunications is independent of natural monopoly regulation.

In the telecommunications context, the predominant economic rationale for a universal service obligation is that pervasive access increases network system benefits for all customers (Lemley & McGowan, 1998). Basically, the idea is that a service obligation on providers of telecommunications service enhances the value of network service for all customers to such a degree that customers are willing to pay a premium to subsidize universal access. The FCC, in its 1997 universal service order, recognized this economic rationale:

> Universal service support mechanisms that are designed to increase subscribership by keeping rates affordable will benefit everyone in the country, including those who can afford basic service. At the simplest level, increasing the number of people connected to the telecommunications network makes the network more valuable to all its users by increasing its usefulness to them. Increasing subscribership also benefits society in ways unrelated to the value of the network per se. For example, all of us benefit from the widespread availability of basic public safety services, such as 911. (In re Federal-State Joint Bd. on Universal Serv., FCC Docket No. 96-45, slip op. at p. 8, ¶ 8 (May 7, 1997).

Because the value of telecommunications service increases to customers with greater degrees of system interconnectivity, universal service is regarded as economically valuable by telecommunications firms and customers, even those who can afford market-priced services. Put another way, universal service creates a positive externality, which inures to the benefit of all customers through pervasive interconnectivity. For example, the more pervasive access to the Internet, the more valuable the Internet is as a communications tool, everything else being equal.[21]

While intuitively attractive, this rationale is not without problems. First, clearly there is some limit on the amount the average consumer is willing to pay to subsidize universal service. At some point, the marginal benefits of enhanced access will not justify the additional cost. For example, expansion of a network initially financed by middle-class customers to include the poor, particular those with whom middle-class customers rarely interact, will likely provide few benefits of the sort that the average middle-class customer will be willing to pay for. The average-middle class customer who can afford to pay for his or her own access will likely not be willing to pay a significant premium to enhance access for others unless there is some cognizable benefit to the network system or to the value of service. Empirically, it unclear how much the average consumer is willing to pay to subsidize universal service. Clearly there are some limitations on the willingness of consumers to pay for system benefits but, without empirical study, this theory fails to provide a clear criterion for limiting its extension. For example, taken to its extreme it could require not only subsidization of the network, but a redistributive tax to pay to provide computers or other electronic communications devices to customers who cannot afford to pay for these. While such a tax may seem desirable as a matter of fairness or distributive justice, it is hardly required by economic efficiency.

A second limitation with this rationale for universal service in the telecommunications context is that it does not factor in network congestion costs. If the infrastructure is already in place to accommodate additional customers at a low incremental cost, the positive externality rationale provides a powerful rationale for enhancing access. However, with limited infrastructure, additional participants may actually cause the value of service for incumbent customers to decline if congestion ensues or if the quality of service is otherwise adversely affected. In the Internet context, for example, the congestion bottlenecks resulting from mass access to system networks are obvious.

These problems aside, while this positive externality rationale for universal service might explain why consumers, in a nonregulated context, may be willing to pay for cross-subsidization of universal service in telecommunications, it is a tenuous argument, at best, for supporting a duty to serve in the natural gas and electricity industries. Under traditional public utility regulation, the consumption of gas and electricity commodities, unlike communications services, do not depend on interconnectivity for their value. Additional customers might make certain secondary markets possible – Circuit City would not exist if customers did not have circuits[22] – and this may stimulate demand for electricity or natural gas. Moreover, as is discussed above, increasing the number of customers on a network have worked to decrease the fixed costs associated with providing electric or natural gas service, reducing the price each customer pays in a rate-regulated environment. However, any individual customer can obtain great value from utilizing electrical or natural gas appliances in complete isolation. An electrical generator, for example, can easily power a home or office, so long as adequate fuel is available. Thus, although some economic benefits to pervasive access can be identified for these industries, they relate primarily to the costs and supply of network service, not to its demand value or the amount customers are willing to pay for universal service. To this extent, the positive externality argument for universal service is weak when applied to commodities like electricity and natural gas outside the natural monopoly framework – or, at least in this context, universal service demands some alternative economic explanation.

Efficiency and Universal Electricity Service in a Competitive Retail Market Framework

To date, most states that have addressed retail competition in power markets acknowledge the potential tension between the common law duty to serve and competitive retail markets without abandoning either goal. For example, California stated in the preamble to its 1996 retail wheeling legislation, "[i]t is the further intent of the Legislature to continue to fund low-income ratepayer assistance programs, ... in an unbundled manner ..." and maintained 1996-level low income and universal service expenditures (Cal. A. B. No. 1890 (signed Sept. 23, 1996), at § 1(d)). New Hampshire, which considered similar legislation, was more explicit:

> A restructured electric utility industry should provide adequate safeguards to assure universal service. Minimum residential service safeguards and protections should be maintained. Programs and mechanisms that enable residential customers with low incomes to manage and afford essential electricity requirements should be included as part of industry restructuring (N. H. State Code, § 374-F:3 VI).

The task of formulating extraordinary service obligations in an era of retail competition is challenging. It should not, however, preclude consideration of retail competition by states, nor should it necessarily lead to the abandonment of extraordinary service obligations. In fact, politically the introduction of retail competition may even lead to enhancement of consumer protection obligations, perhaps from fear of the abuses markets may yield.[23]

Although the rationales applicable to the telecommunications industry are inapposite in competitive electricity markets, there are some plausible economic efficiency rationales supporting continuation of the duty to service in competitive retail power markets. To understand the how extraordinary service obligations will apply in the context of a competitive retail power market, some understanding of this market's operational framework is necessary. While the DisCo is often thought to remain a natural monopolist, generation, power supply, marketing, and brokering, and energy services are today regarded as competitive industries (Fox-Penner, 1997). Since deregulation of the electricity industry acknowledges different market characteristics for different market actors, the traditional approach to implementing service obligations requires some reassessment. Equal application of a duty to every institutional actor providing electric utility services in competitive retail markets will pose significant economic costs and may thwart the development of retail power markets. In particular, from an efficiency perspective, proposals endorsed by many consumer advocates that suppliers or marketers assume extraordinary service obligations (Colton, 1997; Alexander, 1996) are specious, since this aspect of the industry no longer exhibits natural monopoly characteristics. This does not mean, however, that universal service is without any economic efficiency basis.

Current state retail wheeling plans require, at a minimum, that the power distribution sector of the industry assume some extraordinary service obligation. There is little agreement among the states about whether the various market institutions interacting with the DisCo in retail markets should also bear extraordinary service obligations. Extraordinary service obligations *can* facilitate access to power supply without undermining efficiency gains from retail competition, but regulators need to assess carefully the limits of service obligations.

Under most state restructuring plans, for small load customers, such as residential customers, small business and single location offices, power distribution remains a monopoly service. Put another way, a single utility (the DisCo) continues to provide distribution to power supply for the large bulk of power customers. For most smaller customers who do not have access to capital financing markets or own rights of way to build distribution lines, it is cost prohibitive to duplicate distribution lines as long as the incumbent DisCo itself owns the facilities.[24] Thus, even in competitive retail markets, DisCos initially remain monopolies for small residential and commercial customers, at least with respect to the horizontal distribution market.[25] Following California's approach, to date, state retail competition plans define a *de jure* monopoly for distribution, subject to fairly traditional regulation, effectively defining a new regulatory compact for power distribution.

Further, to date states that have seriously considered moving to retail competition in the sale of electricity have determined that a "basic service" option must be provided by the DisCo to those who do not choose an alternative supplier for electricity, are refused service by a retail supplier, or have been disconnected.[26] The DisCo is effectively the supplier of last resort.[27] In some states, basic service will be regulated at a rate established to be less than the rates immediately prior to competition, thus minimizing the impact of stranded costs on small residential customers.[28]

For example, according to Vermont's retail competition restructuring order, "exclusive franchises for distribution" remain necessary. The DisCo "will retain its obligation to plan, build and operate its local distribution system in a manner that ensures safe and reliable service to customers."[29] Vermont defines the "Basic Service Offer" as "[s]ervice offered to customers by the distribution company but provided by a retail service provider through contract." This service "may be priced either to float with the spot market or fixed on a longer term basis."[30] After the transition to retail competition this offer, which is limited to franchised customers of DisCos, "will be made available over a contracted period" and "through a retail service provider."[31]

Since retail competition envisions the fragmentation of utility service into different markets, from generation to transmission to distribution, the implications of continuing the duty to serve will need to be assessed in the context of each of these markets. Given power distribution's *de jure* monopoly status under state retail wheeling plans, with little or no analysis most state regulators have initially looked to the DisCo as the primary bearer of the traditional duty to serve. However, given the inapplicability of the traditional rate regulation framework for understanding service obligations in the competitive market structure, coupled with the mobilization of interests likely to support imposition of new service obligations, the objective efficiency rationales for continuing to impose an extraordinary service obligation on the incumbent utility require reassessment. To the extent regulators can articulate only tentative justifications for service obligation, explicit taxes coupled with vouchers for low income service may be the best route to proceed with updating the duty to serve for a post natural monopoly era.

Cost Spreading and the Efficiency of Universal Power Distribution Service, But Not Generation

Consider, first, the economic rationales for imposing service extension obligations. Since the DisCo maintains a horizontal monopoly with respect to rights of way and essential network facilities, most customers will continue to have a need for access to distribution from it. At the same time, the DisCo will be in a better position than suppliers or others to spread the costs of service extension, minimizing the economic impact of the distribution network on customers, particularly the poor. Society's utility in the aggregate will be higher if resources are expended towards universal service than in maximizing the revenues of the DisCo; conceptually, this poses an aggregation problem and will be very difficult to measure, but the disutility of service discontinuation to at least some consumers will exceed the aggregate utility of a lower DisCo rate for all customers. So even in a competitive retail market, although it is almost impossible to quantify it seems that economic efficiency rationales for requiring the DisCo to extend its distribution network to at least some customers will continue.

It should be noted, though, that in a deregulated environment where power supply is competitive the access and cost spreading rationales for the extension obligation apply to distribution service only, not to competitively provided power supply. Put another way, despite an economic rationale for requiring the DisCo to assume some distribution service extension obligation, economic analysis does not require the DisCo to also provide power supply. Thus, without further exploration of the structure of retail power markets, there does not appear to be a strong economic rationale for requiring the DisCo to build generation facilities or procure power supply to serve customers. Nevertheless, to the extent regulators decide to impose basic service obligations on some institutional actor in competitive power markets, for at least some customers the DisCo may also be in the best position to spread the costs associated with basic service.

Reassessing the Efficiency of Service Continuation Obligations

With respect to service continuation, the second obligation of the traditional duty to serve, the economic efficiency rationales behind the obligation also require some reassessment. Recall that one of the primary economic efficiency rationales for imposing extraordinary service continuation obligations relates to the utility's status as the superior risk bearer vis-à-vis the customer.[32] In deregulated power markets, however, the long-term contract analogy that undergirds application of superior risk bearer analysis to the regulatory compact loses much of its relevance, since customers themselves may select power suppliers on a month-to-month basis.

Further, in a competitive retail market, the same rationales cannot justify imposition of an obligation on a private firm to provide full service at a price below total costs, as often applied under rate regulation. Now, as has been observed, there may be some continuing advantage to avoiding power shut off to the extent that a customer is able to pay the variable portion of the costs associated with the supply and distribution of power. This cost sharing advantage, however, is significantly reduced in a competitive market where power suppliers face alternative customers for their capacity; it may apply to distribution service, but absent excess capacity committed to DisCo customers it does not apply to power supply.

Operational and Reliability Efficiencies

Despite these structural and regulatory differences between a competitive market and the traditional regulated industry, efficiency arguments support imposition of *some* service continuation obligation on the DisCo or other suppliers in a competitive environment. With respect to service discontinuation, the physics of power flow may require the DisCo to bear some responsibility if its grid has not been modernized. Once power is supplied to a distribution grid without computerized customer metering, the DisCo is automatically the supplier of last resort to the retail customer; the customer will continue to receive power until it is physically disconnected by the DisCo. So in certain areas, technology may necessitate some DisCo service continuation obligation.

Informational Efficiencies

Another rationale for imposition of a service continuation obligation is that retail power markets may yield poor information for market actors, precluding consumers or others from enjoying the full benefits of deregulated markets. Assuming that customers have good information about power supply options and the terms of power supply sales contracts, when compared to the DisCo, the customer will be the superior bearer of the risks of service shut off. The customer can purchase supply plans that provide for early warning or, if necessary, insurance to cover the risks of property or other damage due to a loss of power. Many customers, though, may not have adequate information about power supply markets so as to react to the risks of shut off, particularly where shut off is due to technological failure or emergencies. In addition, in competitive power markets, consumers are unlikely immediately to possess the knowledge or experience to react to this information when some reaction, such as the purchasing of power insurance or backup supply options, is in order. Poor information or consumer discounting of risks may require the DisCo or a supplier to assume some service continuation obligation, even in a competitive power supply market. This will especially be true as these markets initially evolve and as regulators embark on the task of educating consumers.

Efficient Welfare Policy

Further, given that a welfare system already exists in our market economy, the imposition of service continuation obligations in a competitive power supply market might work to mitigate the incentives the welfare system produces for taking excessive credit risks. As competitive power markets evolve, consumers are likely to be offered credit financing plans for electricity akin to many of the financing plans available for other purchases, such as purchase of an automobile. Offerers of such sales are likely to provide creative financing options, often offering consumers who are poor credit risks high-cost financing plans. Such risks, to the extent they are repeatedly presented to low-income consumers in a competitive power supply market, will also increase the incidence of default, especially since utilities will not face the same incentives as under rate regulation to continue service with acceptance of partial payment. As customers increasingly default and lose the basic necessities of life, such as electricity service, over time this could both drive up the cost of the welfare system and undermine its poverty reduction goal (Posner, 1995). Thus, imposition of a service continuation obligation, even in a competitive market, might be seen as a way of reducing the costs of public welfare programs.

So, though reassessment is necessary, economic efficiency arguments for continuing with some extraordinary service obligations in competitive markets are not completely irrelevant. To the extent economic arguments exist, though, they relate primarily to horizontal integration and the quality of information consumers will likely possess in the deregulatory environment, as with retail competition the market facilitates many of the transactions which the traditional public utility previously coordinated within a single, vertically integrated firm.

Monitoring Costs

Beyond these efficiency rationales for universal service in competitive electricity markets, most of which focus on the structural nature of efficient power markets, it must be acknowledged that, with deregulation, regulators will bear a heavier monitoring cost in implementing universal service goals for electricity. In contrast to the traditional regulatory structure, where a single natural monopoly firm provided service to all customers within its service territory, multiple firms will now provide a variety of services to these customers. In addition to the DisCo, generating companies, power supply companies, and energy service companies, as well as brokers and marketers, will enter power markets. Any obligation imposed on entities beyond the DisCo will entail significant monitoring costs for regulators.

The Limits of Efficiency: More Explicit Acknowledgment of Fairness and Distributive Justice

To the extent regulators continue to adhere to the constituent obligations of the common law duty, they likely also will need to articulate non-efficiency justifications, such as fairness or distributive justice, to support service obligations in a competitive retail environment. In this sense, retail competition is likely to force more explicit discussion of the costs and benefits of extraordinary service obligations than occurred under the traditional regulatory compact. For example, in Ohio the discussion of consumer service protections has become explicit with the dawn of competition, while previously consumer protections were often built into utility tariffs on a voluntary basis (Johnson, 1998).

Some consumer advocates have proposed that states extend service obligations to suppliers, marketers, and brokers, and that DisCos be required to procure basic service power for consumers through mandated bidding criteria or an allocation plan that accurately reflects market power. While there are legitimate concerns that, in the provision of basic service, the DisCo may tend to favor any generation resources it owns over competitively supplied generation, from an efficiency perspective there is no sound basis for extending utility service obligations beyond the DisCo to power suppliers, marketers and brokers.

Few states have been willing to require complete vertical disintegration but, even absent complete vertical disintegration, unbundling of DisCo power sales and procurement can be achieved financially through requiring DisCos with generation to bid into a power exchange and to meet all basic power needs with power exchange purchases. A power exchange, modeled similar to California's, prices based entirely on the spot market of supply and demand for power. If a DisCo is mandated to bid its power into the exchange before selling basic service to customers, customers purchasing basic service would realize more of the benefits of competition than they would under competitive bidding, because mandatory bidding into a power exchange facilitates decoupling of DisCo basic service power purchases from power sales. Under such an approach, the DisCo has an adequate incentive to purchase from the exchange the lowest cost power or it will risk losing basic service customers to alternative suppliers if those customers opt to participate in the direct retail purchase market. With such institutional reforms, imposition of a duty to serve on DisCos, to be financed through an system benefits charge, can work simultaneously to facilitate the development of robust power supply markets and pass the new efficiencies of these markets on to consumers without sacrificing access goals. Now a notorious example of deregulation policies run amok, California was not an ideal laboratory for this model, since the state's restructuring plan precluded any markets from developing around long-term contracts and burdened the DisCo with a retail price cap (see Chapter 10). Even absent these failures in California's deregulatory experiment, however, its approach to imposing service obligations on the DisCo was not a perfect solution. Regulators still needed to address the issue of how basic service power supply is procured by the DisCo. Without careful attention to market incentives, a DisCo may continue, as utilities did for much of the twentieth century, to see universal service as a way of insulating itself from power supply competition.

States should consider innovating beyond the approach in California's power exchange, which relies on heavily regulated trading protocols to addressing the anticompetitive problems with service obligations, by establishing explicit taxes to support a service voucher program for qualifying customers. A tax, similar to a systems benefits charge, can be imposed on the DisCo. Rather than directly requiring the DisCo to provide default service, a state could make electric service vouchers would be made available to low income customers and others who qualify for universal service based on transparent criteria. Vouchers would allow customers to purchase power supply when needed, but prices would be determined based on the market. Under this approach, it is no longer necessary to impose a per se service obligation on the DisCo, as revenues from vouchers will allow prices signals to work as incentives for service provision. Suppliers could continue to compete for universal service voucher customers, without a state imposing the service obligation on any single market actor, creating a risk for anticompetitive conduct, or attempting to procure power supply for universal service purposes, risking distortion of power supply markets.

To the extent a duty to serve continues to apply to the industry, on whatever rationales, competitively priced retail power markets will work to minimize many of the price distortions of cross-subsidization historically associated with extraordinary service obligations. Under the natural monopoly framework, utility service obligations were paid for through cross-subsidies, but rate regulation helped to minimize the market distortions of this practice. Utilities generally were not opposed to assuming service obligations, especially where they worked to enlarge the customer base, so long as they could recover the costs of these obligations from some customers. With retail competition and a movement to market-based pricing, cross-subsidization will continue to exist, but power supply markets will require DisCos to minimize the impact of subsidies on customers or risk losing customers, especially larger ones, to bypass or other suppliers wheeling on the DisCo system.[33]

CONCLUSION

Cross-subsidies are not without controversy, but the fiction of the regulatory compact coupled with the economics of natural monopoly price regulation have masked the redistributive nature of extraordinary utility service obligations for the past hundred or so years. Under this regulatory framework, public and private interests converged in maintenance of the duty to serve.

Following World War II, public choice theory began to question the orthodox understanding of government regulation generally and utility regulation in particular, providing the intellectual tools for smashing the regulatory compact in a variety of different industries (Mashaw, 1997; Farber & Frickey, 1991). One of the predominant accounts of the growth of utility regulation is regulatory capture – that utilities and other interests, such as consumer groups, secure protection of their interests through the political process by capturing regulation (Becker 1983; Peltzman 1976; Stigler 1971). For example, as Eli Noam (1997) has recently suggested, in the telecommunications context there is a public choice explanation for the existence of a redistributive universal service obligation in the Telecommunications Act of 1996. Consumers and utilities may have formed a coalition to secure legislative endorsement of the universal service requirement; this inures to the benefit of the average consumer, who now has more pervasive access through interconnectivity; it also benefits utilities, as regulators allow recovery of universal service costs by guaranteeing minimum service access charges or rates. If this public choice explanation is applicable to national legislation regulating telecommunications, it would seem even more plausible in the regulation of electricity and natural gas commodities that have developed service obligations primarily at the state level, likely more responsive than the U.S. Congress to the preferences, desires and needs of state consumers and industries. So modern endorsement of the duty to serve in statutes and regulations in the electricity and natural gas contexts may have resulted not from some public-spirited regulatory compact, but from utilities, consumers, and their representatives securing, or capturing, a regulatory benefit from the political process.

As this chapter has suggested, however, there may be some plausible economic efficiency rationales for universal service in competitive telecommunications markets as well as in emerging physical energy markets in electricity and natural gas, even once the regulatory compact has been reassessed as a rationale for regulation. Retail competition in most public utility industries, such as telecommunications, natural gas and electricity, is here to stay. With it the laws and regulatory concepts we have invoked to regulate public utilities since the Gilded Age are undergoing a transformation. It will become important that, in addressing the financing of extraordinary service obligations, regulators avoid building into competitive retail markets structural mechanisms that harm consumers. As I have suggested, in initial restructuring of regulated utility markets, to the extent regulators or courts extend the duty to serve beyond incumbent distributors, to suppliers and marketers, new inefficiencies may result. Imposition of basic service obligation on the DisCo, to be fulfilled through voluntary procurement of power supply and financed through an system benefits charge, minimizes the inefficiency of imposing a service obligation in a competitive market.

Despite efforts to maintain the *de jure* monopoly status of power distribution, though, in the long run competition may prove inevitable for even this segment of the electricity industry. Increasingly, the availability of distributed generation threatens the need for power distribution, as adequate substitutes may be available to customers who can afford generation. Due to the growth of distributed generation, the power generation industry may be set for a future similar to the current main frame computer industry, which has been seriously threatened by the desk-top personal computer industry (Carolan & Keating,

1997; Zuckerman, 1997). Some have suggested that power distribution may ultimately become a competitive or contestable industry.[34] To the extent these developments occur, the ability of a single DisCo to recover the costs of its extraordinary service obligations through a system benefits charge for a geographic area will be weakened significantly. In competitive distribution markets, a more efficient way to finance service obligations may be through a national sales tax on power distribution or supply, coupled with federal voucher and service extension grant programs to guarantee minimum service quality (Rossi, 1998).

Absent federal regulation of electric service, customer service obligations will remain a matter of state law. Enhanced retail competition in historically regulated markets will not mean the end of traditional doctrines of public utility law, such as the duty to serve. Yet regulators must be bold and creative in approaching the content and financing of extraordinary service obligations for new actors in these markets, with a keen eye towards minimizing the structural inefficiencies they pose. Careful study and appreciation of the distinct economic and institutional structures of various utility service markets will be necessary to provide sound guidance as regulators apply the duty to serve to competitive retail industries. At each step of this analysis regulators must not only ask whether there are efficiencies to be gained. Clearly there are, but these must be balanced against the political challenge of passing these new efficiencies on to the average consumer. To the extent that the economic rationales for the duty to serve are lacking in the deregulatory era, increased political transparency for what are predominantly social welfare programs will be inevitable. As I have argued in this chapter, an explicit voucher program for low income consumers, financed through a state tax on the DisCo, holds greater promise for enhancing efficiency and the accountability of regulatory policy than imposing obligations on market actors through regulation.

NOTES

1. See Pipeline Service Obligations and Revisions to Regulations Governing Self-Implementing Transportation and Regulation of Natural Gas Pipelines After Partial Wellhead Decontrol, 57 Fed. Reg. 13,267 (1992), *order on reh'g*, 57 Fed. Reg. 36,128 (1992), *order on reh'g*, 57 Fed. Reg. 57,911 (1992), *reversed and remanded, United Distribution Companies v. FERC*, 88 F.3d 1105 (D.C. Cir. 1996), *order on remand*, 78 F.E.R.C. (CCH) ¶ 61, 186 (1997). Order No. 636 is codified at 18 C.F.R. Part 284 (1997).

2. The case, brought by consumer taxpayers and a consumer advocate nonprofit group alleging illegal expenditure of public funds under the state finance law, was dismissed for lack of standing. See *Public Utility Law Project of New York, Inc. v. New York State Public Service Commission*, 681 N.Y.S.2d 396 (App. Div. 3d Dep. 1998).

3. The development of competition in electricity is hardly a U.S.-specific phenomenon. Many other countries have also deregulated the electricity industry. Electricity competition is also the subject of a recent directive of the European Communities. *See Directive 96/92 Concerning Common Rules for the Internal Market in Electricity*, 1996 O. J. (L27) 27. Also see Klom, 1997.

4. There is little, if any, disagreement that retail wheeling is incompatible with an obligation to serve. A utility cannot be obligated to meet the energy needs of potential customers within its service territory without some guarantee of recovering the costs associated with that obligation. To do otherwise would clearly result in economic inefficiencies. It would also lead to further inequities, since the costs and risks of meeting a standing obligation would be borne either by the utility's remaining customers or its stockholders (Lesser & Ainspan, 1994, pp. 34, 40–41).

5. Of course, civil rights laws may preclude service exclusion for some groups of individuals, (Singer, 1996), but their scope is limited. Also, to the extent a public utility is a state actor (e.g. a municipal utility), the Due Process and Equal Protection Clauses of the U.S. Constitution may impose some limitation on service exclusion. Apart from these exceptions, under antitrust laws ordinary private businesses may unilaterally refuse to deal with particular customers and set the terms and conditions under which they contract. See *United States v. Colgate & Co.*, 250 U.S. 300, 307 (1919). The duty to serve, however, imposes significantly more rigorous dealing and service terms and conditions on utilities than other private actors.

6. George Priest (1992) describes utility regulation as evolving not from regulatory capture, but from a pragmatic negotiation between utilities and local governments that gave utilities the power of eminent domain.

7. There is, in principle, no need for the market to organize around firms. Instead, market actors could organize through arms-length transactions with the guidance of price mechanisms. A firm simply bypasses (or internalizes) the system of market prices and coordinates production without the use of explicit prices. Essentially, Coase was taking exception to the then-dominant understanding that the "natural" evolution of the firm was defined by technology and its costs and could be taken as given.

8. As Platt (1991, pp. 22–25, 69–70, 74–82) suggests, such horizontal integration was dependent on the development of AC current, allowing the extension of electricity transmission beyond a mile and a half, and the technology of central station coordination. In addition, a large degree of horizontal integration has been externally established through informal coordination and contractual pooling (Platt, 1991, pp. 72–74). For example, it is commonplace for vertically-integrated utilities to functionally and operationally integrate with other separately owned utilities through long-term cooperative activities and long-term contractual arrangements governing transmission (Joskow & Schmalensee, 1983).

9. Investor-owned utilities commonly integrate distribution with generation and transmission. It is typical for cooperative and municipal utilities to separate distribution from generation and transmission. Although distribution facilities may be separately owned, they are typically linked with the generation and transmission firm by long-term requirements contracts. Joskow and Schmalensee (1991, p. 113) observes that "[v]ertical integration between generation and transmission is virtually universal."

10. *Missouri Pub. Serv. Co. v. Peabody Coal Co.*, 583 S.W.2d 721 (Mo. Ct. App. 1979); *Iowa Electric Light & Power Co. v. Atlas Corp.*, 467 F. Supp. 139 (N. D.Iowa

1978).11. *Accord* U. C. C. § 2–306, comment 2. This comment notes that requirements to "curtail losses" may constitute breach.

12. With respect to service continuation the utility is not only the superior risk bearer, but also the superior cost spreader. In most cases it will be desirable to impose continuation obligations on the utility, except in those instances where the customer is, on average, the superior risk bearer and the gains from requiring customers to bear the risks of shut off exceed any loss spreading gains from imposing the obligation on the utility.

13. Since FERC's Order No. 888, wholesale access and supply competition occur under FERC's open access policies, which require a transmission utility to offer transmission service to customers and suppliers at terms and conditions comparable to the service it offers its own power supply. *See* Promoting Wholesale Competition Through Open Access Non-Discriminatory Transmission Services by Public Utilities and Transmitting Utilities, 61 Fed. Reg. 21,539 (May 10, 1996) (codified at 18 C.F.R. Parts 35 & 385 (1997)). During prior times, competition at the wholesale level may have had potentially adverse impacts on service obligations. Bouknight and Raskin (1987, p. 239) notes "to the extent that existing obligations are inconsistent with a system of free and fair competition the Congress and the FERC must address the issue."

14. Re Proposed Policies Governing Restructuring of California's Electric Services Industry and Reforming Regulation, 151 P.U.R.4th 73, 92 (Cal. Pub. Util. Comm'n, 1994).

15. Uneconomic bypass has been defined as bypass that reduces costs to one customer but increases overall average network costs, thus creating costs for other customers (MacAvoy, Spulber & Stangle, 1989).

16. Some suggest that traditional rate regulation has had an adverse effect on the average quality of service. Carron and MacAvoy (1981), chronicles a decline in service quality throughout the 1970s. Notably, in England, which deregulated its electricity industry through privatization in 1991, service disconnections fell by 95% over the first few years of deregulation (Costello & Graniere, 1997, p. 14).

17. For example, express and implied warranty protections appear in both state and federal law. See U.C.C. § 2-313 (express warranty); § 2-314 (implied warranty of merchantability); § 2-315 (implied warranty of fitness for particular purpose); § 2-318 (extension of warranties to third party beneficiaries expected to use goods); see also 15 U.S.C. §§ 2301-2312 (Magnuson-Moss Warranty Act, regulating explicit and implied warranties). In addition federal law prohibits "unfair methods of competition and unfair or deceptive acts or practices in or affecting commerce." 15 U.S.C. § 45(a). All states have similar statutes protecting against unfair trade acts. The federal Equal Credit Opportunity Act, 15 U.S.C. § 1691-1691e, and the Fair Credit Reporting Act, 15 U.S.C. § 1681, establish minimum standards that prevent discrimination in the granting of credit and consumer safeguards. See also 15 U.S.C. ch. 41 (Consumer Credit Protection Act); 15 U.S.C. §§ 1692-1692o (Fair Credit Debt Collection Act); 15 U.S.C. § 1637 (Fair Credit Billing Act). State regulation of finance charges, credit terms and the federal Truth in Lending Act (TILA), 15 U.S.C. § 1602(f), have historically not applied to public utilities because these laws contain a stricter definition of credit designed to capture transactions in which both parties intend that payment will be delayed and finance charges imposed as a part of a lengthened payment schedule. In competitive markets, though, retail electricity suppliers and distributors may devise payment plans that resemble credit sale transactions or sponsor open-ended credit plans for the sale of electricity which could trigger TILA disclosure and disputed bill procedures.

18. The FAIR plan was created under the Urban Property Protection and Reinsurance Act of 1968, Pub. L. No. 90-448, 82 Stat. 555 (codified as amended in scattered sections of 5, 12, 15 & 42 U.S.C.). For discussion, see generally Austin (1983).

19. The Hill-Burton Act conditioned the funding of hospital construction on the provision of uncompensated care to indigent citizens. See 42 U.S.C. § 291. In addition, a federal law called the Emergency Medical Treatment and Active Labor Act, adopted in 1986, required Medicare-participating hospitals to examine and treat all emergency room patients and women in labor. See 42 U.S.C. § 1395dd.

20. Telecommunications Act of 1996, § 254, Pub. L. No. 104–104, 110 Stat. 56 (Feb. 8, 1986) directed the Federal Communications Commission (FCC) to define "universal service," consistent with principles in statute. This provision was the subject of deliberations of a joint federal/state board and FCC rules issued in 1997. See In re Federal-State Joint Board on Universal Service, FCC Docket No. 96-45 (May 7, 1997). These rules have been clarified in several orders on reconsideration, most recently in December 1997. See In re Federal-State Joint Board on Universal Service, FCC Docket No. 96-45 (Dec. 31, 1997). For criticism of this new statutory provision, see Mueller (1997). Additional papers and comments regarding universal service are available through the Benton Foundation website (visited Feb. 1, 1998) <http://www.benton.org/>.

21. So too with the fax machine, an appliance that only became valuable once it was distributed among multiple persons connected by a network (Kelly, 1997).

22. Thanks to my colleague Larry Garvin for putting it to me this way.

23. In Ohio, for example, the consideration of retail competition has mobilized consumer protection interests, leading to the proposal of minimum electricity service standards for the first time in the state's history (Ohio 1998; Johnson 1998, p. 4E). Simpson (1997, p. 1) notes that Illinois' restructuring legislation contains new low-income customer assistance charges.

24. As Vernon Smith (1993) has argued, however, joint ventures may work to solve this problem.

25. Fox-Penner (1997, p. 88) cites recent reports by FERC and the U.S. Office of Technology Assessment, as well as the conclusions of Joskow and Schmalensee (1983). However, not everyone agrees (Smith, 1993). As I suggest elsewhere, with the growth of micro-turbines and distributed generation, some competition in power distribution will likely be inevitable.

26. Basic service or the standard offer is independent of a "safety net" provided in many states for low income customers. Unlike the safety net, basic service or the standard offer is designed to provide stable electricity service without major price fluctuations while, at the same time, providing sufficient education about the available options and benefits of retail competition in electricity – to stimulate consumer choice and interest. This approach to ensuring service access is similar to the minimum standard of coverage recommended in health care reform (Rockefeller, 1991, pp. 2507, 2509).

27. A similar model is emerging in the natural gas industry (Merrill, 1999, p. 18).

28. See, e.g. R. I. Gen Laws ch. 316, § 39–1–27.2(d) & (f); Re Electric Utility Industry Restructuring, Maine Pub. Util. Comm'n, Docket No. 95–462, July 19, 1996.

29. Re Restructuring of the Electric Utility Industry in Vermont, 174 P.U.R.4th 409, 434 (Vt. Pub. Serv. Bd. 1996).

30. Ibid, p. 488.

31. Ibid, p. 427.

32. Of course, to the extent that utility risk bearing is desirable, a cost spreading rationale applies as well.

33. Most DisCos are not willing to accept the service obligations absent some compensation guarantee. "The most dangerous position for the disco would be as the backstop provider to customers not effectively served by the market. This scenario is almost assured if the disco does not convince those in power to remove the obligation to serve." (Pleatt, 1998, pp. 44, 48).

34. More than thirty years ago, Harold Demsetz (1968, pp. 55, 59) observed that the history of utilities has been characterized by competition for service areas. (See Chapters 2 and 3.) Of course, the availability of distributed generation may make power distribution competitive in the sense that for some customers switching to self-generation may make distribution unnecessary, so distribution markets will begin to compete with the availability of affordable self-generation, as they already do for some large industrial customers. In addition, some economists suggest that power distribution networks can operate in a competitive manner if property rights are defined so as to facilitate the development of joint ventures (Smith, 1993).

REFERENCES

Alexander, B., & The National Consumer Law Center (1996). *Consumer Protection Proposals for Retail Electric Competition: Model Legislation and Regulations.* National Consumer Law Center.

Arteburn, N. (1927). The Origin and First Test of Public Callings. *University of Pennsylvania Law Review, 75,* 411–428.

Austin, R. (1983). The Insurance Classification Controversy. *University of Pennsylvania Law Review, 131,* 517–583.

Becker, G. (1983). A Theory of Competition Among Pressure Groups for Political Influence. Quarterly *Journal Economics, 98,* 371–400.

Bouknight, J., & Raskin, D. (1987). Planning for Wholesale Customer Loads in a Competitive Environment: The Obligation to Provide Wholesale Service Under the Federal Power Act. *Energy Law Journal, 8,* 237–264.

Burdick, C. (1911). The Origin of the Peculiar Duties of Public Service Companies. *Columbia Law Review, 11,* 514–531.

Carolan, M., & Keating, R. (1997). Microturbines: The Engine of Deregulation. *Investor's Business Daily,* (Dec. 15), p. A40.

Carron, A., & MacAvoy, P. (1981). *The Decline of Service in Regulated Industries.* Washington, D.C.: American Enterprise Institute.

Casson, M. (1997). *Information and Organization: A New Perspective on the Theory of the Firm.* New York: Clarendon Press.

Coase, R. (1937. The Nature of the Firm. *Economica, 4,* 386–405.

Colton, R. (1991). A Cost-Based Response to Low-Income Energy Problems. *Public Utilities Fortnightly,* (Mar. 1), p. 31.

Colton, R. (1997). *The 'Obligation to Serve' and a Competitive Electric Industry.* Report of DOE Office of Economic, Electricity and Natural Gas Analysis, May.

Costello, K., & Lemon, J. (1996). *Unbundling the Retail Natural Gas Market: Current Activities and Guidance for Serving Residential and Small Consumers.* National Regulatory Research Institute.

Costello, K., & Graniere, R. (1997). *Deregulation-Restructuring: Evidence from Individual Industries*. National Regulatory Research Institute.

Demsetz, H. (1968). Why Regulate Utilities? *Journal of Law and Economics, 11*, 55–65.

Epstein, R. (1997). A Clear View from *The Cathedral*: The Dominance of Property Rules. *Yale Law Journal, 106*, 2091–2120.

Farber, D., & Frickey, P. (1991). *Law and Public Choice: A Critical Introduction*. Chicago: University of Chicago Press.

Fox-Penner, P. (1997). *Electric Utility Restructuring: A Guide to the Competitive Era*. Vienna, VA: Public Utility Reports.

Goldberg, V. (1976). Regulation and Administered Contracts. *Bell Journal of Economics, 7*, 426–448.

Haar, C., & Fessler, D. (1986). *The Wrong Side Of The Tracks: A Revolutionary Rediscovery Of The Common Law Tradition Of Fairness In The Struggle Against Inequality*. New York: Simon & Schuster.

Hall, G., & Pierce, R. (1997). Retail Gas Reform: Learning from the Georgia Model. *Public Utilities Fortnightly*, (April 15), 22.

Johnson, A. (1998). State Board Sets Service Standards for Ohio's Electric Companies. *Columbus Dispatch*, (Feb. 6), p. 4E.

Joskow, P. (1977). Commercial Impossibility, The Uranium Market, and the Westinghouse Case. *Journal of Legal Studies, 6*, 119–176.

Joskow, P., & Schmalensee, R. (1983). *Markets for Power: An Analysis of Electrical Utility Deregulation*. Cambridge, MA: MIT Press.

Kelly, K. (1997). New Rules for the New Economy. *Wired*, September.

Klom, A. (1997). Effects of Deregulation Policies on Electricity Competition in the EU. *Journal of Energy & Natural Resources Law, 15*, 1–22.

Lemley, M., & McGowan, D. (1998). Legal Implications of Network Economic Effects. *California Law Review, 86*, 479–611.

Lesser, J., & Ainspan, M. (1994). Retail Wheeling: Deja Vu All Over Again? *The Electricity Journal*, (Apr.), 34–48.

MacAvoy, P., Spulber, D., & Stangle, B. (1989). Is Competitive Entry Free? Bypass and Partial Deregulation in Natural Gas Markets. *Yale Journal on Regulation, 6*, 209–247.

Mashaw, J. (1997). *Greed, Chaos & Governance: Using Public Choice to Improve Public Law*. New Haven: Yale University Press.

Merrill, T. (1999). Supplier of Last Resort: Who, What, Why? *Public Utilities Fortnightly*, (July 15), 18.

Mueller, M. (1997). *Universal Service: Competition, Interconnection, and Monopoly in the Making of the American Telephone System*. Washington, D.C.: American Enterprise Institute.

Noam, E. (1997). Will Universal Service and Common Carriage Survive in the Telecommunications Act of 1996? *Columbia Law Review, 97*, 955–975.

Norlander, G. (1998). Retail Choice: A Race to the Bottom. *Public Utilities Fortnightly*, (Jan. 1), p. 8 (letter to the editor).

Norton, F., & Spivak, M. (1985). The Wholesale Service Obligation of Electric Utilities. *Energy Law Journal, 6*, 179–208.

Ohio Regs Set Service Standards (1998). *Electricity Daily*, (Feb. 9).

Pace, J. (1987). Wheeling and the Obligation to Serve. *Energy Law Journal, 8*, 265–302.

Peltzman, S. (1976. Toward a More General Theory of Regulation. *Journal of Law and Economics, 19*, 211–240.

Pierce, R. (1988). Reconstituting the Natural Gas Industry from Wellhead to Burnertip. *Energy Law Journal, 9*, 1–57.

Platt, H. (1991). *The Electric City: Energy and the Growth of the Chicago Area 880–1930.* Chicago: University of Chicago Press.

Pleatt, G. (1998). Should Metering Stay at the Stand-Alone Disco. *Public Utilities Fortnightly*, (Feb. 1), 44.

Posner, E. (1995). Contract Law in the Welfare State: A Defense of the Unconscionability Doctrine, Usury Laws, and Related Limits on the Freedom to Contract. *Journal of Legal Studies, 24*, 283–319.

Posner, R., & Rosenfield, A. (1977). Impossibility and Related Doctrines in Contract Law: An Economic Analysis. *Journal of Legal Studies, 6*, 83–118.

Priest, G. (1992). The Origins of Utility Regulation and the 'Theories of Regulation' Debate. *Journal of Law & Economics, 36*, 289–323.

Robinson, G. (1928. The Public Utility Concept in American Law. *Harvard Law Review, 41*, 277–308.

Rockefeller, J. (1991). A Call for Action: The Pepper Commission's Blueprint for Health Care Reform. *JAMA, 265*(19), 2507–2510.

Rossi, J. (1998). The Common Law 'Duty to Serve' and Protection of Consumers in an Age of Competitive Retail Public Utility Restructuring. *Vanderbilt Law Review, 51*, 1233–1321.

Sidak, J., & Spulber, D. (1997). *Deregulatory Takings and the Regulatory Contract: The Transformation of Network Industries in the United States.* New York: Cambridge University Press.

Simpson, C. (1997). Thousands Without Heat in Area. *Chicago Sun-Times*, (Dec. 9), 1.

Simpson, J., & Strum, S. (1991). How a Good Samaritan? Federal Income Tax Exemption for Charitable Hospitals Reconsidered. *University of Puget Sound Law Review, 14*, 633–670.

Singer, J. (1996). No Right to Exclude: Public Accommodations and Private Property. *Northwestern University Law Review, 90*, 1283–1497.

Smith, V (1993). Can Electric Power – A 'Natural Monopoly' – Be Deregulated? In: H. H. Landsberg (Ed.), *Making National Energy Policy.* Washington, D.C.: Resources for the Future.

Speidel, R. (1981). Court-Imposed Price Adjustments Under Long-Term Supply Contracts. *Northwestern University Law Review, 76*, 369–422.

Stigler, G. (1971). The Theory of Economic Regulation. *Bell Journal of Economics and Management Science, 2*, 3–21.

Williamson, O. (1976). Franchise Bidding for Natural Monopolies-In General and with Respect to CATV. *Bell Journal of Economics, 7*, 73–104.

Williamson, O. (1979). Transaction Cost Economics: The Governance of Contractual Relations. *Journal of Law & Economics, 22*, 233–261.

Williamson, O. (1996). *The Mechanisms of Governance.* New York: Oxford University Press.

Wyman, B. (1903). The Law of the Public Callings as a Solution of the Trust Problem. *Harvard. Law Review, 17*, 156–173.

Zuckerman, L. (1997). Tiny Turbine: The Next Generator? Company Hopes Its Small Unit Will Dominate Power Market. *New York Times*, (Dec. 2), p. D1.

8. STRANDED BENEFITS VERSUS STRANDED COSTS IN UTILITY DEREGULATION

Reed W. Cearley and Daniel H. Cole

INTRODUCTION

A central controversy in electric utility deregulation concerns the treatment of so-called "stranded costs," which are costs of investments undertaken in reliance upon the pre-existing regulatory regime, with its guaranteed rate of return. Utilities argue that if they are not allowed to recover investment costs – if those costs are left "stranded" – they (and their shareholders) will suffer losses estimated at between $10 and $500 billion.[1] At worst, such losses could threaten the existence of some investor-owned utilities; at least, they would place post-regulatory utilities at a competitive disadvantage to new entrants to their markets.

To avoid this prospect, utilities have successfully lobbied the Federal Energy Regulation Commission and several state legislatures to permit them to recover their stranded costs in the process of utility deregulation.[2] This seems only fair. But the discussion of the stranded-cost issue has been one-sided. The real issue concerns not just stranded *costs* but all stranded *investments*, which can result in either stranded costs for utilities or stranded *benefits* for utility customers. While utilities have complained about the prospect of the former, they have been rationally silent about the later, which would accrue to their benefit and to the detriment of electricity consumers, who have had little voice in discussions of deregulation.

The End of a Natural Monopoly: Deregulation and Competition in the Electric Power Industry, Volume 7, pages 169–190.

ISBN: 0-7623-0995-4

This chapter assesses the issue of stranded investment in full, attending to both stranded costs *and* benefits. An analysis of stranded-cost and –benefit estimates for utilities in Indiana, California, and other states, reveals that, for many utilities, stranded benefits are likely to exceed stranded costs. If that proves to be the case, then deregulation creates greater risks for consumers than for utilities and their investors. Consumers may actually pay more for electricity in the new environment and incur substantial lost benefits from deregulation, without compensation.

DEREGULATING THE ELECTRIC POWER MARKET

The electric power industry is in an uneasy state of transition from a regulated industry to a competitive market in power generation. This may be a result of technological innovations that have greatly reduced the capital-intensity of power production. In the past, utilities spent billions of dollars constructing huge coal-fired and nuclear power plants to take advantage of economies of scale that minimized average production costs. These large units required many years to build and put into service. Today, advances in combustion turbine technology have allowed smaller, low-cost plants to achieve even greater savings then the large generators of the past. Older, large power generating units are becoming less competitive in the move to a deregulated power industry.

Non-utility investors are banking on the move to competition. In Indiana alone, plans and construction are under way to build approximately 12,000 megawatts of new merchant plants.[3] Across the country, approximately 200,000 megawatts of new capacity are currently in the planning process for future development.[4] These merchant plants cost only a fraction of traditional generators, and can be put into service far more quickly.[5] They are fundamentally altering the electric power market, turning giant coal-fired power plants into artifacts of the past.

STRANDED COSTS, STRANDED BENEFITS, AND EQUITY IN TRANSITION

The shift to competition in utility generation may generate wealth transfers between investors and utility ratepayers. "Stranded costs" – a wealth transfer from investors to ratepayers – occur when expected revenues from utility ratepayers are insufficient to cover all operating costs and a fair return on invested capital. Investors would not receive the total revenue required to support the market value of their generating assets. This situation is depicted in Fig. 1a. "Stranded benefits" – a wealth transfer from consumers to investors

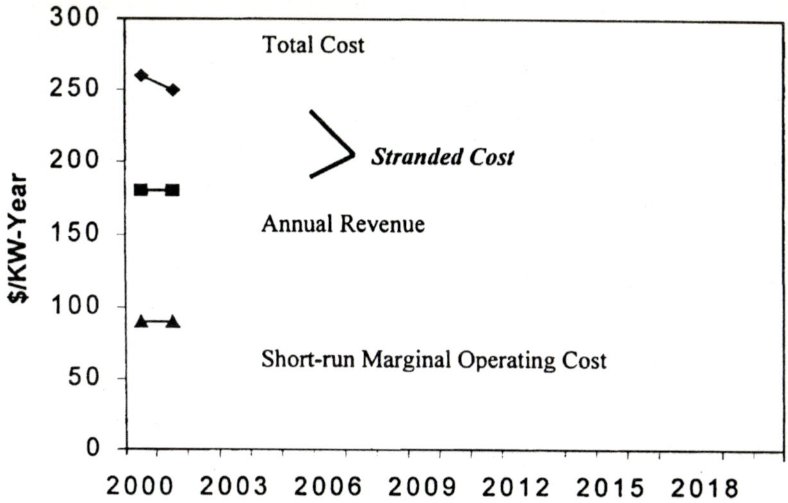

Fig. 1a. Stranded Costs.

– occur when expected revenues received after restructuring exceed the total revenue required under traditional regulation. Fig. 1b depicts these lost benefits to utility consumers. These wealth transfers do not occur under regulation because the regulators adjust the utility's revenue stream from time

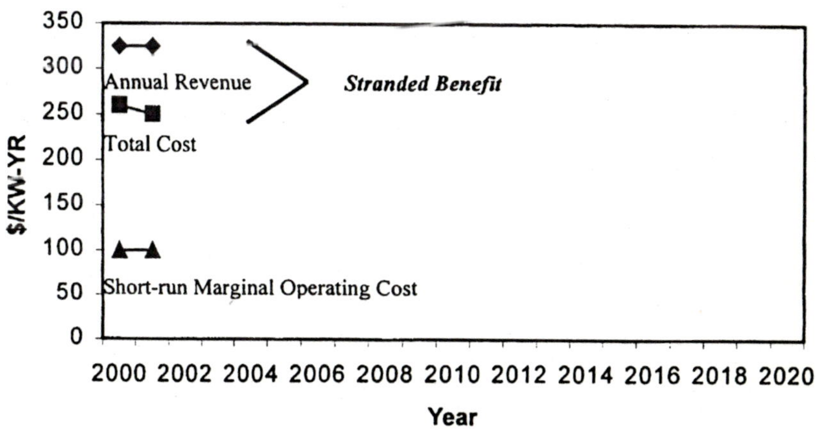

Fig. 1b. Stranded Benefits.

Source: Cearley and McKinzie (1995, p. 19, Figs 1a and b).

to time, insuring that sufficient *but not excess* revenues are collected from the ratepayers, so that utilities recover only a "fair rate of return" on the book value of their assets (see Maloney, McCormick & Sauer, 1997, p. 61).

"Stranded investment" is the flow of both stranded costs and benefits through time. Stranded costs or benefits arise when, in the process of deregulation, risks and benefits of utility investments are reallocated between utility shareholders and customers. Under traditional regulation, ratepayers received the economic benefits of the utility assets, and were expected to bear the economic risks of prudent utility investments (see Cearley & McKinzie, 1995, pp. 16–23).[6] After utility restructuring, however, customers will no longer be required to pay for the utility's generating assets; but neither will they reap the benefits of guaranteed service. In effect, all investment risks and benefits will be transferred to the utility's investors.

Reallocating the risks and benefits creates transition costs and potential stranded investments. Investments undertaken prior to deregulation may yield stranded costs because the investor is no longer guaranteed a reasonable rate of return on those investments. But they may also generate stranded benefits if, in the post-deregulation market, utilities can charge customers more for past investments than they would have received under regulation.

Regulators can minimize the transition costs and potential stranded investments of deregulation by applying certain equitable principles. One such equitable principle, promoted all along by utilities, is that they and their investors should be compensated for stranded costs (see Energy Information Administration – Electricity Prices in a Competitive Environment: Marginal Cost Pricing of Generation Services and Financial Status of Electric Utilities). But this equitable principle will actually have *in*equitable impacts unless it is accompanied by a reciprocal equitable principle that utility customers should be compensated for stranded benefits. These two principles can be merged into one: when electricity markets are restructured, all parties sustaining losses should be compensated. However, this equitable principle should only be implemented if the benefits from compensation outweigh the substantial transaction costs entailed by any compensation scheme. If the expected costs and benefits of stranded investments are both minor, or sufficiently close as to be almost offsetting, then the best policy may well be to leave the costs and benefits where they fall.

MEASURING STRANDED INVESTMENTS

There are two ways to measure a utility's stranded investment: (1) by current market price; or (2) by projected revenue and costs. Both methods provide a reasonable prediction of stranded investment. The first method is best at accurately determining stranded investment for a particular asset because it places a value on stranded investment at the time the asset is sold. However, few assets will be sold by utilities precisely when electricity markets are restructured. Consequently, the second method may be a more realistic approach to determining a utility's level of stranded investment over time.

The Current Market Price Approach

To accurately measure a stranded investment, future changes in annual revenues and costs must be accounted for (see Cearley & McKinzie, 1995, pp. 16–23) because future expectations influence the current market price of a utility's investment. Investors are not myopic; if they expect future costs to exceed expected revenues, market price will decline and some amount of the investment will be "stranded," that is, unrecovered. This is typically reflected in the ratio of market value to book value of the utility's assets. If the market to book ratio is less than 1 – that is, if the market value of the asset is less than the remaining book value – that means investors expect future costs, including a reasonable return on investment, to exceed future revenues. Conversely, if the market-to-book ratio exceeds one, then investors expect that future revenues will exceed future costs, plus a reasonable return on investment.

Stranded investments, under this current market approach, are simply the net difference between the market value of the asset and its book value. Table 1 lists the market to book ratio for utility generating assets that have recently sold, and demonstrates that net stranded benefits of approximately $11 billion exist for utilities, to be borne by current consumers. It is not clear, however, whether consumers will ever recoup these stranded benefits in the form of rate reductions or offsets against recovery of utilities' stranded costs.[7]

The Projected Revenue and Costs Stream Approach

The most accurate way to measure a stranded investment is by comparing the current market price of a utility's asset to its remaining book value. For example, in Table 1 current sales of generation assets have yielded considerable value to investors – selling for approximately 2.16 times their remaining book value. However, these asset sales of approximately 60 thousand megawatts represent but a small fraction of the total existing generation market, and do not accurately predict the total potential level of stranded investment for several reasons. First, in all likelihood only assets whose market value exceeds book value will be sold. The potential liabilities of large nuclear plants, for example,

Table 1. Plant Divestitures: Market Price and Book Values.

Seller/Buyer	Capacity (mW)	Price $MM	Price ($/kW)*	Book ($MM)	Book ($/kW)*
Bangor/PP&L	96	80	833	24	250
BEC/Sithe	1,983	536	270	450	227
CMP/FPL	1,185	846	714	240	203
Cmwlth Energy/Southern	984	462	470	79	80
ConEd/Southern & Dynergy	814	135	166	151	186
ConEd/NRG	1,456	505	347	220	151
ConEd/Key Span	2,168	597	275	330	152
ConEd/Orion	1,855	550	296	250	135
DQE/AYP	276	N/A	N/A	N/A	N/A
EIX/AES	3,956	781	197	N/A	N/A
EIX/Houston	2,276	237	104	N/A	N/A
EIX/NRG & Destec	1,020	88	86	N/A	N/A
EIX/Thermo Ecotek	280	10	34	N/A	N/A
EIX/Houston	1,500	43	29	125	83
EIX/NRG & Destec	530	30	56	N/A	N/A
Energy East/AES	1,424	950	667	662	465
Energy East/Edison Mission	942	900	955	219	232
EUA/Southern	280	75	268	40	143
EUA/NRG	160	55	344	30	188
GPU/Edison Mission	942	900	955	219	232
GPU/Sithe	4,117	1,680	408	814	198
GPU/FirstEnergy	83	43	518	16	193
MainePSCo/WPS-PDI	92	37	405	12	127
Montana Power/PPL	1,556	892	573	552	355
NEES/USGen	3,960	1,590	402	1,100	278
NiMo/Orion	661	425	643	250	378
Orange & Rockland/Southern	976	345	353	179	183
PG & E/Duke	2,745	501	183	380	138
PG & E/Southern	3,065	801	261	432	141
PG & E/FPL	1,224	214	175	160	131
PG & E(Enron)/PPL	323	49	152	32	99
PPL/WPS-PDI	467	106	227	64	137
Puget/PPL	735	549	747	354	482
Sempra/NRG & Dynegy	1,218	356	292	94	77
Sempra/San Diego Unified PD	693	110	159	40	58
Unicom/Southern & Dominion	1,598	250	156	250	156
Unicom/Edison Mission	9,772	4,813	493	1,300	133
United Illuminating/Wisvest	1,056	272	258	217	205
Total or Average	59,844	21,170	346*	9,835	160*

* Per-Kilowat values are calculated by backing out the capacity figures for plants with unknown prices or book values.

Source: Stavros (1999).

could create a risk so large that investors would be unwilling to purchase those assets at a price greater than the remaining book value. Second, guaranteed stranded-cost recovery for utility assets creates a considerable cash flow problem when customers are forced to repay the investors for the remaining undepreciated book value.[8] For large generating assets, therefore, where stranded-cost recovery is assured, the utility will likely hold on to the assets, investing recovered costs from stranded investments in other markets. In other words, guaranteed stranded-cost recovery creates an incentive for the utilities to hold on to presently non-economic assets. In order to measure stranded investment for unsold assets, therefore, future changes in cost and revenues (comparing traditional regulated market rates and projected competitive market prices) must be considered. In a regulated market, annual utility fixed costs decline.

Under competition, by contrast, annual revenues follow the long-run marginal cost curve. Since annual revenues follow the annual costs, the revenues will be equal to annual operating expenses when the plant is fully depreciated.[9] At some point, annual revenues received under regulation will be less than those received under competition. Stranded costs occur when competitive revenues are less that regulated revenues. Stranded benefits occur after regulated revenues fall below competitive revenues. Stranded investment for these assets is represented by the difference in net present value of annual stranded costs and benefits (Cearley & McKinzie, 1995, pp. 16–23). A utility's potential level of stranded investment then depends on whether or not the long-run marginal costs and corresponding market prices paid for electricity exceed the average costs of producing electricity, i.e. the regulated prices. Three questions therefore, must be answered before a utility's potential level of stranded investment can be determined:

(1) What would be the traditional regulated price for existing assets?
(2) What will be the long-run marginal cost and the future price of electricity?
(3) How would traditional regulation revenues compare with competitive revenues?

Regulated Price Projections for Existing Assets

Figure 2 depicts estimated future revenue requirements for electric generating asset under continued regulation. Regulated prices for existing assets are based on the cost of providing service, that is, on fuel, operation, maintenance, and capital costs. Capital costs are associated with a utility's rate base, which is its invested capital, taxes, and depreciation. Fixed charges for existing assets typically decline through time because of depreciation. Regulators, in setting utility prices, usually account for the declining value of the existing asset

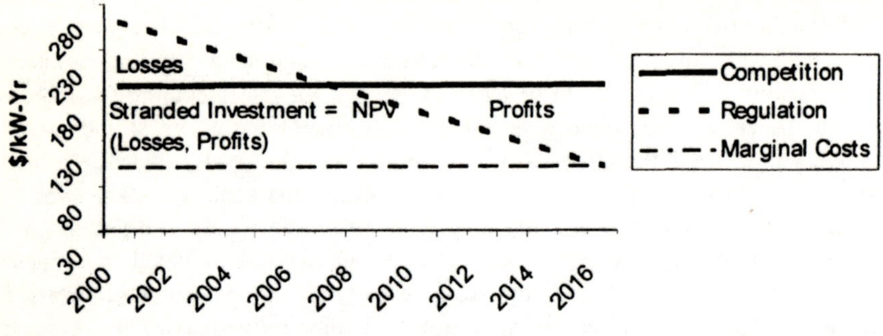

Fig. 2. Competitive Revenue versus Regulated Generation Revenue Requirements.
Source: Stranded Costs, Stranded Benfits – A Two Way Street, *The Electricity Journal*, *8*(9), 20.

base. In effect, historical cost determines the value of the regulated asset base. Regulated prices, then, are based on the average cost of the utility's assets, and do not reflect the marginal cost of providing service on a seasonal or time-determined basis.

Market Prices

Competitive prices for all assets will be set at the marginal cost of the most expensive unit. Once the utilities' assets are no longer regulated, they will receive this market price. Whether utilities earn an economic profit or not will depend on whether or not the competitive market price exceeds their average cost of production.

Figure 2 also depicts competitive market price projections. Expectations of future prices are determined, of course, by the expected interaction of demand and supply over time. Prices could increase due to (real) fuel price increases or increasing environmental costs; or they could decrease due to declining (real) fuel costs or improved productive efficiency. New assets enter the market either to meet increased demand or to replace older, less efficient units. To accurately predict future market prices, therefore, analysts must be able to accurately forecast fuel, operation, maintenance, and capital costs for the least efficient generator needed to meet peak demand at various times of the year. Forecast uncertainty yields substantial economic risks (see Cearley & McKinzie, 1995, pp. 20, 21).

Long-Run Marginal Costs Pricing

Generally, regulated rates exceed marginal costs only when utilities possess excess capacity.[10] In practice, regulators have tended to allow utilities to recover *all* costs of operation, including the fixed costs of excess capacity. Consequently, average rates have tended to be higher than marginal costs.

Conversely, marginal costs and market prices may exceed average embedded costs of generation when demand greatly exceeds capacity. For example, during the summer of 2000 wholesale prices for electrical power in California increased by 270% on average over the same period in 1999, resulting in over $1 billion in additional payments for electricity. During the week of June 14, 2000, purchasers of California power spent $1.2 billion on electricity, 300% more than they paid during the same period in 1999, and one-eighth of their cost of power for all of 1999. Residents of San Diego – the first to be exposed to unregulated electricity prices – saw their June electricity bills double.[11]

In the Midwest, during the summer of 1999, wholesale electric prices were $7.50/kWh – a price that clearly exceeded both contemporary marginal costs and contemporary regulated rates (see State Utility Forecasting Group, 1999, pp. 1–13).[12] This situation, where market prices exceed average embedded rates, generally indicates that the market is acting more as a clearinghouse, providing information about the value of scarce resources, rather than actually allocating resources according to costs.

This cycle of insufficient and excess capacity must be understood in order to fully grasp the stranded investment problem. If the timing of deregulation is such that the newly competitive market possesses surplus capacity, then downward pressure on electric prices from non-utility generators with lower marginal costs could result in significant stranded costs for the newly deregulated utilities. However, this excess supply with its higher-than-marginal-cost rates is likely to be only a temporary phenomenon; over time, increasing consumer demand is expected to eliminate the excess supply condition.[13] Conversely, if deregulation occurs when capacity is tight, putting upward pressure on generation prices, then the possibility exists that electricity prices may rise above regulated rates, resulting in a significant level of stranded benefits for utilities, to the detriment of customers – as happened in California during the summer of 2000.

Figure 3 presents an actual forecast of this long-term cycle of insufficient and excess capacity for utilities in the State of Indiana. The regulation line projects continued regulated rates for all of Indiana's utilities. The Competition line projects the long-run marginal costs for the ECAR/MAIN combined regions.[14] The rates and prices represent average annual rates and prices without consideration of seasonal variations in demand and capacity. Thus, it is possible that short-term price spikes will occur when demand exceeds capacity, as they did in fact in the summer of 1999.

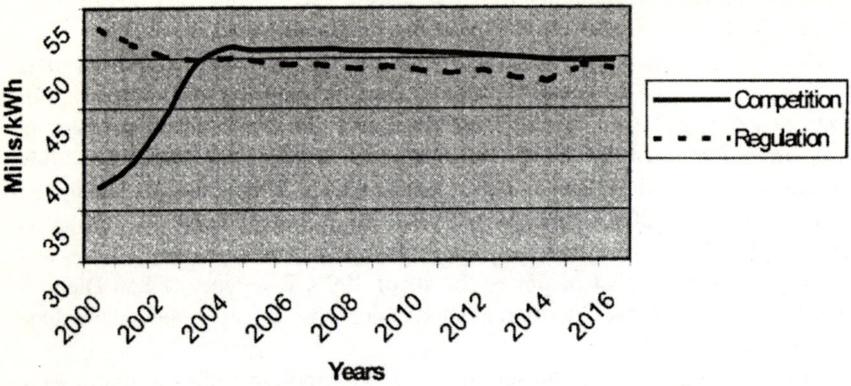

Fig. 3. Indiana Electricity Price Projections.

Source: State Utility Forecasting Group (1999, Fig. 1-8).

Figure 3 indicates that during the initial period of surplus capacity in Indiana's electricity market, market prices may be considerably lower than pre-existing regulated rates. By 2004, however, current capacity surpluses are projected to evaporate, at which point market prices are projected to rise above regulated rates. This transition is expected to occur because the long-run regulated price is based upon an abundance of older, depreciated generation equipment. This older equipment has smaller associated fixed investment costs because of depreciation, resulting in lower regulated prices (see State Utility Forecasting Group, 1999, pp. 1–14).[15]

Some proponents of stranded-cost recovery claim that new generation is significantly cheaper than existing assets. They assume, therefore, that the market price of electricity will trend downward.[16] Implicit in this assumption is that new assets will be price leaders instead of price takers – that is, that the competitive market price will be based on the new assets as they come into the market. However, this assumption runs contrary to the conventional economic wisdom that new investors will seek to profit by accepting higher market prices instead selling their electricity at marginal cost.[17] Further, it is unlikely that new investments (whether in non-utility generation or traditional units) will set the market price for many years to come. Future market prices will probably remain higher than the cost of new generation because the new investments will only make up a small percentage of the generation market. New plant investment proposals in the ECAR, for example, amount to 8,900 megawatts, which represents just 8% of ECAR's total estimated capacity by

2008.[18] Another reason to suppose that new investment might not set the market price is that, in all likelihood, it will only account for growth in demand. In fact, ECAR's new investment does not even keep pace with demand, and projected capacity margins are expected to decline over the next ten years.[19] There is good reason, therefore, to expect that existing high marginal-cost units, rather than the new lower cost units, will be setting the price in ECAR, at least for the foreseeable future. There is an important caveat, however: the newer units may become price-setters if there is a dramatic increase in their marginal costs, resulting perhaps from an unexpected spike in fuel costs, so that they become the higher cost units. In ECAR, as in most other regions, the new units of choice are the combustion turbine or the combined cycle units, both of which use natural gas as their primary fuel choice. A dramatic, short-term increase in natural gas prices could raise the cost of generation at these new plants so much that they would have higher total costs of generation than traditional coal-fired units in the regions.[20] They would, in that circumstance, become price setters, but market prices would be rising.

Other factors can also be expected to affect market prices in competitive electricity markets. The early retirement of nuclear or coal-fired capacity and increased environmental regulations could decrease existing capacity and result in higher market prices. In ECAR, approximately 1,000 megawatts of nuclear and coal-fired capacity will be withdrawn from service over the next ten years. The early retirement of nuclear capacity alone will significantly reduce the level of low-cost ECAR generation resources – leaving the market price to be set by other higher cost units. Moreover, ECAR projects that significant reductions in capacity margins could occur because of increased environmental regulations (see: Assessment of ECAR-Wide Capacity Margins, 1999–2008, pp 35–37). Again, reduced margins would leave the remaining higher marginal cost units to set the market price. The net result is that the marginal costs and competitive prices could be significantly higher after deregulation, resulting in less stranded investment for the existing utilities. This possibility is depicted in Fig. 3, according to which ECAR's projected competitive market prices are expected to exceed the projected regulated prices between 2004 and 2015 in Indiana.

Projected Revenue Streams: Competition versus Continued Regulation

Table 2 provides a possible measure of stranded investment for Indiana's utilities, where market prices are expected to exceed the rates that would prevail if regulation continued. The figures presented in the table indicate the net difference between competitive and traditional regulated revenues for Indiana's utilities.[21] Competitive revenues and prices are based on the long-run marginal cost of all existing and projected assets in the ECAR/MAIN combined regions.

Regulated rates and revenues are based on the estimated cost of providing service for Indiana's electric utilities (as would be the case under a "reasonable-rate-of-return" approach to ratemaking).

The figures in Table 2 have serious implications for the treatment of stranded utility investments in Indiana. As previously noted, the potential exists for near-term stranded costs of approximately 3.4 billion dollars. But there is also a potential for stranded benefits to Indiana's consumers of at least 2 billion dollars over the next sixteen years. And that figure could be higher if competition does not materialize and existing utilities continue to wield substantial market power.[22]

Surely, if equity requires that utilities (and their investors) be able to recover stranded costs, e.g. through near-term rate freezes, then equity must also require that ratepayers recover stranded benefits. However, the State of Indiana has yet to enact legislation that would ensure the recovery of either stranded costs or

Table 2. Difference in Continued Regulated and Competitive Revenues for Indiana.

Year	Competition $/MWh	Regulation $/MWh	SUFG Indiana Forecast GWh	Competition Revenue $MM	Regulation Revenue $MM	Difference $MM
2000	37.31	52.98	96,867	3,614	5,132	–1,518
2001	39.39	51.55	98,922	3,897	5,099	–1,203
2002	43.69	50.24	101,170	4,420	5,083	–663
2003	49.39	49.83	103,298	5,102	5,147	–45
2004	50.94	49.97	105,179	5,358	5,256	102
2005	50.90	49.79	107,058	5,449	5,330	119
2006	50.89	49.35	108,833	5,539	5,371	168
2007	50.86	49.36	110,601	5,625	5,459	166
2008	50.79	49.05	112,433	5,710	5,515	196
2009	50.71	49.26	114,148	5,788	5,623	166
2010	50.60	48.84	116,124	5,876	5,671	204
2011	50.48	48.52	118,291	5,971	5,739	232
2012	50.43	48.87	120,130	6,058	5,871	187
2013	50.09	47.96	122,389	6,130	5,870	261
2014	49.88	47.80	124,797	6,225	5,965	260
2015	49.81	49.30	126,406	6,296	6,232	64
2016	49.79	49.03	128,237	6,385	6,287	97
Total						–1,208
Total 2000–2003 potential stranded costs						–3,429
Total 2004–2016 potential stranded benefits						2,221

Source: State Utility Forecasting Group: Indiana Electricity Projections: The 1999 Forecast.

benefits. Several other states, including Illinois, have enacted legislation providing for recovery of stranded costs, e.g. through near-term rate freezes, but not stranded benefits.[23] This legislation provides a safety net for utility investors but completely ignores the legitimate interests of consumers.

STRANDED INVESTMENTS AND COLLECTIVE ACTION

Stranded investment is typically represented in the literature as the stream of stranded costs without reference to the stream of stranded benefits (see, e.g. Sidak & Spulber, 1998; Maloney, McCormick & Sauer, 1997). Authors account only for the stream of future utility losses without considering the possibility that customers may pay more for electricity in the future. When the market value exceeds the book value no mention is made to the potential adverse effects on current customers.[24]

What explains this disparate treatment of stranded costs and benefits in utility deregulation? One does not have to be a staunch advocate of Public Choice theory to recognize that collective action problems play a prominent role in the explanation (see Olson, 1971). Utilities, not surprisingly, have lobbied state legislatures for stranded-cost recovery; but they have no interest in pushing for reciprocal stranded-benefit recovery for ratepayers. Meanwhile, utility ratepayers represent the type of diffuse interest group that has difficulty coalescing around an issue to effectively pursue its collective interest.

Theories of collective action cannot, however, explain the lack of attention to potential stranded benefits in the academic literature. Even more puzzling is the lack of attention to stranded benefits by utility commissions. Traditionally, regulators and courts have been careful to protect the interests of ratepayers (i.e. consumers) when utility assets have sold for prices above book value. For example, in *Illinois Public Telecom Assoc. v. FCC,* 117 F.3d 555 (D.C. Cir. 1997) the court stated,

> As a general rule, utility service ratepayers "pay for service" and thus "do not acquire any interest, legal or equitable, in the property . . . of the company. Property paid for out of moneys received for service belongs to the company" [citation omitted] However, we have held that neither ratepayers nor the company (and thus its shareholders) are necessarily entitled to increases in the value of assets employed in the utility's operations. [citation omitted] Rather, such increases are to be allocated under a two-step test in which the court first asks which party "bears the risk of loss" on the assets [citation omitted] The party that bore the risk of loss is the party entitled to the capital gains on the assets. [citation omitted] Only if it is difficult to determine who bore the risk of loss will "the second principle come into play, namely, 'that those who bear the financial burden of particular utility activity should also reap the benefits resulting therefrom' " [citation omitted].

The court further stated:

> Under a rate-of-return system, a company "can charge rates no higher than necessary to obtain sufficient revenue to cover" the costs of regulated activities and "achieve a fair return on equity" [citation omitted]. The provision of payphone service traditionally has been treated as a regulated activity [citation omitted]. Thus, LEC shareholders were protected against losses from depreciation expenses on the assets of regulated activities; it was ratepayers who bore the risk of loss on such assets. However, in October 1990, the Commission switched to a "price cap" system of regulating the larger LECs (i.e. the BOCs and GTE companies) [citation omitted]. Under a price cap system, "the regulator sets a maximum price, and the firm selects rates at or below the cap" [citation omitted]. Cost reductions under the price cap scheme "do not trigger reductions in the cap," but rather increase the company's profits [citation omitted]. Thus, after 1990, the ratepayers no longer bore the risk of losses from payphone operation assets. To the extent a BOC incurred expenses in connection with payphone operations, company and shareholder profits declined. As a result, at least since 1990, investors rather than ratepayers have borne the risk of loss on payphone assets (tangible and intangible), and thus, under Democratic Central, investors should reap the benefit of increases in the value of such assets.

The court in *Illinois Public Telecom Assoc.* understood that the party who bears the risk of loss for the utility's investment should also receive the benefit of a market gain, if the asset is sold for a price above book value. Indeed, the court's understanding reflects the central question in utility restructuring: who bears the risk of loss. If it is unfair for utilities (and their investors) to bear the risk of loss for costs stranded as a result of deregulation, then it remains to be explained why it is not similarly unfair for ratepayers to bear the risk of loss for stranded benefits. Nevertheless, the disparate treatment of stranded costs and benefits persists.

Consider, for example, California's recently enacted restructuring legislation.[25] Under this law, stranded costs (but not benefits) are recovered through a non-bypassable transition-cost recovery mechanism, which allows electric utilities (but not consumers) an opportunity to continue to recover various costs for generation-related assets.[26] California's electric consumers bear the risk of loss from non-economic assets.

To illustrate how California's deregulation bill allocates the risks stemming from deregulation consider the treatment of the gains from sales of utility assets in recent California Divestiture Proceedings:

SDG&E Sec. 851 "Divestiture" Application 97-12-039

SDG&E filed its divestiture application on December 19, 1997 to divest all of its fossil plants, its 20% interest in SONGS nuclear power plant as well as all of its long term power purchase contracts. On February 18, 1999, the Commission approved (D. 99-02-073) the sale of the Encina power plant and 17 combustion turbines by SDG&E to a consortium comprised of Dynergy Power Corporation and NRG Energy Inc. Encina and the combustion turbines had a combined net book value as of December 31, 1997 of $94.8 million. The sale price was $ 356 million.

D. 99-03-015 issued on March 4, 1999, approved the sale and donation of the South Bay Power plant to the San Diego Unified Port District. Under the agreement, the Port District will pay $110 million for the plant to SDG&E and SDG&E will provide the Port District with a charitable donation of the main plant site land, the LNG Parcel, the Transmission parcel and the value of the South Bay plant facilities, which exceeds $110 million. The Port District has leased the plant to Duke Energy for operation.

PG&E, Sec, 851 "Divestiture" Application 98-01-008

D. 99-04-026 issued on April 1, 1999 approved the sale of PG&E's second batch of plants. Southern Energy purchased the Potrero and the Delta plants for $801 million. The net book value of these plants was $318.394 million. Calpine purchased the Sonoma County Geysers and the Lake County Geysers power plants for a total of $ 212.8 million. The combined net book value of these plants was $272.73 million.

Earlier, PG&E (A. 96-11-020; D. 97-12-107) had sold a total of 2645 MW of capacity (Morrow Bay –1002 MW, Moss Landing-1478 MW and Oakland Power Plant-165 MW) to Duke Power Services for $501 million. The net book value of these plants was $390 million.

Southern California Edison, Power Plant Divestiture A. 96-11-046

Edison offered all of its 12 oil/gas fired power plants for sale through an open auction process approved by the CPUC. 10 of these plants were sold in November of 1997. The sale was approved by the CPUC on December 16, 1997 (D. 97-12-106). The two remaining units – Long Beach and Ormond Beach power plants were sold earlier this year. The total capacity of all 12 of these plants was 9562 MW. The first 10 plants sold for a total of $ 1.115 billion, which was 2.65 times the net book value of those plants. Long Beach (530 MW) plant was sold to NRG Energy and Destec Energy for $29.9 million. Ormond Beach was purchased by Houston industries for $40 million. The net book value for this plant was $125 million.[27]

After these generation assets are sold for a combined 1.88 times book value in California, they will supply energy at market prices, which means that consumers receive none of the stranded benefits from the divestitures; only the utility and its shareholders profit from selling assets previously paid for by ratepayers. According to the California Public Utility Commission, the gains from these asset sales can be used to offset utilities' stranded costs (transition cost balancing accounts or "TCBA"),[28] which substantially reduces the unfairness to consumers. Still, under California's approach, consumers bear the risk of *net* losses from noncompetitive generation assets.

This situation is not unique to California. Restructuring legislation in Maine and Ohio similarly provides that stranded benefits may offset current stranded costs, but any net gains accrue to investors.[29] Utilities are required to offset stranded costs up to the point where stranded benefits equal those costs. Any excess stranded benefits simply become additional contributions to capital – a windfall for investors.

The California, Maine, and Ohio restructuring laws all violate the equitable principle enunciated in *Illinois Public Telecom Assoc.*: that the party who paid the cost for the asset should receive current and future benefits associated with it. At best, utility customers who paid for utility assets through rate paying can only expected to benefit from future sales of those assets to the extent that any profits offset other stranded costs; if there are net stranded benefits, they cannot recover the excess benefits. By contrast, if stranded costs exceed stranded benefits, utilities and their investors can recover the excess. To make matters worse, California's electricity consumers will have to pay utilities a small "Competitive Transition Charge" ("CTC") for costs associated with nuclear power contracts and industry restructuring. These CTCs, which will be set by the Commission, further shift the risk of loss to consumers. By transferring the costs of noncompetitive assets to consumers during restructuring, utilities and their investors are protected. In fact, they are *more* than protected. The CTCs virtually guarantee that investors in California's utilities will be *over*-compensated for generation assets.[30] Consumers, in effect, will be paying twice for the same generation assets – first, through the recovery of stranded costs and, again, by paying market-based prices after restructuring.

CONCLUSION: STRANDED INVESTMENTS, EQUITY, AND THE TRANSACTION COSTS OF COMPENSATION

In the process of electric utility deregulation it is clear that there will be stranded investments, both costs and benefits, which if left uncompensated would effect unjustified wealth transfers between consumers and investors. If utilities are not compensated for stranded costs (from noncompetitive generating assets built with the understanding of a guaranteed reasonable rate of return), investors will suffer potentially sizeable losses, while consumers will benefit from not having to pay for uneconomic investments. Many scholars have noted that such a wealth transfer from investors to consumers is unjustified. Few have paid any attention, however, to the converse problem of stranded benefits, which arises if consumers are not compensated after utilities profit from selling (at higher than book-value prices) generating assets that consumers previously paid for under regulation. But such a wealth transfer from consumers to investors is certainly no more justified than a wealth transfer from investors to consumers.

The California, Maine, and Ohio deregulation statutes exemplify how effective utilities and their advocates have been in lobbying to ensure that they will be able to recover stranded costs. Consumer interests, by contrast, have hardly been considered in the process. Utility customers will be required to shoulder the transition costs of the most inefficient utilities, while paying market prices for electricity that may, for the foreseeable future, exceed traditional regulated prices.

If stranded cost recovery is allowed, then equity dictates that stranded benefit recovery should be allowed as well. The most efficient way to implement such an equitable principle would be to allow stranded cost recovery only where a utility's stranded costs exceed the sum of stranded benefits and the transaction costs associated with the compensation system. Similarly, electricity customers should be allowed to recover stranded benefits where those benefits exceed the sum of stranded costs and the transaction costs associated with the compensation system. Where the difference between expected stranded costs and expected stranded benefits is small, then the best policy may be to allow no recovery of either. In that case, the expense of implementing a compensation system may exceed the benefits. Indeed, given the substantial *ex ante* uncertainty about who will gain and who will lose from investments stranded by changes in the regulatory system, the best overall policy may be to leave stranded costs and benefits where they lie.

NOTES

1. The figure cited is at the high-end estimate of investor-owned utilities. Other estimates range between $10 billion and $160 billion in total stranded costs. See Thierer (1997). However, as Cearley and McKinzie (1995, p. 16) have cautioned, estimating stranded costs "is essentially a shot in the dark at a moving target."

2. 78 FERC 61,220 United States of America Federal Energy Regulatory Commission 18 CFR Part 35 [Docket Nos. RM95-8-001 and RM94-7-002; Order No. 888-A], Promoting Wholesale Competition Through Open Access Non-discriminatory Transmission Services by Public Utilities; Recovery of Stranded Costs by Public Utilities and Transmitting Utilities (Issued March 4, 1997).

3. Indiana Utility Regulatory Commission Cause No. 41757 – testimony of Reed W. Cearle, September 20, 2000.

4. Electric Power Supply Association See http://www.epsa.org/competition/merchant.cfm. Many of the new generating units are or will be owned by local gas utilities, large global energy companies, and energy cooperatives. The deregulation of generation has yielded significant new generation investment, which will benefit the Midwest generally during times of peak demand and will likely benefit Illinois customers in the future. See http://www.icc.state.il.us/icc/home/ec.asp. It should be noted, however, that not everyone believes that this new capacity will be built. See testimony of Benjamin H. Sisson, witness for the petitioner in PSEG Lawrenceburg Company LLC's request to build a merchant plant in Indiana, IURC Cause No. 41757: Mr. Sisson stated: "As of March 2000, 24,100 MW new capacity for the entire ECAR region has been announced. IN all of ECAR only 3,863 MW of the 24,100 MW announced is either operating or under construction. Given the challenges associated with power plant development, it is reasonable to conclude that only a portion of the 24,100 MW currently announced is expected to be built."

5. Combustion turbine plants of approximately 150 MW cost about $330/KW; Combined Cycle plants of approximately 200 MW cost about $490/KW; Conventional Coal plants of approximately 500 MW cost about $1150/KW. See Purdue University, State Utility Forecasting Group, " Indiana Electricity Projections: The 1999 Forecast." According to recent plans for merchant plants in service in Indiana (similar to other regions as well), it takes approximately two to two and a half years to build and place in service a peaking turbine using natural gas; it takes approximately three to four years to build and place in service a combined cycle intermediate plant. Currently there are no plans to build a base load generator, but it usually takes seven years to build and place in service a base load generating plant.

6. Implicit in the argument for allowing for stranded costs recovery is that consumers bear the economic risk of the utility's assets. However, what is typically lost in this argument is that if consumers bear the economic risk then they should also reap the economic benefits from those assets.

7. See "Plant Valuation: Book Value and Beyond", *Public Utilities Fortnightly*, September 1, 1999 p. 60. "In general, Central Maine Power Co. appears to have implemented a good strategy in divesting its generation assets. In 'Valuing an Electric Utility: Theory and Application,' we assumed that the company's return on invested capital was approximately 13%, which was likely to significantly exceed its after-tax weighted average costs of capital. It is not clear, however, how much of the gain, if any, will be shared with the company's customers."8. If the selling utility is guaranteed stranded costs recovery after the sale then the sale of these assets will not be impeded. However, it is unclear which party to the contract will receive the stranded cost recovery – buyer or seller. Current utility holding company mergers (American Electric Power with Central and South West) tend to indicate that the stranded cost recovery will tend to accrue to the buyer. In the AEP-CSW merger any stranded costs recovery will accrue to the electric operating companies and thus, the new entity, i.e. the remaining corporation after the merger, American Electric Power. See Central and South West Corp., Form 10-K December 31, 1997.

9. This follows from the construction of a utility's rate base with the inclusion of generating assets subject to stranded-cost recovery. The rate base (noted in Chapter 5) is defined as the sum of plant costs (for structures and improvements, boiler plant equipment, generators, and capitalized interest incurred during construction, etc.) net of

accumulated depreciation and accumulated deferred taxes. Accumulated deferred taxes are the timing difference between book and tax depreciation rates. This is not a factor in calculating stranded investment. The rate base is calculated at a particular point in time, i.e. a rate case – usually when a large generating asset is placed in service. Once the rates are set the rate base is frozen in time for rate-making purposes and will not be set again until the next rate case. However, the utility's rate base undergoes continual change – decreases due to changes in accumulated depreciation and deferred taxes – increases from new capital assets (usually referred to as ongoing capital – investment in transmission and distribution plant and investment in capitalized maintenance for existing generators).

It should be noted that stranded investment does not require negative utility investment. The only requirement is that the existing asset's value, for which stranded investment is calculated, declines through time. The value of all other assets, e.g. of transmission or distribution plants, may increase or decrease in value according to the relation between depreciation and continuing investment. Existing generation assets subject to stranded investment recovery will have a set value as of the time that stranded investment recovery is granted. From that time forward this set value and associated returns must decline because of depreciation. This is a situation where the revenue requirement (as they would receive through rate base/ rate of return regulation) for existing generation assets declines through time and probably will be less than market determined revenues.

10. In fact, past utility-sponsored Demand Side Management ("DSM") programs were a direct result of this regulated utility average base rate pricing structure. When the utility's marginal costs were greater than the utility's average costs, i.e. regulated rates, there was an incentive to reduce costs by reducing customer demand. Generally this incentive exists when there is a shortage of generation capacity to meet expected demand. In a sense, utility sponsored DSM was an adjustment to consumer demand in order to maintain marginal costs within the range of fixed regulated average-based rates.

11. See President Loretta Lynch and EOB Chairman, Michael Kahn's, Summer 2000 Report to Governor Davis regarding California's Electric System. http://www.cpuc.ca.gov/

12. According to the State Utility Forecasting Group (1999, pp. 9-9, 10), these astronomical prices have caught the attention of the FERC and State regulatory commissions. In late June 1998, wholesale electricity prices reached $7,000/MWh in the Midwest. For the California independent system operator, replacement power prices were approximately $5,000/MWh in early July 1998 and settled at $9,999/MWh on July 17, 1998. These real world departures of electricity prices from marginal costs may be artificially induced by dominant suppliers withholding production capacity, i.e. market power abuses. The California report to Governor Davis also indicated that market power abuses may be the cause of the extreme price increases in the summer of 2000. If this is the case then it appears very unlikely that any stranded costs for the utilities may actually exists.

13. Rates are generally fixed for a period of time and do not change unless the utility goes before the commission and requests rate relief. However, fixed rates do decrease in real terms over time.

14. This figure does not represent stranded investment for Indiana for two reasons. First, competitive price projections are based on a perfectly competitive market. Introduction of non-competitive market restrictions may increase competitive prices by as much as 30%. Second, the projected continued regulated rates include new generation capacity additions.

Stranded investment only applies to existing generation capacity and not new capacity after the transition. This tends to increase the regulated price beyond that necessary to compensate investors of existing capacity. On the subject of imperfect markets, Haarmeyer et al. (1998) discussed the reason why U.S.Gen's bid for the NEES power plants could prove a bargain, even if the price exceeded book value. The authors cited several factors for the high purchase price: the region's high rate, high capacity costs, transmission constraints, unit locations. All of the factors cited represent impediments to competition.

15. It should be noted that the SUFG projects that over this time period that anywhere from 8,000 MW to 11,000 MW of additional capacity will be needed in Indiana. Although SUFG projects that this capacity will be provided by traditional utility generation, in all probability, much of this capacity will be met by new merchant plant development. See SUFG report Table 4-2 p. 4-11.

16. See Energy Information Administration – Annual Energy Outlook 2000 – Electricity Prices – http://www.eia.doe.gov/oiaf/forecasting.html

17. A recent report of the State Utility Forecasting Group (1999, pp. 1–13) casts doubt on the competitiveness of the electricity market in Indiana, where the summer 1999 price, which averaged $7.50/kwh, was clearly unrelated to any known marginal cost.

18. Assessment of ECAR-Wide Capacity Margins – 1999–2008, 99-GRP-57, East Central Area Reliability Coordination Agreement, August 1999. http://www.ecar.org/publications/ GRP/default.htm It should be noted that the ECAR assessment does not include projections of new merchant plant development – which could be sizeable. Others have indicated that within ECAR an additional 24,000 MW to 50,000 MW of new merchant plant capacity may be built. This spread of forecast tends to indicate the state of flux the current market is experiencing.

19. See ECAR report page 19. Capacity margin is that portion of capacity resources that exceeds peak demand. ECAR members capacity margins are expected to decline from 11.6% in 1999 to 1.8% by 2008 (Table 4a on page 23 of the ECAR report).

20. The Annual Energy Outlook 2000 report by the Energy Information Administration projects a real increase in natural gas prices over the next 20 years. See page 74 EAO2000. In 2000, natural gas prices increased dramatically. The price of natural gas was approximately 50% greater than it had been the previous year. See http://www.eia.doe.gov/oil_gas/natural_gas/info_glance/prices.html

21. Unfortunately, the table does not present a complete picture of stranded investment for two reasons. First, competitive price projections are based on a perfectly competitive market. Introduction of non-competitive market restrictions may increase competitive prices by as much as 30%. Second, the projected continued regulated rates include new generation capacity additions. Stranded investment only applies to existing generation capacity and not new capacity after the transition. This inclusion tends to increase the regulated price beyond that necessary to compensate investors of existing capacity.

22. Potential market problems may be significant. For example, since opening its electric markets in March of 1998 through 2000, only 1.2% of California's eligible customers took advantage of their much-touted new choices by switching electric suppliers. This means that just under 99% of California's customers were still captives of their old utility. (see Citizens Action Coalition Web page: http://www.citact.org/). Moreover, The California Commission was concerned that market power may have played a role in recent supply and pricing problems in the summer of 2000. The Commission concluded:

(A) The price increase is not explainable by increased costs, weather, volumes or even the existence of much higher wholesale price caps in 2000.
(B) Total energy usage on June 29, 1999 was 763,000 MW-h, at a cost of approximately $45 million dollars. On June 29, 2000 Californians used 795,000 MW-h, that cost over $340 million.

The California Commission suggested that sellers may have been withholding power from the market in order to drive up prices in other parallel markets. See http://www.cpuc.ca.gov/ and a discussion in Chapter 10.

23. Illinois's recently passed legislation imposes a transition charge, which allows utilities to collect stranded costs until December 31, 2006 (see Illinois Commerce Commission Webpage: http://www.icc.state.il.us/icc/home/ec.asp).

24. Ibid.

25. See California Assembly Bill No. 1890 Chapter 854 Article 6: Requirements for the Public Utilities Commission. Sections: 367 and 368.

26. Ibid. Section 330.

27. State of California: Public Utilities Commission memorandum, October 6, 1999: Status of Electric Restructuring Matters, and Upcoming Milestones, for Commissioner Reports Discussion.

28. See California Public Utility Commission: Decision 97-12-039, December 3, 1997.

29. Electric Industry Restructuring in Maine, Section 3208. Stranded cost recovery

(1) *Stranded costs defined.* For the purposes of this section, the term "stranded costs" means a utility's legitimate, verifiable and unmitigable costs made unrecoverable as a result of the restructuring of the electric industry required by this chapter and determined by the commission as provided in this subsection.
(2) *Calculation.* For each electric utility, the commission shall determine the sum of the following to the extent they qualify as stranded costs pursuant to subsection 1:
    (A) The costs of a utility's regulatory assets related to generation;
    (B) The difference between net plant investment associated with a utility's generation assets and the market value of the generation assets; and
    (C) The difference between future contract payments and the market value of a utility's purchased power contracts.

When determining the market value of generation assets and purchased power contracts, the commission shall rely to the greatest extent possible on market information, including, but not limited to, market valuations that become known as generation assets and the rights to power under contracts with qualifying facilities are sold.

Electric Industry Restructuring in Ohio: Section 4928.39. Upon the filing of an application by an electric utility under section 4928.31 of the revised code for the opportunity to receive transition revenues under sections 4928.31 to 4928.40 of the revised code, the public utilities commission, by order under section 4928.33 of the revised code, shall determine the total allowable amount of the transition costs of the utility to be received as transition revenues under those sections. Such amount shall be the just and reasonable transition costs of the utility, whose costs the commission finds meet all of the following criteria:

(a) the costs were prudently incurred.
(b) the costs are legitimate, net, verifiable, and directly assignable or allocable to retail electric generation service provided to electric consumers in this state.

(c) the costs are unrecoverable in a competitive market.
(d) the utility would otherwise be entitled an opportunity to recover the costs.

30. The proof of this is determined by the constructed returns in a regulated market and competitive market. Under a regulated environment, utility investment costs, i.e. fixed charges, decline through time as the rate base is depreciated. Once fully depreciated, the return on the investment is zero because the investors' initial investment has been returned. Returns in a competitive market are determined by market prices. Shifting from a regulated market to a competitive market may lead to a situation where market-based returns are paid on a fully depreciated asset, a situation that could not occur in a regulated market. In effect, the transition to competition may be comparable to the customers paying twice for the utilities assets – once under regulation and again under competition.

REFERENCES

Cearley, R., & McKinzie, L. (1995). The Economics of Stranded Investment – A Two-Way Street. *The Electricity Journal, 8*, 16–23.

Haarmeyer, D., McWhinney, R., & Moe, R. (1998). The New England Auction Regional Strategy for Competitive Generation. *Public Utilities Fortnightly*, (Feb. 15), 34–39.

Maloney, M., McCormick, R., & Sauer, R. (1997). On Stranded Cost Recovery in the Deregulation of the Electric Power Industry. *Natural Resources Journal, 37*, 59–123.

State Utility Forecasting Group (1999). *Indiana Electricity Projections – The 1999 Forecast*. West Lafayette, IN: Purdue University.

Stavros, R. (1999). Generation Asset Divestiture: Steal of the Century. *Public Utilities Fortnightly*, (September 1), 42–56.

Thierer, A. (1997). Electricity Deregulation: Separating Fact from Fiction in theDebate Over Stranded Cost Recovery. The Heritage Foundation Talking Points No. 20.

EDITORS' FOREWORD TO CHAPTERS 9 AND 10

The preceding chapters have presented the history of the development of the electric power industry and the regulatory system governing it – both based on the economic concept of natural monopoly. But clearly, we are at the end of natural monopoly as the guiding paradigm of the electric power industry.

What will this mean for the future?

Two views are expressed in the following chapters. The first, by Andrew Morriss, a legal scholar, takes a pessimistic approach in a mostly polemical argument about why the law-making and law-enforcing processes will produce nothing like deregulation and competition in the electric power industry.

The second, by Peter Grossman, an economist, looks at the widely publicized events of California from the summer of 2000 to the spring of 2001, and then draws some conclusions about the possible future of the electric power industry. Though California set back efforts at deregulation, Grossman is less pessimistic about the future. There has been an end to natural monopoly in the electric power industry, and a competitive model seems most likely to replace it. The regulatory system, Grossman surmises, likely will, no doubt slowly, take account of that change in paradigm.

9. WHY THE MUSIC IS OFF-KEY WHEN LAWYERS SING FROM ECONOMISTS' SONGBOOKS OR WHY PUBLIC UTILITY DEREGULATION WILL FAIL

Andrew P. Morriss

INTRODUCTION

Although public utility regulation has passed through a series of regulatory paradigms, and is currently settling on some form of "deregulation," economists have never thought it particularly difficult technically. Implementing the technical solutions suggested by economists, however, has proved far more difficult. Once lawyers take possession of the straightforward regulatory concepts offered by economists, the laws that result contribute to high levels of inefficiency. These inefficiencies in turn spur the creation of new regulatory paradigms. Time and again, the law, or at least public utility law, has proved inadequate to the task of implementing the economists' visions.

In this chapter, I will argue that public utility regulation in the U.S. follows a cyclical pattern in which economists identify problems with a utility industry, economists offer a solution, lawyers imperfectly implement the solution, and the imperfections create inefficiencies that restart the cycle. The question is therefore whether deregulation is the end of this history or merely

The End of a Natural Monopoly: Deregulation and Competition in the Electric Power Industry, Volume 7, pages 193–213.

ISBN: 0-7623-0995-4

the beginning of a new cycle. I argue that it is the beginning of a new cycle for three reasons. First, we can already observe the complications being created in deregulatory laws. Real deregulation does not involve complicated statutes or regulations; it requires the opposite: clearcutting the existing forest of statutes and rules. We do not observe a lessening of regulatory complexity. "With few exceptions, Congress refused to repeal outright its regulatory statutes or abolish regulatory agencies" (Aman, 1998, p. 812). Indeed, as Joseph Kearney and Thomas Merrill observe, many of the modern 'deregulatory' statutes are undeserving of that name and are better characterized as "a system of regulatory transformation" (Kearney & Merrill, 1998, pp. 1324–1325). Second, powerful political interests have a great deal at stake in maintaining their influence in regulated industries. With enormous amounts of plunder at stake, it is nearly impossible for political interests to forswear the opportunity for influence. And such influence is the dominant feature of many utility regulatory regimes: As one utilities commissioner put it, "when the Governor says jump, I say how high" (Stalon et al., 1995, p. 841). Third, past regulation has created interests that depend on the continuation of regulatory intervention. The gains from deregulation, on the other hand, are dispersed and relatively small in magnitude. The most likely coalitions are not, therefore, those in favor of true deregulation.

Note that no one is to blame in this story, not even the lawyers. The flaw lies with the nature of regulatory law, a crude instrument shaped by many forces other than economic theory. For example, regulators continue to attempt to redistribute wealth through price level regulation despite clear proof that they cannot do so without imposing intolerable costs on society (Arrow & Kalt, 1979). Imperfect implementation of efficiency ideals is thus a foregone conclusion. Why? "Because it is there" seems to be the main response. Redistribution via utility regulation may be costly but it is possible; cheaper forms of redistribution might not be politically possible. While we can always hope that it will do better, the economists' vision of efficiency will thus remain out of reach. Second-best solutions are not necessarily bad things – they are better than, for example, third-best or eleventh-best solutions. If second-best is the best we can do, we ought to aim for it. The problem, however, is not simply that we will fail to reach the ideal. Rather the problem is that our pursuit of the ideal is likely to lead us farther astray by offering new opportunities to engage in costly behavior with no discernable net social benefits.

It is possible that the current trend toward "deregulation" will yield better results than past attempts that centered largely on "improving" regulation. The history of public utility regulation, however, suggests powerful reasons to be cautious in accepting the widely forecast improvements. After all, the most recent cycle of regulatory reform efforts before deregulation fever took hold centered on the discovery of public utility regulation's potential by previously uninvolved interest groups such as environmental pressure groups (Stalon et al., 1995, pp. 831–832). These interests are unlikely to be willing to give up their newly discovered regulatory tools without a struggle. Older interests also are likely to resist loss of their influence, not the least of which are lawyers. The result, I suspect, will bear far too close a resemblance to prior cycles of utility reform. I will even predict that the authors of this volume can be reassembled in twenty to thirty years for a new volume explaining whatever regulatory trend follows "deregulation."

This chapter is structured as follows: First, I will briefly sketch the history of public utility regulation in the United States to make the case for my cycle of regulatory pain. Following that, I will briefly discuss some of the reasons the legal system is incapable of implementing economists' regulatory prescriptions without creating new problems that start the cycle anew. Finally I will examine the recent trend toward "deregulation" and argue that it is no different from earlier regulatory reform movements and thus does not represent "the end of history" for regulatory law.

HISTORY

The history of public utility regulation can be roughly described as six part cycle:

(1) Utilities' behavior sparks calls for regulatory action.
(2) Economists prescribe regulatory actions based on economic theory.
(3) Lawyers imperfectly translate economists' prescriptions into laws.
(4) Utilities and others discover and exploit imperfections in regulatory laws.
(5) Inefficiencies grow as a result of imperfections.
(6) Repeat.

American public utility regulation has followed this pattern from its earliest beginnings.

Cycle One

What we regard as utility services were often provided on a competitive basis in the late nineteenth and early twentieth century. Indeed, a surprisingly high degree of competition remained even into the 1960s and 1970s in the electric power market. Forty-nine communities in 16 states had direct competition among electric utilities in 1966, for example (Primeaux, 1985, p. 130). Nonetheless, parallel distribution networks were costly and the possibilities of reducing costs by consolidating into a single firm were obvious. The "natural monopoly" in gas distribution was identified as early as 1848 (Pierce, 1988, p. 2). Firms rapidly sought to achieve those cost savings by the creation of local monopolies. These new monopolies did not stop at cutting costs, however, but proceeded to act like monopolies, stifling competitors, raising prices, and reducing quality. Both business and residential customers quickly sought relief from state legislatures (Merchants Association of New York, 1905, pp. 4–14).

Economists offered a clear explanation of the problem and a prescription for curing it. Utilities were "natural monopolies" and the solution was a regulatory framework that captured the benefits of the monopoly's reduced costs and restrained its exercise of bad behavior. A 1926 text on utilities for New York high school students, *The Story of Public Utilities*, explained the problem thus:

> to prevent such useless and utterly wasteful duplication and competition, particularly in the case of electric light, gas and telephone companies, the regulatory commission steps in. It creates virtual unification in the utilities, gives, as it were, exclusive franchises, a protection against ruinous competition, to the existing companies in which great sums of money have already been expended (Hungerford, 1926, p. 343).

Similarly, and only slightly more technically, the standard pre-World War II textbook on public utility economics summed up the problem for regulators as simultaneously restraining monopoly pricing and using monopoly "as a beneficent principle of organization" (Glaeser, 1927, p. 634).

The first round of utility regulation was thus based on behavior by companies holding local monopolies in various industries. The primary solution quickly identified by economists was to use public regulation by local governments to restrain bad behavior while obtaining the benefits of efficiencies in the private sector. Although this seems naïve today, it was a perfectly respectable analysis and solution by the standards of the time. Indeed, with the New Deal's alphabet soup of regulatory laws and agencies just around the corner, this first round was, if anything, insufficiently ambitious.

Economists developed the theory but lawyers wrote the laws that implemented it. The first attempts at translation of natural monopoly theory into law took two main approaches: public ownership and rate regulation. The public ownership school of thought saw the solution of the problem in removing the profit motive from utilities. Public managers could achieve the technical gains of a monopoly but, freed from the demands of stockholders, would have no incentive to gouge the customers. The rate regulation advocates pinned their hopes on control of rates by public commissions, typically giving commissions broad authority and vague instructions.

Unfortunately, both types of attempts to capture the benefits of utilities' natural monopoly status while avoiding the perils of monopolistic behavior floundered. Public ownership failed to capture the benefits of the monopolies' management as the utilities became subject to political forces. Attempts at rate regulation ran into problems with the legal frameworks set up to control rates. The U.S. Supreme Court's 1898 attempt to detail the constitutional requirements for ratemaking, *Smyth v. Ames*,[1] produced an unworkable framework for regulators based on a four factor analysis without guidance on how to weigh the factors against each other. The result was regulatory chaos. One ratemaking proceeding in Illinois in 1914–1916, for example, generated 24 hearings over 62 days, with 10,000 pages of testimony and 283 exhibits (Groninger, 1928, p. 201). Worse, some of the definitions of the criteria were themselves circular, which caused "regulatory policy to be determined by regulatory policy" (Sherman, 1983, p. 66).

Cycle Two

Early commission regulation proved unsatisfactory to both the regulated and the regulators. Utilities suffered as regulators' guesses about appropriate rates swung between too little and too much. Regulators suffered as regulatory proceedings stretched into interminable hearings.

In part, the problem was due to a lack of clarity in the concept of "public utility." Even economists were never entirely clear about just what defined a natural monopoly. Henry Hazlett traced the intellectual history of the concept of natural monopoly and found that it "entirely reversed its rationale, yet the policy recommendation lives on: political agency is the solution to the natural monopoly problem" (Hazlett, 1985, p. 22). The elasticity of the term "public utility" can be seen today in claims that Microsoft is a public utility and should be regulated as such.

Nonetheless, even with this lack of clarity economists were usually certain that the changing set of industries labeled "public utilities" fit whatever the definition of natural monopoly was. Despite the lingering confusion about the definition of natural monopoly, economists had created a powerful justification for regulatory action. As George Priest recently noted, the social welfare justification offered by natural monopoly theory "is so widely accepted that the natural monopoly case is viewed as the prototypical context for governmental regulation. Virtually all public interest justification for regulation in industries not characterized by natural monopoly consist of claims that the alleged market imperfection in the particular industry will generate an effect resembling natural monopoly" (Priest, 1993, pp. 295–296). Armed with this powerful intellectual tool, economists were able to show that social welfare could be improved through regulations designed to achieve "beneficent" organization.

Technical change in the utility industry brought changes in regulatory tools as the development of public utility economics brought greater sophistication to the economic analysis of the problem. Rate regulation grew more elaborate and generated treatises on the topic hundreds and even thousands of pages long (Morriss, 1998, p. 159).

Utilities rapidly outgrew their original municipal boundaries and interconnections began to appear. Regulators thus faced regulated entities operating beyond their jurisdictional boundaries. In the gas industry, for example, the "logical and universally beneficial" expansion of the market beyond municipal boundaries "created stress in the traditional institutional structure of regulation through municipal franchise" (Pierce, 1988, p. 3). The utilities thus transcended the ability of local government bodies to regulate them and by the mid-1920s regulatory focus shifted up to the state level (Pierce, 1988, pp. 3–4). State bodies were better able to collect data, to protect residents in one locality from harm from the actions of regulators in another, and to gain the attention of state legislators for necessary statutory solutions to new problems (Morriss, 1998, p. 162; Hungerford, 1926, p. 345).

Once again, the solution to the problem was seen as straightforward. Federal and state regulators stepped in to replace or supplement local regulators. Indeed, the solution was so obvious that theorists like Glaeser (1927, p. 752) worried that regulatory commissions "no longer bear aspects of novelty; they have, accordingly, lost much of the original glamour which attended their establishment."

As before, however, implementation was another story. Consider the natural gas industry. Congress initially sought to address the "natural monopoly" in distribution but soon allowed the gas pipelines to use the regulatory process to gain protection from competition in the sale of gas as well (Pierce, 1988). To implement these provisions, Congress instructed the Federal Power Commission to also regulate construction of new facilities, initiation and abandonment of service, and sales "in the public interest" in the Natural Gas Act of 1938 (Pierce, 1988). All this came about in response to the "natural monopoly" of distribution systems!

The strains placed on the legal framework by the new regulatory tools and the vast expansion of regulatory subject matter in the New Deal brought a temporary retreat by the courts from the field. In a 1944 decision, *Federal Power Commission v. Hope Natural Gas Co.*,[2] the U.S. Supreme Court signaled its withdrawal from the field of second guessing regulators from a constitutional perspective. So long as the result of ratemaking was "reasonable," the Court held, it would no longer inquire into the methodology that was used to produce it.

Getting the federal courts out of the business of reviewing the substance of ratemaking proceedings helped the regulatory process proceed more smoothly. For a time after *Hope* utility regulation enjoyed relative quiet as a backwater of mostly state regulatory effort. Technological advances in the post-War period brought steadily declining utility costs in most areas, some of the benefits of which regulators got to distribute among the ratepayers. As one regulator put it, "Not bad work if you can get it" (Phillips, 1983, p. 34).

The lengthy regulatory peace of the post-World War II era was bought, however, by sharing the gains from increasing technical efficiencies among ratepayers and shareholders. Since, in an era of declining costs, regulatory delays tended to provide the utilities with an advantage, utilities could live with the process. Consumers, the group disadvantaged by the regulatory process's delays, nonetheless experienced declines in real prices for most utilities. In the natural gas market, for example, federal rate regulation cost consumers billions (Pierce, 1988). Since the loss was simply that prices might have declined faster or further, however, public interest in the subject remained low. The excruciatingly boring nature of rate making proceedings further dampened public interest.

The courts' withdrawal from constitutional oversight did not mean that regulators were left free to pursue pure-efficiency goals. Public utility regulators in the post-World War II period began to gradually accumulate additional responsibilities as regulatory statutes' scope expanded. The short lists of goals economic theory provided regulators proved an irresistible target for lawmakers seeking ways to influence utility behavior. By 1961, for example, leading utility economist James Bonbright was already telling students through his textbook that utility regulation served four, sometimes conflicting, purposes: "(1) the producer-motivation or capital attraction function; (2) the efficiency-incentive function; (3) the demand-control or consumer-rationing function; and (4) the income-distribution function" (Bonbright, 1961, p. 49). Although Bonbright saw any conflicts among these four goals as resolvable through "wise compromise," it would not be too long before legislators' realization of the potential offered by utility regulation greatly expanded the number of conflicts. When the growth of technological efficiencies was overwhelmed by outside price shocks, the regulatory peace was ultimately destined to collapse. Thus, although a long period of stability was made possible by several decades of steady technological improvements, the distribution of those gains attracted legal complications. The presence of those complications made the system vulnerable to price disruptions. A system built around a division of the spoils, after all, could not be expected to survive the disappearance of the spoils.

Cycle Three

Utilities and regulators received a number of jolts in the late 1960s and early 1970s. Energy price fluctuations shook up the energy utilities, disrupting the calm that the prior decades' production efficiency increases had bought. Increasing controversy over nuclear power brought intense public scrutiny of energy utilities' behavior. Environmental and social pressure groups discovered utility regulation and began to demand that regulators use their oversight powers to force utilities to adopt more environmentally or socially sensitive techniques. Indeed, environmentalists and utilities were soon making common cause before state regulatory boards to jointly advocate the subsidization of conservation efforts through increased utility rates (Black & Pierce, 1993, pp. 1356–1357). Technological advances in telecommunications began to put stress on the complex array of cross-subsidized pricing plans. Regulators responded with increasingly complex regulatory schemes designed to promote multiple goals.

The intellectual climate also changed in an important way. Utility issues were no longer left to men like Bonbright who believed in "wise compromise." Public utility economics generated ever-greater numbers of schemes to improve the efficiency of regulation by adding considerations to regulators' analyses. For example, the 1970s brought the Public Utility Policy Reform Act ("PURPA") that mandated that utilities buy electricity from outside suppliers, who were often relatively high-cost. Generating and selling high-cost electricity in a rate-of-return environment was one thing, being forced to purchase it from a competitor was another, and utilities began to experience serious regulatory pain.

In the 1980s, the idea of using "environmental adders" began to gain support among public utility economists as a means of internalizing environmental costs. Instead of simply requiring utilities to charge their customers for the actual costs incurred, additional charges could be added to customers' bills to reflect the "true" social costs of various forms of energy use. Unfortunately since these "costs" were really simply guesses, the concept only reinforced the political nature of utility pricing. Moreover, since adder programs violated basic principles of economics and environmental science, their adoption despite such "obvious" flaws can be explained best as the result of institutional incompetence and political pressure (Black & Pierce, 1993). Again, politically determined prices were not unacceptable to utilities in and of themselves, but politically determined prices set by interest groups with quite different objectives from the utilities' objectives were often painful.

The new interest groups changed the political calculation for utilities. Having been battered in the nuclear regulatory process in the 1970s and early 1980s, utility executives could now see that regulated rates themselves would be transformed into a battleground over issues they could not control. Their experience with PURPA showed them the disadvantages of remaining in the regulatory framework. Moreover, the due process revolution of the 1960s also began to affect economic regulation. Regulators came under pressure to provide opportunities for outsiders to participate and to change their own procedures. As one regulator put it, "judicialization of the [regulatory] commissions became intense" (Stalon et al., 1995, p. 790). The federal courts' withdrawal from oversight of economic issues in regulation became overshadowed by those same courts' increasing activism in other regulatory areas that affected utilities. Environmental regulations, for example, had a major impact on energy utilities' businesses. In this changed environment, regulatory lags no longer favored the regulated. Indeed, by 1995 one regulatory expert estimated the deadweight losses of electricity regulation at 20% (Stalon et al., 1995, p. 863).

Around the same time, on the market-oriented-side, Harold Demsetz, George Stigler, Claire Friedland, and Richard Posner led the charge by a new group of economists who argued for rethinking the entire rationale for utility regulation (Morriss, 1998). This frontal theoretical assault provided the intellectual foundation for widespread deregulatory efforts, although most proposals centered on relatively limited and partial deregulation.

The reaction to regulatory pain and the rise of outside interest groups was a shift to a somewhat different paradigm for utility regulation. Rather than trying to squeeze the maximum advantage out of scientific design of rates, regulators and economists now focused on injecting the maximum amount of competition into the system while ensuring "fair" competition (Burns et al., 1999). The new paradigm accepted that there might be natural monopoly aspects to some utility industries. These aspects could be minimized, however, by promoting competition among utilities (encouraging electric utilities and cable TV companies to use their lines to offer telephone services while encouraging telephone companies to offer cable TV services) and by restructuring utilities to segregate out the irreducible minimum of natural monopoly services (splitting electric utilities into separate distribution and generation companies).

Utilities also began to have second-thoughts about the regulatory "bargain" they had lived under. Pressed on one side by non-efficiency-oriented regulation, such as regulation to achieve environmental goals, and on the other by market-theorists pushing for greater reliance on incentives and competition, utilities began to feel the pain of regulation through adverse selection. Indeed, because much of traditional regulation was built around the use of cross-subsidies, competition created serious problems for the regulated industries. With new, deregulated competitors "cherry-picking" profitable market segments out from under them, utilities could no longer rely on profitable market segments to recoup losses from segments where regulatory policy dictated below cost pricing. For the first time, utilities had an incentive to seek to free themselves from regulation.

The Next Cycle

Despite the new emphasis on deregulating as much of the market "as possible," regulators show no signs of withering away. Although the new theory nominally accepts competition as a playing a central role, the devil lies in the details. It is one thing to recognize a network; it is another to see the existence of a network as a basis for regulation. Yet this is precisely the direction network theory is taking. For example, state regulatory commissions have a particularly important role to play, according to a National Regulatory Research Institute paper, "as we evolve toward the intermeshed networks or 'network of networks' model" (Burns et al., 1999, pp. 8–9).

Natural monopoly theory is still around as well: Distribution networks are natural monopolies according to many regulatory theorists.[3] Although power generation or long distance or natural gas production or cable TV content can be deregulated, almost everyone agrees something – the electric grid or the 'last mile' of cable and pipe – remains to be regulated to ensure a competitive market place. At a series of "National Association of Regulatory Utility Commissioner Summits," state regulators concluded that "special attention should be given to market analyses so that state commissions can identify workably competitive markets, emerging competition, tight oligopolies, and residual monopoly markets or services." "Workably competitive markets," the Commissioners determined, were those "free from internal market failure resulting from any of the following categories of unfair trade practices that are also violation of consumer protection laws in most states: covert coercion, undue influence, deception, incomplete information, or needlessly confusing information" (Burns et al., 1999, pp. 1–2).

This is the Achilles heel of modern deregulatory efforts. Commission lawyers sing the economists' song – competition is the key: "the new public utility environment should be consumer driven." The notes are flat, however, because the lawyers' focus is on issues such as the need to make markets be "workably competitive" (Burns et al., 1999, p.1) and on process issues. Indeed, lawyers' focus on process is a major problem with "market-oriented" reforms' implementation. For example, the director of the Harvard Electricity Policy Group summed up the impact of judicial review as "what all of us do naturally when faced with an issue, particularly an arcane one. You retreat to what you know. And what are lawyers trained in? They are trained in process. They know process" (Stalon et al., 1995, p. 819). For us the problem is that lawyers focus on process because that is what lawyers do.

Process and markets do not mix, however. Markets, at least when they work, rely on nimble competitors adjusting their behavior continuously to meet changing conditions. When we read about successful reform at a large corporation, it is not a story about adding process to corporate decisionmaking but a story of rooting out process to empower decisionmakers. Process requires time for consultation, appeals, neutral decisionmakers – all things that inhibit entrepreneurial behavior. It requires those things for a reason: when we clothe an activity with the powers of the state, we want deliberation, consultation, and appeals. These are not, however, the attributes of successful private decision makers. Public decisionmakers understand this. A major theme at the 1995 Harvard Electricity Regulatory Project meeting, for example, was the horrors of process as experienced by regulators (Stalon et al., 1995).

Moreover, regulators, almost by definition simply do not understand markets. Many regulators even now cling to ideas like the one expressed by a former federal and state regulator at a 1995 conference: "Public Utility Commissions are essential parts of the U.S. economic management system. And economies have to be managed as firms have to be managed" (Stalon et al., 1995, p. 790). For every Alfred Kahn there are hundreds like the one quoted above.

While it is hard to imagine how anyone familiar with the history of the twentieth century, let alone anyone in a position of authority, could make the claim that "economies have to be managed," such claims are more the rule than the exception. Even when regulators do not cling to such outdated views, they often have unusual ideas about the circumstances that justify intervention. For example, one category of evidence of anticompetitive behavior is often stated as "engaging in price wars to deter or repel competitive entry" (Burns et al., 1999, p. 12). With such a definition it is difficult to imagine circumstances under which regulators will not be able to justify their continued roles. Similarly, according to a paper commissioned by a regulatory interest group, regulators must take care to avoid unintended effects on "'nonjurisdictional' parties" – or those outside the usual regulatory process (Schoengold, 1996, p. 4).

One result of this confusion over the rationale for the regulatory state is complexity. Economists Anne O. Krueger and Roderick Duncan argued that "Economic policy analyses may be correct as formulated *on the assumption that the initial policies will be adopted and not be altered,* but be wrong if it is recognized that increased complexity may be an inevitable cost of the policy" (Krueger & Duncan, 1993, p. 1). A good example of this is the 1978 attempt to deregulate interstate natural gas sales through a process that regulatory policy expert Richard Pierce described as "extremely complicated and gradual" (Pierce, 1988, p. 11). Again, this leaves enough room to squeeze an elephant through in reregulating utilities.

SLIPPERY SLOPE OR FLAWED IMPLEMENTATION?

Why do lawyers' implementations of economic theory go wrong? One possibility is that the dynamic of the regulatory process leads to error. An alternative is the familiar legal argument about the "slippery slope." One foot on this dreaded ground and society is plummeting downward toward disaster at an ever-increasing rate. In some ways my sketch of regulatory history sounds like a slippery slope argument – if any regulatory activity continues, more will inevitably follow. This may be true, but the argument here is different. Rather than a slippery slope, the problem with regulatory measures taken by lawyers is that they do not address an important aspect of the problem of monopoly – the monopoly on decision-making asserted by the regulators.

In a competitive industry, by definition, no one actor can force the others to act in any particular way. Anyone is free to spot an arbitrage opportunity, a new way of doing business, or a modification to a product and use it to out-compete incumbent firms. In a regulated industry, on the other hand, regulators are in a position to force, using the full power of the state, market actors to behave in ways the regulators think are most appropriate. When market actors make a mistake, they lose money. When regulators make a mistake, consumers and investors lose money. And regulators regularly make major mistakes. For example, Richard Pierce (1988, p. 12) attributes the "abysmal failure" of the 1978 Natural Gas Policy Act to "five fundamental flaws," all of which are mistakes by Congress in understanding market conditions and the nature of regulatory processes.

In this sense, regulators are in a position analogous to the classic industrial organization metaphor of a monopolist in nuts entering the competitive market for bolts. It does not matter that the bolt market is full of enterprising competitors so long as the monopolist has a secure grip on the market for nuts. The nut-monopolist is still able to extract his full measure of monopoly profits from both markets. Similarly, regulators can lack authority over a firm's activities in a hundred markets so long as they have authority to regulate one. Modern regulators, of course, retain far more than one aspect of utility firms within their control. One study of regulators' future roles in the electric industry concluded that merely to "monitor" deregulated electricity markets, regulators would:

> need to know whether and under what conditions firm service might be interrupted and under what conditions interruptible service will be interrupted. Regulators also need to know

> the price of each type of generation service, each ancillary transmission service, and each type of transmission service under a variety of market conditions. This information needs constant monitoring (Burns et al., 1999, p. 17).

The same study listed 10 broad areas in which regulators would need information on natural gas firms (Burns et al., 1999). Such information demands suggest that a "market-based" approach to energy sales will be far from the competitive model.

Regulators also seek to retain control over important aspects of utilities. For example, most states require government permission to site transmission facilities at particular locations. "Typically, these siting reviews require the developer to justify that the facility is needed by the state where it will be located, and that it is consistent with providing energy at the lowest cost and minimum environmental effect" (Tierney, 1998, p. 2).

The characteristics that prompted the initial designation of utilities as "natural monopolies" will also provide regulators with considerable leverage. The electric power system, for example, requires "precise, continuous and near instantaneous balancing of generation at power plants and customer demand at different locations around the regional grid" (Tierney, 1998, p. 2). Competing telephone systems will require interconnection and both law enforcement and public safety concerns (e.g. wire tapping and 911 systems) will provide openings for state intervention.

Why will regulators seek to retain control? A number of forces push in the direction of continued state involvement in utility regulation. First, the existence of state and national bureaucracies devoted to regulation ensures a continual presence in state and national legislatures of lobbyists seeking continued oversight powers. Second, utilities have proven a remarkably lucrative and compliant target for state and local tax authorities, which will be reluctant to see the end of their gravy train.[4] In 1994, before state level deregulatory efforts began in earnest, state and local governments collected over $13.4 billion from investor owned utilities (Deloitte & Touche, 1996). Since utilities traditionally were allowed to pass taxes along to their customers, utilities did not resist the myriad taxes imposed upon them. Without regulatory protection, however, many utilities will be able to avoid such exactions in the future by locating facilities in low tax jurisdictions. As a study of the tax implications of deregulation concluded, competition is likely to both reduce state and local tax revenues and affect the competitive balance between electricity providers through differential taxation (Deloitte & Touche, 1996).

Third, utility regulation offers politicians opportunities to provide services through distortions. Tierney (1998, p. 3), for example, notes that "[in] the new deregulated environment, states will continue to have a clear interest in the performance of the bulk power system. When consumers lose power for any length of time, they typically do not care if it is a local distribution problem or a problem with the larger regional system; they take their complaints to the local regulators and politicians." This offers an incentive for politicians to ensure that "system operators have the correct incentives" (Tierney, 1998). Of course, the "correct" incentives from a politician's point of view may differ substantially from the efficient incentives – if a politician bears the blame for system outages and can affect the system, but does not pay the full cost of additional safeguards, one would expect the system to overinvest in reliability.

There are several possible responses to the regulatory monopoly. Supreme Court Justice Stephen Breyer, for example, sees merit in lawyers' roles in transforming economic theory into rules capable of enforcement.

Because economists excel in the use of theory, some of them may be tempted to believe that theory alone will lead a regulator to correct results. Economic theory may do so, however, only when it takes account of an important fact well known to lawyers and civil servants, namely that the regulatory process is an *administrative process*. Any decision must create or embody administrative rules. Those rules must be simple; they must be uniform; they must remain unchanged over fairly long periods of time; they must also be capable of application by nonexperts and, above all, they must be capable of resolving disputes. Lawyers are likely to be more sensitive to the needs of administrability than are economists (Breyer, 1985, pp. 205–206).

Others have more hope for the future: Professors Kearney and Merrill sum up the new regulatory paradigm as built around contractual choice by consumers. They define it partly in terms of what it is not (no cross-subsidies, no filed tariffs, no mandated bundle of services) and partly in terms of the regulatory focus on relations among providers (Kearney & Merrill, 1998). In essence, regulation assumes the form of common carrier regulation of bottlenecks rather than of the traditional price or profit level regulation. Both views are, I believe, over-optimistic.

The translation errors created when lawyers' translate economic theory into rules is not a virtue but a vice. To see why consider the following. I speak Spanish badly. Suppose I translated a passage from the classic *Don Quixote* into English. Then suppose someone else, even someone fluent in both Spanish and English, retranslated the passage to Spanish. The result: what was once a beautiful piece of prose would be lifeless and unreadable. Lawyers "speak" economics less well than I speak Spanish. The economic theory expressed by today's regulatory statutes would be insufficient to gain a passing grade from even a third rate economics program if "retranslated" into economic theory.

Moreover, even if some regulators have gotten a good dose of economic religion, and their conversions are genuine and not simply matters of convenience, the adoption of more congenial forms of regulation, as Kearney and Merrill suggest may be happening, does not prevent the problem. The multiplication of regulatory goals beyond efficiency creates unresolvable tensions.

DEREGULATION AND "THE END OF HISTORY"

Francis Fukuyama (1992) created quite a stir when he announced the end of history in his 1992 book of the same name. Fukuyama argued that history had "ended" because the world had come to accept the western notion of a liberal democracy and market economy as the ideal. It is tempting to see the widespread embrace of deregulation of public utilities as signaling something similar for public utility regulation. Seemingly everyone now embraces deregulation of one form or another as vital to the reform of regulated industries. Have we at least reached the end of regulation, if not the end of history? Sadly the answer is no.

Regulation is not over because even many deregulation advocates see core natural monopolies as requiring a continuing regulatory presence. Yet, as Richard Pierce noted, "the form and scope of government intervention appropriate in a market is not static because no market is static" (Pierce, 1988, p. 53). Today's network is tomorrow's obsolete technology – the monopoly in mainframe computers that inspired the government's massive antitrust assault on IBM ultimately fell to Microsoft, not regulators.

While there is widespread agreement on the need for deregulation (at least among the intelligentsia), there is no such agreement on the means by which deregulation will occur. Knotty issues remain – allocating "stranded costs" of white elephants like nuclear power plants, defining what is a "stranded cost," ensuring "comparable" services are offered to rural and urban customers alike through special fees to consumers to name just a few. Judge Richard Cudahy summed up the problem neatly when discussing the problem for telecommunications regulators caused by "competition and its tendency to drive rates down toward cost" and the resulting conflict between cost minimization and "equity." "We have a thing called universal service that means everybody is entitled to some kind of a service, which may be a broad super highway or it may be a dial tone. I do not know which it is but they are entitled to it, and at an affordable price . . . . So what is equity? It is whatever the regulators say it is, I think. Of course, it is what the courts say it is." (Stalon et al., 1995, pp. 828–829).

Legislatures faced with these issues are sometimes opting to pass a general call for deregulation and leave the controversy for someone else to resolve, as when the Ohio legislature "deregulated" the Ohio telephone industry without specifying how to handle the "problem" of the higher cost of serving rural customers. It all begins to sound like the 1920s debate over defining the rate base or the 1950s discussion of "fully distributed costs." Expanding regulatory control to deal with these "problems" is likely to lead to disaster – Richard Pierce (1988, p. 16) concludes his survey of the natural gas industry by noting that "To a large extent the regulatory distortion of the gas market of recent decades is attributable to a single generic error in policymaking – failure to limit government intervention to that required to respond to a demonstrated market imperfection." Moreover, two major trends are likely to spark the next round of regulatory behavior: globalization of utility companies and increased attention to utility regulation by environmental and social pressure groups.

Internationalization

Cross-jurisdiction sales by utilities already pose problems beyond the abilities of most regulatory bodies. Indeed it was the expansion of utility markets across municipal lines that led to a state role and the expansion across state lines that led to a national role in regulatory efforts. The expansion across state lines, however, also helped create the impetus for competition (Tierney, 1998). Utilities today, however, are increasingly international bodies. Even simple issues threaten the structure of state and national regulation. Professor Alfred Aman, for example, noted the presence of "innumerable fundamental but hidden issues in seemingly simple cases" that will force governments to alter their regulatory approaches (Aman, 1998, p. 815).

Even within the United States, cross-jurisdictional issues threaten to make state regulatory bodies irrelevant. A 1996 regulators' policy study group report, for example, warned that there would be "significant impacts" on state regulators from neighboring states' deregulatory efforts (Schoengold, 1996, p. 14). Tierney (1998, p. 1) notes that "[p]olicy decisions made and actions taken by those in one state can dramatically affect conditions in neighboring and distant states."

State-level regulation grew out of the inadequacies of municipal regulation of utilities that had outgrown local government boundaries. In today's environment, where utilities are frequently multinational companies spread across continents, regulators face an equivalent challenge without the opportunity to correspondingly kick regulatory authority up to the next level. Even national level regulation cannot hope to effectively regulate a British owned Texas utility buying power from a Mexican generating subsidiary and selling it across a

French owned distribution line into Ohio. Even worse, that same company (or interlocking family of companies) may also be selling natural gas, water, and communication services to some of its customers.

The particular set of transactions described above is merely a hypothetical as I write this, but may not be by the time you read this chapter. International utility companies are becoming the norm rather than the exception, in part because international utility customers are demanding one stop shopping. General Motors, for example, operates plants across the United States, Canada, and Mexico, and GM executives have expressed a desire to reduce to a minimum the number of companies they purchase electricity.

The result of this shift is not hard to predict. Tax authorities around the world have struggled for years to resolve the problem of allocation of costs and profits among subsidiaries of multinational companies. Regulated firms have "a natural incentive to engage in self-dealing with unregulated affiliates" to evade regulators (Pierce, 1988, p. 44). As interconnections among power and communications networks grow, as capital and research costs are increasingly easy to shift among different subsidiaries, utility regulators will find themselves in a similar bind.

The result need not be a total failure of regulatory efforts. It will be enough that utilities gain an advantage in structuring their operations to advantage their best customers. Because industrial customers are often more price sensitive in their purchase of utility services than residential consumers, it is not unlikely that the former will reap the lion's share of the efficiency gains from introducing competition into the market for utilities. (These gains will, of course, indirectly benefit their customers.) This disproportionate benefit to corporations will, in turn, serve as the entry point for complaints about "unfair" consumer rates and the like. The need to regulate various aspects of these businesses to prevent "predatory" or similarly labeled business practices will follow as surely as night follows day.

These attempts will ultimately simple create new problems to replace old ones. For example, a government's "reaction to nationally perceived problems cannot create a level playing field for all who do business within its borders, since integrated global markets mean that a variety of other legal regimes are involved in such a company's processes" (Aman, 1998, p. 784).

Environmentalism

The second major entry point into diluting market-oriented reforms will be environmental regulation. This is already happening: "The interstate transport of pollution from electricity production and use provides a fundamental rationale for regional approaches to regulation .... [R]egulators in some states are exploring ways to introduce environmental objectives into the competive market structures they are creating for the electric industries in their states" (Tierney, 1998, p. 4). Among the methods being considered are several that merely change the name of old regulatory methods: adopting "non-bypassable" charges to fund development of alternative energy sources, creating generation performance standards, monetizing values for environmental externalities, using restructuring agreements to subsidize the upgrading of older plants' environmental equipment (Tierney, 1998, p. 5). Environmental regulation of the power industry utilities (gas and electric) is thus fairly certain; regulation of communications utilities (cable, telephone) is less likely although far from impossible. (Both are crucial to, for example, telecommuting). Functionally similar concerns concerning creating "equal access" to information could play the same role for those industries.

How would environmental regulatory concerns lead to broader reregulation? Again, regulatory history suggests the mechanism. There are two possible scenarios with respect to environmental concerns' expression in regulation. The first is that outcomes will be the metric by which utility performance is judged. If this is true, new relatively clean "greenfield" utility plants will have a significant advantage over retrofitted, existing "brownfield" plants. The owners of those existing plants will thus be at a significant cost disadvantage and be headed for significant financial losses. The second is that requiring action to protect the environment will be held to be more valuable than actual results. Environmental regulators will thus require costly and pointless (for new plants) actions to protect the environment. This was the case with the requirement of the use of scrubbers on all coal fired power plants, even those burning low sulphur coal, by the 1977 Clean Air Act Amendments (Ackerman & Hassler, 1981).

In the first case, large costs will be imposed upon a well-organized group of existing interests (current stockholders in existing utilities) for the benefit of a dispersed group of unorganized interests (those planning to build new greenfield power plants). It does not take a particularly sophisticated public choice analysis to predict that the existing group will be successful in achieving mitigation through the regulatory process. And indeed, the second case described above is simply one of the possible regulatory outcomes that one might expect to appear from the political process. Other forms of reregulation are possible, of course, such as taxes on energy to fund remediation efforts or pay for "stranded costs." The important point is that environmental regulations that actually change behavior are costly and will lead to efforts to spread those costs through the regulatory process.

CONCLUSION

Let me conclude by doing an unlawyerly thing: I will make a bold prediction. Deregulation will fail. That is not to say that something called "deregulation" will not occur; that most, if not all, states will pass laws with titles like the "Public Utilities Deregulation Act of 2000;" and that the various industries today called public utilities will look radically different in twenty years. Some customers will pay more, some will pay less, services will be bundled into different bundles than they are today. But deregulation will fail nonetheless.

Deregulation will fail in the following sense: twenty or thirty years from now, a new regulatory reform debate will begin. Inefficiencies in utility operation will be discovered. Consumers of utility services will bemoan problems they have with their utilities. Legislators will make speeches on the subject and discover a campaign issue. Hearings will be held, laws passed, and the cycle will start anew.

Deregulation will fail at least in part because lawyers will implement it. Lawyers will write the deregulation laws and interpret them. Deregulation will fail because lawyers will fail to grasp what economists mean when they say deregulate. The lawyers will be unable to refrain from creating multifactor balancing tests, tweaking statutes to cover problems like stranded costs, and discovering public policies sitting on top of deregulatory statutes that no one ever noticed before. The next wave of regulation may be called deregulation again or it may get a new name like the "third way" terminology popular in Britain and some parts of Washington today, but it will come.

Lawyers love remedies – virtually every law review article on every subject (and that is a lot of articles!) ends with a policy reform. It is precisely this love of remedies that will doom deregulation – we can't seem to keep our hands off public utilities (or employment relations or consensual behavior among adults or anything else).[5] "Problems" in the industries known as public utilities will inevitably appear and, rather than seeing them as entrepreneurial opportunities for a profit making business, some lawyer will draft a statute to "correct" the problem and that will be the end of the "de" part of "deregulation." Thus the cycle will begin anew. The remedy here is obvious: really deregulate, rip out the regulatory statutes by the roots and burn them all. Abolish the regulatory agencies, layoff their staffs, tear down their offices, and salt the earth where their buildings stood. It will never happen.

NOTES

1. 169 U.S. 466 (1898).
2. 320 U.S. 591 (1944).

3. One might ask why it is that we need so many natural monopoly distribution networks – my house has phone lines, electric lines, and water, sewer, and gas lines as well as a dormant television cable line. While it is difficult to imagine how gas and telephone signals might be transmitted across the same physical connector, it is not hard to imagine a small scale gas fired power plant competing for my electricity business with other providers, eliminating the need for the gas line. Certainly electricity, telephone, and cable service could be provided with fewer than three distribution networks.

4. Many interests benefit from the existence of monopoly utility dependent upon regulatory agencies, as was made dramatically clear at a Public Utilities Commission of Ohio hearing that I attended. The hearing was to gather input on a proposed local telephone service deregulatory plan. Attendance was sparse, except for two groups. First, the lawyers (from PUCO, from the local Bell operating company, and from the potential competitors) far outnumbered the members of the public present. Second, the local Bell operating company had "encouraged" attendance by board members and officers of several local non-profits, all of whom testified that they had been provided with free and cut-rate equipment and services from the local Bell operating company and that they hoped its ability to provide them with such discounts would be protected.

5. Faced with objections (and probably good ones) during the early period of the Russian Revolution, Lenin is reputed to have rejected a proposal to add lawyers to the list of classes to be liquidated by noting that there would be just as many the next day.

REFERENCES

Ackerman, B., & Hassler, W. (1981). *Clean Coal/Dirty Air*. New Haven: Yale University Press.

Aman, A. (1998). The Globalizing State: A Future-Oriented Perspective on the Public/Private Distinction, Federalism, and Democracy. *Vanderbilt Journal of Transnational Law, 31*, 769–870.

Arrow, K., & Kalt, J. (1979). *Petroleum Price Regulation: Should We Decontrol?* Washington, D.C.: American Enterprise Institute for Public Policy Research.

Black, B., & Pierce, R. (1993). The Choice Between Markets and Central Planning in the U.S. Electricity Industry. *Columbia Law Review, 93*, 1339–1432.

Bonbright, J. (1961). *Principles of Public Utility Rates*. New York: Columbia University Press.

Breyer, S. (1985). Economists and Economic Regulation. *University of Pittsburgh Law Review, 47*, 205–218.

Burns, R., Costello, K., Rosenberg, E., & Darr, F. (1999). *Market Analyses of Public Utilities: The Now and Future Role of State Commissions* Columbus: The National Regulatory Research Institute NRRI 99-14.

Deloitte & Touche LLP (1996). *Federal, State and Local Tax Implications of Electric Utility Industry Restructuring*. Washington: National Council on Competition and the Electric Utility Industry.

Fukuyama, F. (1992). *The End of History and The Last Man*. New York: Free Press.

Glaeser, M. (1927). *Outlines of Public Utility Economics*. New York: The Macmillan Company.

Groninger, T. (1928). *Public Utility Rate-Making*. Indianapolis: Bobbs-Merrill.

Hazlitt, T. (1985). The Curious Evolution of Natural Monopoly Theory. In: R. Poole (Ed.), *Unnatural Monopolies: The Case For Deregulating Public Utilities* (pp. 1–25). Lexington, MA: Lexington Books.

Hungerford, E. (1928). *The Story of Public Utilities.* New York: G. P. Putnam's Sons. New York: Arno Press Reprint 1972.

Kearney, J., & Merrill, T. (1998). The Great Transformation of Regulated Industries Law. *Columbia Law Review, 98*, 1323–1409.

Krueger, A., & Duncan, R. (1993). The Political Economy of Controls: Complexity. NBER Working Paper 4351.

Merchant's Association of New York (1905). *For An Investigation of the Conditions Surrounding Gas and Electric Lighting in the City of New York.* January 11.

Morriss, A. (1998). Implications of Second-Best Theory for Administrative and Regulatory Law: A Case Study of Public Utility Regulation. *Chicago-Kent Law Review, 73*, 135–188.

Pierce, R. (1988). Reconstituting the Natural Gas Industry from Wellhead to Burnertip. *Energy Law Journal, 9*, 1–57.

Phillips, C. (1983). The Changing Environment of Public Utility Regulation: An Overview. In: A. Danielsen & D. Kamerschen (Eds), *Current Issues in Public Utility Economics: Essays in Honor of James C. Bonbright* (pp. 25–39). Lexington, MA: Lexington Books.

Priest, G. (1993). The Origins of Utility Regulation and the 'Theories of Regulation' Debate. *Journal of Law and Economics, 36*, 289–323.

Primeaux, W. (1985). Total Deregulation of Electric Utilities: A Viable Policy Choice. In: R. Poole (Ed.), *Unnatural Monopolies: The Case For Deregulating Public Utilities* (pp. 121–146). Lexington, MA.: Lexington Books.

Schoengold, D. (1996). *The Unintended Impacts of Restructuring.* Washington: National Council on Competition and the Electric Utility Industry.

Sherman, R. (1983). Is Public-Utility Regulation Beyond Hope? In: A. Danielsen & D. Kamerschen (Eds), *Current Issues in Public Utility Economics: Essays in Honor of James C. Bonbright* (pp. 41–75). Lexington, MA: Lexington Books.

Stalon, C. et al. (1995). Harvard Electricity Policy Group: Regulatory Decisionmaking Reform. *Administrative Law Journal, 8*, 789–911.

Tierney, S. (1998). *Regional Issues in Restructuring the Electric Industry.* Washington, D.C.: National Council on Competition in the Electric Industry.

10. DOES THE END OF A NATURAL MONOPOLY MEAN DEREGULATION?

Peter Z. Grossman

INTRODUCTION

How likely is genuine deregulation in the U.S. electric power industry? Events at the time of this book's completion are not encouraging. As Professor Morriss has argued in the previous chapter, much of what had been touted as deregulation is simply re-regulation. Moreover, problems and failures under these new forms of regulation have led to calls for a return of the old regulated monopoly system (Goozner, 2001). The motivation this time is not the alleged natural monopoly characteristics – falling average costs as output increases – of the technology, although some argue that at least with respect to distribution, the industry is indeed still a natural monopoly, needing substantial regulation (see Chapter 6).

More typically, proponents of the old-style regulatory process advance new arguments. One common argument stands the old natural monopoly idea on its head. As noted in Chapter 2, competition was thought unsustainable in electric power because one producer would be able to supply the market at a lower cost than any combination of smaller firms (strict subadditivity). The result was that a monopoly firm would inevitably prevail. This firm would then price at the level that maximized its own profits – a level that would create hardships for consumers, a drain on economic functioning generally because too little

The End of a Natural Monopoly: Deregulation and Competition in the Electric Power Industry, Volume 7, pages 215–243.

ISBN: 0-7623-0995-4

power would be available at too high a price, and excess profits for the power providers. Thus government was needed to step in and moderate prices. While this model and its assumptions were shown in other parts of this book to be grossly oversimplified, and probably wrong, it was the textbook – and often public – rationale for regulation.

Now the argument for old-style regulation is a variation on the old "ruinous" competition argument (see Chapters 3 and 4): Competition will drive down *supply* to levels that barely meet the average demand on a system, since competing firms in normal times will make scant profits.[1] Competing forces will drive prices down, which is good, but in the event of a change in demand, for example in peak times during hot summers, there will inevitably be shortages. This will also force up prices to exorbitant levels. Indeed, power providers will be able to gouge customers by simply taking away some generating capacity at peak times to raise prices and make excessive profits. (This assumes of course that someone cannot step in with more supply.) And since it does take time for new generating capacity to be installed – there is no free entry in the short run – there are no answers to the gougers and potential gougers. Either competitive firms will be able to enjoy excess profits temporarily or consumers will face inevitable shortages, or both. Thus *competition,* once thought unsustainable but desirable, now is pictured as undesirable but sustainable.

There is a technical problem (noted in other chapters) that also is still raised as a barrier to a functioning competitive market for electric power, according to those who oppose free markets: Electricity cannot be efficiently stored and has to be produced at the moment of use. Therefore, no one can, so the argument goes, stock up on power to utilize it in the event of a shortage. The only solution is for: (1) government to require that capacity be sufficient; (2) government to make sure that power is available to meet peak demands; and (3) government to guarantee power providers a "reasonable" return on capital so that no one be tempted to gouge or profit unduly from demand spikes. This protects consumers from gouging and shortages; it protects producers' profits; and in general it protects the economy as a whole. This "solution" is of course quite familiar. It is none other than the old system of natural monopoly regulation, which was critiqued in earlier chapters. Only now the rationale has changed: we need this system specifically to protect us from competition not from monopoly.

As of the turn of the twenty-first century, opponents of free electricity markets had what seemed a good case against deregulation: a disastrous set of regulatory changes in California. The woes faced by that state – including shortages, blackouts, and high price spikes – brought calls (even from the state's governor) to reverse course, and it slowed movement toward deregulation in the country as a whole.[2] But as the next section will argue, that case was not by any definition "deregulation," but a peculiar mess of new regulatory rules that set the stage for disaster. The section following will argue that the new rationale for a regulated system is based on flawed and dubious assumptions, and that, from an economic perspective, deregulation is most likely to provide the highest benefits at the lowest costs. A final section will sketch a scenario somewhat more optimistic than that presented by Professor Morriss on how we might get genuine deregulation in the electric power industry.

THE CALIFORNIA POWER CRISIS[3]

Assembly Bill 1890

While California officials touted their 1996 restructuring of the state's electric industry[4] as deregulation, some observers recognized at the outset that the legislation, Assembly Bill 1890, was generated by the demands of politics not the electricity market. It promised something positive for all "stakeholders." First, it guaranteed (or tried to) that utilities could recoup their stranded costs. Second, the retail price was fixed at the relatively high price of 9¢/KW-h. For consumers, while the price was not low initially, at least it was predictable, but this measure was really intended for the electric industry since the "high" fixed price would guarantee full realization of stranded costs. Consumers were to receive their greatest benefits later: the legislation declared, in the future consumers would *necessarily* pay a lower price; indeed, the law stipulated that prices were to fall "by at least 20%," with a 10% cut coming in 1998. Finally, the legislation promised benefits for outside independent generators. These firms would have a really competitive market and no one would deny them access to the grid. All of this was to be managed by government regulators. Indeed it was referred to not as "free market" competition but rather as "managed competition" (Taylor, 1997).

Overall, the effort to provide benefits for everyone apparently without costs suggests that the bill was meant for immediate political gain and had little to do with an assessment of either economic or technical reality. Indeed, any bill that legislates falling "market" prices is necessarily connected more to political markets than economic ones. And it hardly qualified as a change from government control to market orientation. As one expert (cited by Taylor, 1997) noted, "none of this [California's new energy law] should be called deregulation."[5]

There were several other important components of the package. Distributors, the old monopoly utilities, were to divest themselves of at least 50% of their fossil fuel generating capacity, to open the market for "competition" and to focus on serving the retail customer through a continuing regulated monopoly of local distribution.[6] The state government would run a "day-ahead" spot wholesale market for power, and through this market all electric power would be bought and sold. No purchase could be made forward more than one day; no long-term contracts for power provision were allowed.

Power would be produced by independent competitive generators, and would be purchased by the distributors. Then they would distribute the power (buying at lowest cost) to retail customers at the fixed price 9¢/KW-h price. This level was well above the expected wholesale price[7] and was designed to compensate the old utilities for 100% (or actually even more 100%) of their stranded costs.[8] As the authors of Chapter 8 argued, the stranded cost argument was dubious (or at least incomplete) at the outset, but it was part of the rationale for the fixed price. The old utilities were very much in favor of the fixed retail rate, which appeared to guarantee them several years of high profits through protection against lower-priced competition.

To call such a program "deregulation" was certainly a misnomer. Clearly A. B. 1890 left the industry more, not less, heavily regulated by state authorities (Taylor & Van Doren, 2001b). The industry that emerged bore no relationship to a free market.

Characteristics of a Free Market

If a market goes from regulated to "free," what does that imply? Consider the basic components of a free market as economists generally understand them:

First, in a free market parties can freely contract with each other. Voluntary exchange, agreed on prices, and mutually acceptable terms – different lengths and conditions – are fundamental aspects of markets. In market settings, participants can enter into a long-term contractual relationship, and by contracting, both consumers and producers can hedge against future swings in demand and supply – the factors determining market prices.

Second, producers can enter and exit the market. That is, if someone wants to start a competing company and has the wherewithal to produce, he or she can get into the market, produce and try his or her luck. There may be rules about collusion, quality, discrimination, pollution and so on, but those who abide by the rules of the game are permitted entry or exit from the market.

Third, firms have property rights in the means of production. Property rights – fairly well defined ones – are basic to market exchange. Providers of electric power can sell their output (or purchase output from others) to sell to end users.

Fourth, (and above all) prices *at all levels*, for both outputs and inputs, are set by the market forces of supply and demand. There cannot be functioning "markets" in which there is one price set by the forces of supply and demand and another price set by government fiat, without there being the potential for, indeed the likelihood, of conflict.

In California, none of these conditions for a free market were fulfilled. The 1996 deregulation bill in fact made most of these impossible. Actually, in one case, the new law was not the problem: there was nothing in it that prohibited the second condition, entry and exit. But these could not be affected either because of other state rules. Firms could in theory enter the market but in fact because of environmental rules and NIMBY protests, virtually no new generating capacity was, or could be, added (Seltzer, 2001; Taylor & VanDoren, 2001a).[9] This led to a peculiar result for the state. Though entry was allowed, there were no additional generating assets created. In other words, the divestiture requirement of the state law meant only that assets were shuffled from one firm to another. So a firm could enter if it could buy an existing asset, but industry output was basically frozen, and competitive entry was essentially impossible.

Though the NIMBY problem was real, clearly the "deregulation" bill itself was the main barrier to the transformation of the regulated "natural monopoly" industry to a competitive market-based industry. Indeed, if supply is frozen, there still should be a free market with no reason for failure. The market-clearing price would simply rise as demand increased, and fall as it decreased. But then California bore no resemblance to a free market.

Consider again the facets noted above of a free market:

Right of contract?

Not in the California system. The deregulation bill set up a market for spot sales of wholesale power to be administered by the state. But firms were not just *allowed* to buy and sell in the spot market, they were *required* to trade in that market. That is, spot sales were mandatory. Any contract term beyond a single day was forbidden. Though some distributors and end users alike might have benefited from long-term arrangements, they could not make them. This effectively meant that there could be market competition but only on one dimension: the wholesale price of power. Parties could not hedge risks of long-term reliability through direct contracts between buyers and sellers or through some kind of futures markets in forward power contracts.

The bill also limited who could own power distribution facilities. Distributors who owned most of the generating assets to begin with had to exit – or at least sell off 50% or more of their fossil-fueled generating assets. In fact, for the most part, they sold more than 50% (and sometimes 100%) of those assets, often to unregulated subsidiaries of other former natural monopoly power providers. They also used the proceeds to purchase assets for their own unregulated subsidiaries operating outside the state. One result of this was that the holding companies of California's distributors (including the unregulated generating assets) reported profits in early 2000, while the distributing subsidiaries filed for Chapter 11 bankruptcy protection or at least reported devastating losses.

Moreover, the fact that all trades had to go through a state controlled central dispatch organization meant that no end user could contract directly with a producer and no producer could create a separate parallel system even if there was a market demand for it.

All of these barriers were serious and probably would have made it impossible for a well functioning market to have taken root. But the eventual crisis in California was due especially to one particular feature of the 1996 bill. The state government fixed retail prices while the wholesale price was freed. This was a recipe for disaster. If the wholesale price ever rose above the retail price, then there had to be either massive losses for the distributor or there had to be shortages for users. In the end, California managed to create both. For some reason no one quite believed that such a scenario was even possible. The distributors took on enormous risk but it appears that they did not see their behavior as risky. Indeed, they expected to realize substantial benefits (Easterbrook, 2001).

The system was supposed to work as in Fig. 1.

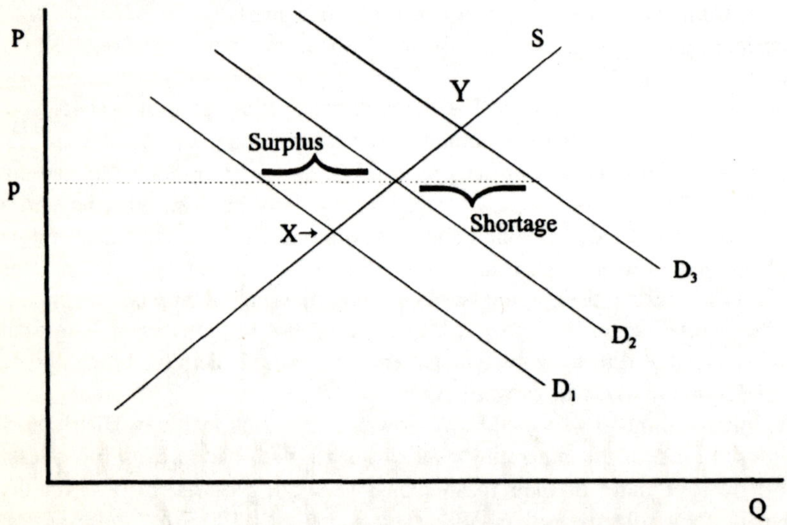

Fig. 1.

Note: At fixed price {p}, there is surplus power to meet unexpected increases in demand. However, if demand increases beyond D_2 without an increase in supply, a shortage will ensue.

Note in the figure that the fixed retail price (P) is above the market equilibrium level (X), the point where $S = D_1$. Because the price is set at a high level, it would be expected to lead to a surplus of electricity over that needed to satisfy demand. That is, the amount that producers will generate at that price will be greater than the amount that consumers will demand. From the consumer's (and regulator's) standpoint, this should mean that there will be a reserve margin of electric power to cover contingencies that suddenly raise demand to D_2, for example especially during hot days in the summer that put pressure on power systems. Since electric demand does move around and not just from day to day but hour to hour, this reserve allows power providers to meet a range of shifting needs.

The problem arises of course if demand shifts to D_3. Now the equilibrium price in a free market would be where $D_3 = S$, point Y, above the fixed price. An equilibrium above the fixed price would also occur if the supply curve shifted to the left, which it would do in the event that input costs increased or some generating capacity went out of service unexpectedly. In either case, because the retail price must remain at the fixed price, demand will exceed supply and there will be a shortage. Note in the figure (where a demand shift is shown), the amount that will be supplied at the fixed price is the point where the price line intersects the supply curve at $S = D_2$, but the quantity demanded will be the amount indicated where the price line intersects D_3. Since there are no price signals to tell consumers that supply is less than demand (retail prices cannot change because they are fixed), consumers demand too much and so a shortage ensues – which is a blackout or brownout when applied to electric power.

Actually the situation in California was more complex and in fact more problematic from theoretical standpoint than the above discussion suggests. If there had been simply a fixed retail price, then the distributors would have bought power at no more than the retail price. If power were offered at a price above 9¢, no distributor would have acquired it. Shortages would have appeared in short order as the distributor made clear that it could no longer find adequate supply at the fixed price. Consumers faced with limits to supply would have had to adjust their behavior because of the shortages, perhaps shifting some peak demand to off-peak times.

But in California, the regulated distributors were supposed to provide power to all users, in accord with the duty to serve concept (see Chapter 7). In these circumstances, the distribution companies would be forced to pay the wholesale price *no matter what it was* even if it rose substantially above the fixed retail price. In this case, however, consumers would fail not only to receive any price signals pointing to greater scarcity, they would also fail (initially) to experience any shortages to change their behavior. If this state of affairs persisted, of course, the distributing company would soon be faced with the problem that every kilowatt-hour (KW-h) it purchased would cost more than any KW-h it sold.

This situation also created the temptation for market manipulation on the part of generators. If a distributor *must* buy to meet demand, and quantity demanded is determined by price, but there are no price signals to consumers, then quantity demanded at any given moment will not change. Consider the situation in Fig. 2.

Two different demand curves are shown. The solid line (D_1) depicts demand in the case where consumers could react to price. It is downward sloping and shows that the quantity demanded will decline as price rises, and will rise as price declines. The broken line (D_2) is completely inelastic and reflects the demand curve that distribution companies effectively faced. Since they could not convey signals to consumers, there was no way that supply prices could influence final market prices.

Now consider a situation where the supply curve shifts upward to the left either because the cost of inputs rises (e.g. natural gas) or because supply is simply withheld, again shifting the supply curve upward to the left as shown

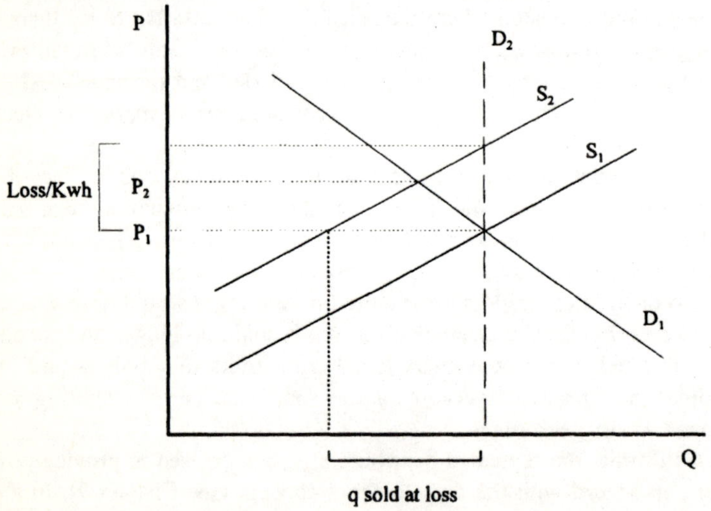

Fig. 2.

Note: This illustrates the problem for the electricity market in California. Demand was unaffected by wholesale price increases. But distributors had to buy at high wholesale rates and sell at fixed retail prices {P_1}, absorbing huge losses in the process.

in Fig. 2. If this were a market situation, the supplier would raise prices to consumers from P_1 to P_2, and quantity demanded would fall as consumers faced a higher price of power. But if the demand curve is the vertical broken line, then the cost of supply rises but the quantity demanded and retail price in the market are unchanged. The more power that is withheld from the market by generators, the more the wholesale price is squeezed higher. It only stops when the distributor decides it can no longer pay the price wholesalers are asking and there is simply isn't enough power anymore in the system to meet demand. Blackouts develop signaling finally that there is a problem. In a sense, the temporary result looks in effect like Fig. 3.

Note that demand and supply curves now are both vertical. Supply is being withheld deliberately or is otherwise constrained and there is no price signal to consumers to cut back so demand remains fixed at the quantity demanded at the fixed price. Since supply does not equal demand, there is a shortage.

Given the above, some or all of the following consequences would be expected in a situation like that of the California "deregulation":

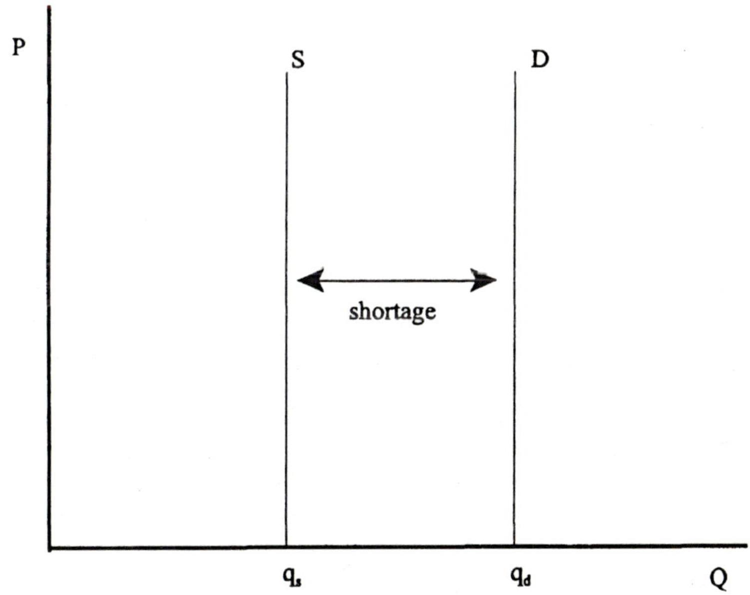

Fig. 3.

Note: In essence, the California market could not increase supply and there were no signals to mitigate demand.

- the distributors would face insolvency since they are buying every kilowatt at a loss (shown in Fig. 2);
- power generators would be reluctant to sell at any price to the distributors for fear they would not be paid, increasing the shortage problem;
- consumers, after receiving no real signals that they needed to alter their behavior, would suddenly experience severe shortages and/or higher prices (if price hikes were allowed); then they would need to change their behavior dramatically and quickly to adapt.

All of these problems were in fact observed.

In the event of continuously growing demand, this set of consequences would be inevitable regardless of the behavior of generators unless there was a stream of new supply that would be added at a comparable rate. Indeed, the novelties of the California law notwithstanding, there had been conditions of rapidly growing demand and temporary shortages before. In the post-World War II period, demand soared in the Pacific Northwest leading to problems with insufficient supply. Throughout the country, in fact, (as noted in Chapter 5) demand for nearly three decades after the war grew at about 8% per year. But the answer to this problem lay in expanded supply, which included many new large base-load coal-fired (and sometimes oil-fired and nuclear-powered) plants, giant hydroelectric facilities and new networks of transmission lines. For this to occur there had to be a commitment by the government (as there was with respect to construction of large hydro facilities) or incentives to build for private firms. Regulators, however, assumed that the latter meant that utilities had to have a guaranteed return on capital regardless of whether the investment proved prudent or necessary (see Chapter 5). But it was moot in the California case since supply was not expanding during this period.

As it turned out, the problems developed mostly as the theory would suggest. California experienced an economic boom (as well as a population inflow) in the late 1990s. This alone put pressure on demand, while supply did not increase significantly. Despite increased demand and supply constraints, there was no change in the fixed retail rate, and so there were no signals for consumers to conserve power. By 2000, there were also pressures on natural gas prices – one of the main fuels for California power generation.[10] Drought conditions reduced the availability of some hydroelectric resources as well. All of these factors caused the price of wholesale power to rise. But at some peak times, the increase was dramatic, apparently worsened by market manipulations by a few generators (Woolfolk 2002). While the average wholesale price of electricity during this period was about 15¢/KW-h, it reached as much as $12/KW-h at certain times. This was of course very far above the fixed retail price that the distributors could charge their customers.

Though these price spikes alerted officials and electric companies that there was a potential problem, nothing was done to curb consumption. Some construction of new generating facilities was finally undertaken but the power would not be available for some time. The distribution companies were nevertheless supposed to meet demand – which they did but at a loss. In fact by late 2000 the losses had reached several billion dollars. Two companies – Pacific Gas & Electric (PG&E) and Southern California Edison (SCE) – absorbed most of those losses and by the end of the year, PG&E was effectively (and later actually) bankrupt, and SCE was teetering on the edge.

Moreover, shortages ensued anyway. Actually there was supply available, according to some reports more than California needed to meet demand, but producers were unwilling to provide it. They feared, with good reason, that if they provided power to bankrupt distributors, they would never get paid (Easterbrook, 2001; Jenkins, 2001a, b). Thus the power disaster scenario contained in the California law played itself out.

The response of elected state officials was to blame the power providers who were accused of "gouging" even "raping" California consumers.[11] The fact that many of the corporate centers of the providers were out of state allowed state officials some convenient scapegoats, but the problem was mainly in the law, not in the practices of the power producers.[12]

The governor of California, Gray Davis, gave a speech in January 2001 that properly said that the state's "deregulation (sic) scheme is a colossal and dangerous failure," but he attributed it not to the fact that deregulation had never occurred but rather to the machinations of the power producers. He especially singled out the "out-of-state generators" who were out to maximize "unheard of profits." And he painted a picture of predatory outsiders who had been holding the state "hostage" and he spoke of his determination to gain "control over the power that's generated in California."

The solutions he proposed in his speech were actually quite bizarre and at least one, undoubtedly illegal. The latter was his attempt to prevent any electricity generated in California from leaving California. This was an especially odd idea since California was a net importer of electric power and received power – which it clearly needed – not only from other states but also from Canada; if other states and Canada were to adopt Gov. Davis' plan, California would be far worse off. But more important, it was clearly unconstitutional and so apparently a mere political declaration rather than a serious effort and policy making. He also proposed putting guards at all power facilities to force them back on line if they went off at the wrong time, and to deny plants the ability to go off line for unscheduled maintenance if it was not in the interest of California – assuming the generator was not genuinely disabled. There was to be a criminal statute also that prohibited anyone from withholding power from the California grid.

These ideas seemed mainly the result of political calculation and emotion rather than anything like a set of workable proposals for California's power crisis. However, politicians, energy experts, and consumers generally insisted some action had to be taken immediately. Doing nothing was inconceivable. The federal government took the first step, when the Federal Energy Regulatory Commission (FERC) imposed a series of hard and soft price caps[13] on the wholesale market to prevent large spikes and control market volatility. Those caps went into effect in mid-December of 2000. This was not enough, however, to resolve the crisis, given that California's distributors were near bankruptcy, and rolling blackouts were still occurring regularly. But then the FERC understood that its own measures would not resolve the problem; indeed, the federal agency disclaimed any intention of playing the lead role in ending the crisis. It was not going to deal with the issues of retail prices or contracting procedures between retailers and wholesalers; and it could do nothing about increasing California's sources of supply or the perilous financial condition of the state's utilities. The onus clearly was on the state to act.

California's officials reacted angrily to the FERC's perceived unwillingness to play a larger role in resolving the crisis. By January 2001, however, it was clear that they could expect little more assistance from the federal government. In the meantime, out-of-state suppliers grew increasingly reluctant to export any electric power into California out of fear that bankrupted or nearly bankrupted utilities would not pay them. The State began to act in late January of 2001, when the California Department of Water Resources, as agent for the State, started buying electric power with public funds. Within six months, the agency had spent eight billion dollars. They also began to negotiate long-term supply contracts, which had previously been disallowed under the State's re-regulation scheme. These contracts guaranteed supply, but fixed prices that, by the end of 2001, proved to be as much as 400% higher than spot-market prices. The idea of securing long-term contracts was not a bad one, in and of itself, as noted earlier. However, the State was acting in a panic, and took on far more risk than was warranted to secure future supplies. More sober alternative approaches included entering into fewer long-term contracts to minimize the risk of declining spot-market prices, or drafting long-term contracts that allowed for some adjustment in case spot-market prices fell precipitously, as they in fact did.[14] State negotiators certainly should have been aware that spot-market prices can change dramatically. Just two years earlier, in 1999, suppliers had offered the State long-term contracts at prices 50% or more below prices agreed upon in the panic-induced buying spree of Spring 2001.

California also made great efforts to encourage conservation. In April 2001, the state authorized about $800 million for that purpose. These included a massive education program and incentives such as rebates for homeowners for new, more efficient refrigerators and tax breaks for commercial operations that installed more efficient lighting and air conditioning systems. Low interest loans were also offered to communities for energy efficiency programs in public buildings.

Throughout 2001, demand did decline as the state had hoped. Experts had predicted that demand would grow from an already high level through the spring and summer of 2001 and they expected a summer of rolling blackouts to result. But after months of bleak predictions, demand declined by summer and throughout most of the year.

But just how much this was due to state spending was unclear. First, an economic downturn dampened demand; there was, also, more temperate than normal (or expected) weather, but even so-called "weather-adjusted demand" fell. What was the main reason for the decline? Arguably, it was the market. Retail prices were allowed to rise above the 9¢ limit. They started rising in April and continued upward, seeing the largest part of the increase in June. As *The Wall Street Journal* noted, "Only when retail rates surged in June did customers reduce consumption significantly." Still, as Table 1 shows, those price increases cannot explain all of the demand reduction because demand was already falling prior to April, largely thanks to conservation efforts. In any case, reduced consumer demand for electricity eased the state's supply pressures. So, too, did the addition of 1,800 megawatts generating capacity to the State's power supply during the summer of 2001. This marked the first increase in generating capacity in California since the early 1990s.[15]

The state also increased its ownership and control of the state's electricity system. In April 2001, California acquired the transmission system of Southern California Edison, the near- bankrupt power distribution company, for $2.75 billion,[16] and obtained additional generating and transmission assets in the months that followed. The State also created the California Consumer Power and Conservation Financing Authority to construct, own, and operate electric-power production and transmission facilities.

FERC, meanwhile, was putting into place new price mitigation plans to prevent wholesale prices from soaring, as they had in the previous year. This included a variety of new price and bid caps to control the upward movement of electricity prices. As Joskow (2001) observed, the FERC plan contained many loopholes that allowed for easy evasion of the pricing restraints.

By the fall of 2001, the wholesale spot price of electricity had stabilized at around 3.5 cents per kilowatt-hour, approximately one-fourth of the price during

Table 1. California Electricity Usage January–July 2001.

Month	Expected Demand	Actual Demand	Percent Reduction
January	19.78 million MW-h	18.72 million MW-h	5.4%
February	17.65 million MW-h	16.37 million MW-h	7.3%
March	19.58 million MW-h	17.80 million MW-h	9.0%
April	18.60 million MW-h	14.34 million MW-h	6.9%
May	20.90 million MW-h	17.61 million MW-h	11.0%
June	21.93 million MW-h	18.20 million MW-h	12.4%
July	22.89 million MW-h	21.60 million MW-h	5.2%

Note: MW-h = 1000 KW-h.
Source: California Energy Commission 2002.

September of the previous year and one-tenth of the price in December. By this time, however, the spot market barely functioned primarily because California had entered into long-term contracts or was providing electricity from state or municipally-owned assets.[17] The State had also abandoned the idea of consumer choice among retail power providers. In September 2001, the California Public Utilities Commission formally reversed its previous policy supporting retail competition in power markets (Joskow, 2001).

It's fair to say that the main result of the crisis, apparent by the fall of 2001, was the complete abandonment by the State of California of anything even remotely related to electric utility deregulation. The re-regulatory experiment was deemed a complete failure by state regulators, and especially Gov. Davis who stepped up his attacks on companies like Enron as he began his 2002 re-election campaign. And that failure was taken as conclusive proof against the wisdom and value of deregulation in the future.[18] California ratepayers were paying electricity prices that were much higher than when the re-regulatory process began, and seemed destined to pay high prices for many years to come. This fact was cited as the penalty for a deregulatory policy (Goozner, 2001) that, in fact, was not deregulatory to begin with. Moreover, deregulatory efforts throughout the country were slowed, or even abandoned, in light of what was perceived to be "failed deregulation" in California.[19] Simply put, the entire deregulatory enterprise was tainted by its dubious association with what passed for – but really was not – deregulation in California.

THE "FEAR SCENARIO"

The distortions of the California debacle notwithstanding, some economists (e.g. Paul Krugman, 2001, 2002; Faux, 2001) and various analysts and pundits (e.g. Goozner, 2001; Hawken, 2001; Bradley, 2001), have argued that there are legitimate reasons to be fearful of genuine deregulation of electric power. Their concerns boil down to four related issues: First, competition will cause the retail price of electricity to fall to marginal cost. Second, as a result of the low retail price, reserve capacity will fall to minimal levels or disappear entirely. Third, with little reserve capacity, changes in demand will inevitably lead to shortages. And finally, since capacity is tight and demand is instantaneous, firms have incentives to remove supply to manipulate the market and force prices much higher; again this will guarantee shortages and volatile prices.

These four arguments against deregulation of electric power constitute what I call a "fear scenario." Taken together, they suggest that deregulation means a world of insecure electric power supplies prone to disruption, manipulation and wild price volatility. The fear scenario is not entirely baseless but as I will argue below, is built on an important assumption that is false. Take away this assumption and the fear scenario largely evaporates.

There is a surface logic to the fear scenario. To begin with, if there is retail competition for electricity, prices *should* fall. That is, in fact, a rationale for deregulation. In the event of a change in regulatory regime to permit competition, lower prices are expected, forecast, and even, in the case of California, demanded by law. And that does mean that profit margins should fall ultimately toward a normal rate of return.[20] This is especially true for a market that has the characteristics of something like "perfect" competition and electric power would seem to fit important aspects of that model.

The perfectly competitive market is characterized most notably for our case by product homogeneity. That is, one company's product is essentially the same as another company's. Agriculture is the typical example used in economic textbooks. Throw the soybeans from farm A into a bin with soybeans from farm B and the chances are no one can tell them apart. But this means that it is difficult for any one supplier to claim that it offers any particular reason to choose its product over that of a competitor. Even close substitutes have some basis for market differentiation. McDonald's "Quarter Pounder" may be quite like products at Burger King, Wendy's and other chains, but it is distinct enough so that it can be advertised on various attributes. Pricing power in the fast food business will be limited because of the closeness of substitutes, but it will nonetheless be present.

Not so with soybeans, or on the face of it, electric power. As Borenstein (2001, p.1) argues, since electricity is a homogeneous good the market for it will "clear at uniform or near-uniform prices for all sellers – regardless of the cost of production. . . ." And homogeneity, common generating technology and competition guarantee that it will clear at something close to the marginal cost of production for producers of minimum efficient scale, leaving slim profits for all sellers and driving inefficient operators out of business.

Given these limits on profitability in the sale of a single homogenous good, it would in fact be likely that capacity would be squeezed. Idle capacity produces no revenue and if profits are low, significant amounts of idle capacity would produce losses since it has maintenance and depreciation costs. This would be true of even the most efficient providers; indeed, it is hard to see that any inefficient generators would survive at all. Capacity would in general settle at the average expected peak demand in the market through the year. That would mean that there would be capacity to meet expected daily, monthly and even annual changes in demand, but not ones that were unexpected. Any additional capacity would be risky since it might never generate the revenue to pay for itself. This is especially likely, it would appear from the foregoing argument, because the price of output would continually be driven down to marginal cost and so making the risk of un-reimbursed investment large.

Demand for electric power is notoriously unpredictable, at least with real precision, for the long or even medium term. Unusually hot (or cold) weather, rapid economic expansion (beyond forecast), greater than normal servicing requirements, constraints in fuel supplies, and any number of other problems could lead to greater than expected demand or less than expected supply, a forecast error potentially very substantial. That in turn would mean that there would inevitably be insufficient capacity for at least short periods of time. Periodic outages, due to supply shortages, would then seem likely to be relatively frequent.[21] Of course, if shortages persist and lead to forecast revisions, new capacity could be brought on line. However, it can take years to acquire that capacity. Even standardized gas turbines require several months from order to installation and that rather short time frame presupposes existing facilities to accommodate them.

Moreover, it may be to the generating companies' interests to see to it that those supplies are added as slowly as possible, if at all. The idea here is that if supply-increases trail those of demand, the market-clearing price will continue to rise to the benefit of existing firms. Indeed, as the market approaches the limit of capacity there will be incentives for firms to take generators out of service temporarily (as they apparently did in California) to *force* a price spike. In the longer term this may not be sustainable since outages and high prices (and so profits) will both encourage entry and diminish demand as consumers adjust to higher prices and supply constraints. But squeezing supply may be a frequent ploy, according to the fear scenario, so that firms can earn supernormal profits at least for the short run.

Indeed, in the short term, in the scenario described thus far, firms in the industry *should* earn high profits. The reason is that demand for electricity appears to be very inelastic in the short term; many would argue that the demand curve is probably close to vertical at any given moment in time. As a result, reduced supply translates entirely into price increases (if these are allowed) for all sales, raising overall revenues in the process.

Of course this problem of supply manipulation would be solved if electricity were easily stored. But this is not the case. To the extent that it can be stored at all – through, for example, banks of batteries or so-called "pumped" storage[22] – it is costly and cumbersome. It is typically cheaper to produce electricity on demand. But this means that a system, especially as portrayed in the fear scenario, is particularly vulnerable to demand spikes and/or supply reductions.

In sum, this is the fear scenario in full:

(1) prices fall to marginal cost and profits to "normal" for all generating companies;
(2) the companies, constrained on the profit end, are reluctant to invest in any new capacity unless they have a reasonable expectation of it making money; they will, thus, tend to underinvest;
(3) whenever conditions cause sudden surges in demand the capacity simply won't be there and since supply after a certain point cannot be instantly expanded, there will be insufficient supply and outages and/or price spikes will (must inevitably) ensue.

In the end according to this view, the peril of deregulation is not that there will be one gouging monopoly, but there will be a combination of mini-gougers and chaos. People will cease to rely on their electric switch and this will have untold consequences both for production and for our very sense of well being.

Assumptions and Problems of the "Fear Scenario"

Fortunately, the fear scenario is based on faulty assumptions. As some economists and policy analysts have suggested, the right of contract alone would lead to a significant departure from the fear scenario (Joskow, 2001). That is, if all consumers have the option of contracting for service, whether long, medium or short term, the problems of the fear scenario are likely to disappear.

Consider the fear scenario again now with the right of contract: The price, it is said, must inevitably be bid down to the marginal cost in a power. Again, this might be true if, like California, only spot market sales were allowed. Unless (or until) demand reached the limits of supply, there would be a tendency for the price to be bid downward.

But presumably a contractual price of electric power must account for the extra capacity (or the ability to acquire it quickly) that would be needed to assure the provider met its contractual obligation. The provider would not enter into the contract unless it received some compensation for the risk the company was assuming.

This provision would also mean that capacity would likely be adequate to meet unexpected surges in demand, either through the maintenance of a significant reserve capacity or transmission links with other providers who might be able to fill in quickly.[23] Indeed, there might even be a niche for firms to offer emergency power (sufficiently compensated) that could be transmitted throughout large regions of the country, filling in for demand fluctuations, outages or other problems that could emerge. In fact, while it is true that electricity cannot be cheaply stored it can be transmitted relatively cheaply. Load shifting and transfer of electric power are basic givens (in fact the raison d'etre) of the nation's interconnected electric power pools (see Chapter 5). This, of course, does presuppose adequate transmission facilities, and in California and elsewhere in the U.S. these facilities have often been less than sufficient. But the ability to direct load to a system that needs it, is no less a fundamental feature of electric power than is the difficulty of storage.[24] In all, this implies that while supply problems may arise, there also can be market incentives to solve them.

Contracts would also eliminate the incentives for market manipulation. As Joskow and Kahn (2001) noted with respect to the California case, one power company which had entered into forward contracts with customers, showed no sign ambiguous or otherwise that they withheld supplies from the market to force prices higher. Indeed, it would have been a pointless exercise. Since they were obligated at a specified price to provide power, they would not have benefited from taking generating assets off-line. Indeed, a firm might well face an actionable breach in attempting to do so. Thus contracting alone eliminates the fear scenario, and suggests a basis for genuine deregulation and competitive wholesale and retail electric markets.[25]

The Key Assumption of the "Fear Scenario"

As I noted earlier, in general the fear scenario is based on one important assumption. That is: electricity is an entirely homogeneous good and competition takes place on only one dimension. In other words, the only thing that is sold from the time electricity is generated to the time that it is used is (and can only be) the electric power itself. If this were true, then the fear scenario would probably have some validity. And it was in some sense true for California since the only deregulated market was in fact the wholesale power market, and so there was only one homogeneous good in one market on which "competition" was possible. But of course California had nothing approximating a competitive electric power market generally. And as such it has very little to teach us about how a competitive market in electric power might work.

In fact, in a truly deregulated electric power system, where there is choice for consumers both at the retail and wholesale level, where distribution and transmission facilities are available to all, what would power providers sell? They would sell power, of course, but they would also sell other attributes: reliability would be one. Indeed, after California many customers would be willing to pay a premium for service that is less likely to be interrupted or curtailed regardless of conditions. The additional capacity would be paid for whether or not it was utilized by higher than marginal cost charges on power that is distributed. More to the point, the marginal cost of low-risk power would include the capital fixed charges on reserve capacity that would be necessary to reduce the risk. Of course firms or individuals could opt to buy power at lower prices with higher risk. Thus consumers would weigh choices based on their relative tolerance of risk. And this in turn implies that power is not entirely homogeneous, and because it is not there are opportunities for competitive markets. Pricing would not fall strictly to the marginal cost of producing and delivering a megawatt of electric power.

Firms could also offer maintenance, demand management and other services at the consumer's end. Consumers could utilize power providers to assure technical reliability, vary demand throughout the day, and find means in general of greater efficiency in electric usage. These are just examples of the way in which firms could compete through bundled service packages. In this case electric power itself would be only one component of several that consumers would contract for. Competition would develop in fact for the nature and flexibility of the packages themselves. That is, a consumer might have a menu of options and could pick from them individually. In this case, again, there is no necessary reason why firms would sell only at the marginal cost of production of the power. Moreover, there would be some pricing power for firms the more they could differentiate the packages they offer.[26]

Service bundles could even extend beyond the delivery and utilization of electric power. There is no reason why the delivery mechanism – the wires – could not serve for multiple information and entertainment services. That is, providers could offer electric, phone, cable, internet – a variety of uses over a delivery system now utilized exclusively for electricity. In this regard, besides offering an expanded bundle of services, the power providers would compete in a variety of markets on multiple dimensions.

There is no reason to suppose that this system would be any less reliable than the regulated natural monopoly system. There are some fears that firms facing financial hardship could go bankrupt, leaving their customers without power. But of course, many firms go bankrupt without disruptions of service, although it is the case that courts and governments might well need to play a role in company reorganizations, assuring continuity of at least basic service.

If Consumers Assume the Risks

Of course, there might be those, providers and consumers, who would prefer a relationship whereby the price of power will not be set by long- or medium-term contract. Rather they would prefer a price based on the spot rate, and they would be willing to accept more risk for lower prices. In that case a price above marginal cost (to insure service or to acquire service bundles) would seem unnecessary. But if such customers would prefer a spot-based contract, do they, customers and the power provider, inevitably fall into the fear scenario's potential trap?

The answer to this is no, provided the cost of generating or acquiring power can be passed from the producer to the user. This was the major failing of the California regulatory experiment. Customers never had any signals about the cost of electric power at the wholesale level since the retail rate was fixed. But information technology is today advanced enough so that we can have real-time pricing (Borenstein, 2001c; Faruqui et al., 2001; Taylor & VanDoren, 2001b). That is, the cost of generating or acquiring power through the grid can be transmitted instantly to customers, and the retail price will rise commensurate with the wholesale market. So if peak load is more expensive to produce, consumers should pay more but be aware that they are paying more for it. In some writings about the California power situations there was the implicit argument that consumers, needing power instantly, cannot and will not respond to price signals even if they actually get them.

But this is simply wrong – especially when people see the price alternatives. Those who made this suggestion offered no proof while studies have actually shown consumers do in fact respond to price signals with respect to electric power when they get them (Taylor, 2001). In virtually all markets, people have shown that they will adjust their behavior. If the price of electricity is ten times higher at four in the afternoon, than it is at midnight, it is highly likely that a significant number of individuals and companies will put off power using tasks to the later hour – especially when they observe these cost differences on a regular basis. People can and will turn off air conditioners if it is costly to run them and they have no reason to do so (Faruqui et al., 2001). It is a basic assumption of economics in fact that price changes alter behavior. There is no reason to believe that this economic rule should be suspended for the consumption of electric power.[27]

Some consumers have expressed the fear that real-time pricing would permit power providers to manipulate the price during peak times. That is, the same kind of manipulated outage problem would be possible. The one barrier to this would be the fact that if consumers are alert to price signals then these skyrocketing prices would lead to significant curtailments in demand, reducing, if not eliminating the incentive and the benefit of such an exercise in market power.

It should also be noted that a competitive electricity market does not mean a market in which government plays no role whatsoever. Indeed, some government regulation can improve market efficiency and lower the cost of exchange. While I will return to this point later in the chapter, one point here is that rules, for example antitrust statutes, may also be used as a brake against such opportunistic behavior. Note, too, that unless there is collusion to reduce output, there will be benefits to other firms entering (for example those noted above as potential emergency power providers) as prices rise. Since peak demand would likely fall under a real time pricing system, unless the markets were actively manipulated, the amount of market power that any one firm could achieve would likely be minimal.[28] There would surely be a role for government to enforce antitrust statutes in the event that collusion became evident.

Still in all, a market that freely permits distribution of risks and consumer choice is likely to overcome any perception that we need the natural monopoly system to protect us from alleged flaws in the electric power market. The perception of necessary market failure requiring regulation is not valid. Nor of course is the technical rationale. It has been argued earlier that there is no such thing as a natural monopoly although there may be contingencies when a single firm might be more efficient. But with the possible exception of distribution (and that is disputed, see the Foreword to Chapter 6) there is no part of the electric system that can reasonably be said to be, even accidentally, a "natural" monopoly. There does not need to be a government regulated power company to save consumers either from the perils of monopoly or competition.

If the Fear Scenario is not Valid . . .

In the end, this section suggests the following:

(1) the fears about deregulation *in principle*, while worth noting, are not a valid reason for reversing or preventing the process;
(2) genuine deregulation and the move to competitive markets is a better solution than partial measures (as California amply demonstrated).

Think of the issue this way: the components of the fear scenario were linked. *Because* power was a homogeneous good profits would be driven down. And *because* they would be driven down there would no incentive to maintain adequate capacity. And *because* capacity would be inadequate there would inevitably be shortages both *because* demand might exceed supply. And *because* firms would have incentives to exercise market power, therefore, deregulated competitive electric systems were inherently unstable if not downright dangerous.

But now consider it this way: firms that freely contract with consumers can distribute risk, insure against problem, compete on a variety of dimensions, provide incentives for demand management and have incentives for adequate supplies. Indeed, *if* they compete on various dimensions profits need not be driven to zero and there will be several market participants. And *if* they are able to compete on various dimensions, which include reliability, then there will be some insurance against the inadequacies of supply. And *if* the supply is adequate because there are long term contractual obligations (or short run price risk agreements or both) which would reduce or eliminate incentives to exercise market power, therefore competitive, deregulated electric power markets will be stable, dynamic and no more dangerous than current monopoly markets are.

A DEREGULATED FUTURE?

Though the preceding section has argued that there is no reason to fear a competitive electric power system, it is easy to be pessimistic about the future of electric power deregulation in America. Although there may be no technical reason to maintain monopoly power companies, there seem to be institutional ones. The legislatures are reluctant to take measures against strong lobbying from the monopoly utilities and so for example there are rules over stranded investments that retard progress to competitive markets.

Indeed, as Public Choice economic theory has noted (Mueller, 1989), lawmakers are also reluctant to make large changes to rules that have vested interests within government itself. In California, legislators clearly tried to make everyone happy and in the end made everyone angry. But the result of it all was that state government returned control of the electric system almost entirely to state regulators. This was considered, if nothing else, safe.

The problems of government regulatory muddles are perhaps more acute with respect to energy than anything else. Consumers both individual and corporate experience their dependence on energy supplies daily and feel tremendously discomfited by disruptions or large price fluctuations. This leads political leaders to: (1) meddle in markets even ones that have never been declared natural monopolies;[29] (2) give up control only with the greatest reluctance, unless it be seen to maximize political advantage; and (3) react apoplectically when things go wrong.[30] As one columnist (Hawken, 2001) put it, "Energy is the nation's most politicized commodity; politics and [energy] markets are dreadful bedmates."

But at the same time, there are examples of moves toward competition both in the U.S. and abroad that suggest that the process of transition can be managed successfully. It would be incorrect to suggest that most of these efforts represent more than small steps toward deregulated, competitive markets. But they have shown that competition does not necessarily produce disaster, and indeed can be clearly beneficial. In Pennsylvania, for example, the electric power market was restructured about the same time California's new rules were put into effect. This effort, too, left the state with considerable control in the market. Again the utilities were permitted recovery of stranded, and other transition, costs (without particular regard to stranded benefits) and there were some rules about wholesale and retail prices, duty to serve, and so on. But the state permitted contracting, did not require that anyone sell or buy generating assets, encouraged entry of new suppliers and distributed generation facilities, and made a point of educating retail customers about electric provider choice. The result has been generally lower electric prices (relative to the country as a whole and to Pennsylvania previously), adequate supplies, and general satisfaction with a market-based approach. Indeed, close to 30% of all electric power consumption was choice determined. Those who did not choose had providers chosen for them but typically benefited from the effects of competition on prices (Fischer, 2001).

But of course this is still heavily managed by the state, and it is not clear when or if the system will become one of more or less free exchange and entry where the state plays the more limited role it adopts in the markets for other commodities. But the small successes exhibited in this and several other cases, gives me some reason for optimism about the future direction of deregulation in the electric system. Here is a hopeful scenario:

Success on the margin as evidenced in the Pennsylvania case will encourage others to move in the same direction. Yes, California represented a step back, but there are many positive reasons to go forward. Indeed, the failure in California can perhaps have the benefit of illustrating how poor, contradictory measures can lead to problems, while programs that take care to avoid the same kind of pitfalls can be successful. Success including the benefits of generally lower prices induces other states to press ahead with more competitive models. Rules concerning distribution systems, transmission lines, buying and selling power across state lines and through regions are clarified by federal rules.[31] Of course such rules will undergo refinement and change, but is likely to led to a market system whereby power providers can offer services to local, regional and even national customers, increasing consumer choice and the competitiveness of the market.

Transition will take time, and there probably needs to be management of the process. There will be steps backward, no doubt, as states and vested interests try to gain benefits at the expense of the larger market, but as the benefits of deregulation and competition are proved, there will hopefully be continuous progress forward. Government's role will recede to maintaining general rules of antitrust, discrimination, and so on. There may even be a need for subsidies for those in low-income brackets, maintaining the concept of universal service (see Chapter 7). Eventually, though, people will understand that the electric-power market is a market where goods and services are acquired. They will understand the choices of attributes and the benefits and costs of their choices. Electricity markets will also be harder to manipulate even in the case of where consumers are paying spot prices (Berenson, 2002). With real time pricing, consumers will be able to adjust their behavior as prices change and so market power will be increasingly more difficult to exercise. There is no reason why this system will be any less reliable than one based on natural monopoly since the market incentives should do a better job of directing resources to their highest valued use, than do political commissioners today. Public service commissions may persist although it is not clear why they would. At the very least, their purpose will have to change, as price setting and investment recovery will be left to the markets, where they clearly belong.

Is this scenario as unrealistic as pessimists like Professor Morriss suggest? I think not, given that there are at least partial successes in the deregulation of presumed natural monopolies in other industries. Telecommunications has already been noted, but there have been definite reductions in the regulatory control in trucking and airlines, and government did act – admittedly after more than 100 years to abolish the Interstate Commerce Commission, an early attempt at government control. It is clearly not the case that government is incapable of moving away from regulatory control.

Still, we do seem to be at an important moment in the process given the particular failure (and misinterpretation of that failure) in California. Perhaps the best that can be hoped for at this stage is an adaptive learning process (North, 1990), where there is a slow effort to evolve more efficient institutions for production and consumption of electric power. This might be a fairly long process, given not only the California case, but also the vested interests that benefit from the old natural monopoly system. In any instance of significant institutional change, there are always those who are losers in the process and who seek therefore to thwart it. But signs of success in the U.S. and abroad should lead other interests to move the process toward a more efficient outcome. This must inevitably mean genuine deregulation of the electric power market. There is no real rationale for retaining the old system beyond the argument that new systems, designed badly, produce bad outcomes. It can only be hoped that no one failure becomes an excuse to rely on old inefficient systems or to twist reform into something worse than what it was meant to replace.

CONCLUSION

Natural monopoly, as a concept, is at an end for the electric-power industry. It is an empty concept to a large extent but no longer applies, even as a contingency, to this industry. But now that it is over, what will replace it? It could be largely free, competitive markets. It could be a mishmash of rent seeking control boards, promulgating contradictory rules, and reacting to problems with draconian but self-defeating actions, and boisterous rhetoric. But proponents of deregulation can take some solace from the progress of other industries that have undergone the end of natural monopoly. Telephone service still has evidence of the old monopoly systems, but it has been substantially and fundamentally altered. The level of services and competition has expanded choices and lowered prices for all consumers throughout the U.S., proceeding sometimes fitfully forward, but clearly in that direction. It may take time, but there's hope that electric power will follow the same general path. The end of a natural monopoly should mean deregulation and competition for the production and service of electric power in the United States.

NOTES

1. These are referred to as "zero economic profit;" that is, the cost of production including a "normal" return on capital.

2. Nevada, Wisconsin and Oklahoma were among the states that ceased legislative movement toward regulatory changes because of the California debacle (noted in Smith 2001).

3. There are many valuable analyses of the California Power crisis. Notably, Besant-Jones and Tenenbaum, 2001; Faruqui et al., 2001; Joskow, 2001; Sioshansi, 2001, 2000; Taylor and VanDoren, 2001b.

4. Assembly Bill 1890, signed into law September 23, 1996.

5. The California story would suggest that Prof. Morriss's argument that regulation will fail because of lawyers is not entirely apt – unless all legislators are presumed to be lawyers.

6. It should be noted, however, that the distributors could and did establish independent unregulated generating subsidiaries to produce for other markets.

7. It was generally believed in the industry and apparently by the government that wholesale prices would fall continuously under competition.

8. In practice some were able to recoup *more than 100%* of their stranded costs. The estimate at the time of passage was that the utilities would gain an excess of $28 billion through the fixed price (Taylor, 1997).

9. California producers faced unusually strict environmental rules. In some cases, for example, power producers were required to provide pollution offsets. That is, if a natural gas burning plant were constructed and it produced x amount of air pollutants, then the firm would need to reduce x amount of air pollution elsewhere in the environment. That would mean, for example, a buyout of a certain number of older, more polluting cars; or possibly, retrofitting some other business' burners or smokestacks. In any case, the requirement made it at least very expensive to locate a new plant in California. Nuclear plants, of course, solve the air pollution problem but face other environmental hurdles, and it is not clear that a nuclear plant can be constructed cost effectively. Even alternative, environmentally benign sources such as wind and solar may face environmental challenges because of their lack of aesthetic appeal, interference with migratory birds or some other conflict with nature and appeal wildlife. Additional transmission lines to import power from other states could be another alternative, but these, too, were difficult to affect in California. Indeed, the resistance to any sort of expansion of the power system led some observers to suggest that in California people did not practice NIMBY (not in my backyard); instead they practiced BANANA (build absolutely nothing anywhere near anybody). However, exactly how much impact environmental rules had in contributing to the crisis of 2000–2001 is a matter of some dispute (Taylor & VanDoren, 2001b).

10. The increase in the cost of natural gas represents an increase in input prices. Unless costs are cut elsewhere, it will necessarily mean reduced supply of electricity – that is, a shift in the supply curve to the left. That raises the equilibrium price in a free market situation, but of course, with a fixed price it only widens the shortages that are likely to arise.

11. Some companies, most notably the Enron Corporation, deliberately took advantage of the power crisis to raise prices. Before evidence came to light that Enron had endeavored to manipulate the market, some studies had argued that companies had used their market power to take advantage of California's predicament (Borenstein, 2002; Borenstein et al., 2000; Joskow & Kahn, 2001, 2002), although others, looking at the same data, disputed this conclusion (Harvey & Hogan, 2001). In any event, as argued earlier in this chapter, any opportunity for market manipulation was embodied in a flawed deregulation scheme that was bound to lead to a crisis and set the basic conditions that made manipulation possible. Actually, it was not clear as of this writing exactly how (and how many) generating companies manipulated the market. Enron, for example, most notably created false sales in order to trick the system operators into believing that there was excess demand in the system. Federal rules required operators to pay generators to relieve system congestion. In this case, there was none. But exactly how much of the manipulation involved taking generating assets offline during peak load periods to create price spikes is not presently known.

12. There have been some claims that providers manipulated supply given that the short-term elasticity of demand is very low. That means that revenues will increase in the event supply is reduced. As of this writing no cases of deliberate supply reduction to manipulate the market have been brought to appropriate courts.

13. Hard price caps set a strict limit on prices; soft caps, sometime termed "flexible" rate caps, would be adjusted according to circumstances, allowing power suppliers to charge more when they could demonstrate that costs necessitated higher prices.

14. A group of legal, economics and business scholars in "Manifesto on the California Electricity Crisis" had warned in January specifically against a rush to contract. "Now is precisely the wrong time for the State to commit to long-term contracts . . ." (1/31/02).

15. In fact according to the Department of Energy, capacity in California declined by 2% during the 1990s.

16. According to the *Economist*, it was "an inflated price" ("Lost in California's Haze," April 18, 2001).

17. An interesting feature of the California power crisis was the fact that publicly-owned power assets, particularly those of the Los Angeles Department of Water and Power (LADWP), sold at high profits surplus power to the distribution companies. LADPW, which bought some of its power from the Hoover Dam for about 3¢/KW-h, sold it for as much as 36¢. Its marginal cost of electric power was in fact probably lower than many of the independent generators who were accused by the governor of criminally exploiting the state of California (cited by Republican California State Senator Ray Haynes, "Government Did it Again," 7/6/01, online at: http://republican.sen.ca.gov).

18. As one energy consultant put it, "I don't think one can have a deregulated system if one wants reliable power." Quoted in D. R. Francis (2001).

19. For example, in an Associated Press report, "New Talk of Energy Conservation, "the California electricity crisis was said to be "largely due to a failed attempt at electricity deregulation . . ." May 4, 2001, found at: <http://wire.ap.org>.

20. In economic theory, marginal cost implies also the opportunity cost of investment, so it includes a "normal" profit (see Note 1).

21. Historically, the reliability of the natural monopoly system in the U.S. was high, especially compared with systems in developing countries. But it is also wrong to romanticize the success of that system. As noted in Chapter 5, there were periods of shortage, spectacular power outages and periods of wildly inaccurate forecasts of demand that led to massive overbuilding and huge price hikes for consumers.

22. This entails using power at off-peak times to pump water into an elevated storage holding tank. The water can then be released at peak times to turn a hydroelectric generator.

23. As Joskow has noted, "If a generator has a long-term contract then the financial incentive is to generate steady power in order to maximize sales" (Quoted in Easterbrook, 2001).

24. It is noted in Chapter 7 that power cannot be directed to individual users, but it can be sent to distribution systems simply by opening up a transmission link.

25. It should be noted that a contractual system entails its own transaction costs. The terms must be monitored and measured and the contracts must be enforceable. All of these must be at low enough cost to justify a contract regime. There is no reason to believe that this would be problematic in the U.S. although in other countries with poor contract enforcement, such a system might well be too costly.

26. The cellular telephone industry provides a useful illustration in this regard.

27. There is another type of option called "time of use" pricing. This sets in advance prices for various times of the day, days of the week and seasons of the year. So for example, the price might be set at 5¢ for weekday nights and 10¢ for weekday afternoons, and maybe 15¢ for weekday afternoons in summer. These are improvements over the single price in that they give consumers incentives to plan electric use daily and seasonally. Still, real-time pricing would give a truer picture of the actual cost and availability of electric power.

28. It is important to note that although the technology for real-time pricing exists, it would be costly to provide to all users. Borenstein (2001b) has suggested it would be cost effective to provide the technology to large electric consumers while making

the transition to smaller users, residential and small business customers, over time, perhaps as the cost of the equipment falls. In the meantime, a combination of real-time pricing for large customers and time-of-use pricing for small ones could obtain some of the same benefits that universal real-time pricing would achieve.

29. For example, the government has generally made a hash of policies with respect to oil (see Lee et al., 1990).

30. Again the oil market offers the most pertinent cases. Increasing prices have led to rash statements and proposals by political leaders including presidents. These have included demands to investigate oil companies, arguments to tap into the nation's strategic oil reserves and promises to give large subsidies for various kinds of energy development.

31. FERC is (as of the spring of 2002) in the process of developing a common system of rules with respect to transmission and distribution. These are likely to face strong lobbying opposition, rent seeking amendment, regulatory jurisdictional conflict, and are unlikely to be fully resolved for years.

REFERENCES

Banerjee, N. (2000). Dwindling Faith in Deregulation. *The New York Times*, (September 20), online at: http://www.nytimes.com

Besant-Jones, J., & Tenenbaum, B. (2001). Lessons from California's Power Crisis. *Finance & Development*, *38*(3).

Berenson, A. (2002). Does Energy Deregulation Still Make Sense? *The New York Times*, (May 12), online at: http://www.nytimes.com

Borenstein, S. (2001a). The Trouble With Electricity Markets (and Some Solutions). Working Paper PWP-081, Program on Workable Energy Regulation, University of California, Berkeley.

Borenstein, S. (2001b). Frequently Asked Questions about Implementing Real-Time Electricity Pricing in California for Summer 2001. manuscript, available at: http://www.ucei.org

Borenstein, S. (2001c). Electricity Pricing Should Clue Consumers to Judicious Use. *Los Angeles Times*, (op-ed), January 17.

Borenstein, S., Bushnell, J., & Wolak, F. (2000). Diagnosing Market Power in California's Deregulated Wholesale Electricity Market. Working Paper PWP-064, Program on Workable Energy Regulation, University of California, Berkeley.

Bradley, W. (2001). Power to the People, *The American Prospect*, *12*(11)(June 25), online at: http://www.prospect.org

Easterbrook, G. (2001). Brown and Out: Can California's Energy Companies Change a Lightbulb? *The New Republic*, (May 24), online at: http://www.tnr.com

Faruqui, A., Chao, H., Niemeyer, V., Platt, J., & Stahlkopf, K. (2001). Analyzing California's Power Crisis. *The Energy Journal*, *22*(4), 29–52.

Faruqui, A. (2001). Getting out of the Dark. *Regulation*, (Fall), 58–62.

Faux, J. (2002). American Needs a Future, Not a Tax Cut. speech to the National Press Club, February 28, 2001, online at: http://www.epinet.org

Fischer, T. (2001). Successful Deregulation. *The Dismal Scientist*, (May 24), online at: http://www.dismal.com

Francis, D. (2001). Cooling to Electricity Deregulation. *The Christian Science Monitor*, (April 3), online at: http://www.csmonitor.com

Goozner, M. (2002). Free Market Shock. *The American Prospect*, *12*(15)(February 2), online at: http://www.prospect.org

Grossman, P. (2002). 'Deregulated' Energy Destined to Fail. *Indianapolis Star*, (editorial)(June 11), online at: http://www.indystar.com

Harvey, S., & Hogan, W. (2001). Identifying the Exercise of Market Power in California. Manuscript.

Hawken, P. (2001). Cautionary Advice from California. *The Christian Science Monitor*, (September 5), online at: http://www.csmonitor.com

Jenkins, H. (2001a). Back to the Future in California. *The Wall Street Journal*, (January 17), online at: http://www.wsj.com

Jenkins, H. (2001b). Crisis? What Crisis? *The Wall Street Journal*, (September 5), online at: http://www.wsj.com

Joskow, P. (2001). California's Electricity Crisis. manuscript, Massachusetts Institute of Technology, September 28, [updated].

Joskow, P., & Kahn, E. (2001). Identifying the Exercise of Market Power: Refining the Estimates. manuscript, Massachusetts Institute of Technology, July 5.

Joskow, P., & Kahn, E. (2002). A Quantitative Analysis of Pricing Behavior in California's Wholesale Electricity Market During Summer 2000: The Final Word. manuscript, Massachusetts Institute of Technology, February 4.

Krugman, P. (2001). The Unreal Thing, *New York Times*, (February 18), online at: http://www.nytimes.com

Krugman, P. (2002). The Reality Thing. *New York Times*, (June 25), online at: http://www.nytimes.com

Lee, T., Ball, B., & Tabors, R. (1990). *Energy Aftermath.* Boston: Harvard Business School Press.

Mueller, D. (1989). *Public Choice II.* Cambridge: Cambridge University Press.

North, D. (1990). *Institutions, Institutional Change and Economic Performance.* Cambridge: Cambridge University Press.

Seltzer, I. (2001). Trends. *The Milken Institute Review*, (First Quarter), 6–13.

Sioshansi, F. (2000). California's Flawed Market: What Went Wrong and How to Fix It. *IAEE Newsletter*, *9*(Fourth Quarter).

Sioshansi, F. (2001). California's Electricity Crisis Continues *IAEE Newsletter*, *10*(First Quarter).

Taylor, J. (1997). High Voltage Swindle: Why Electricity Restructuring will Electrocute Ratepayers. *Today's Commentary*, Cato Institute, January, online at: http://www.cato.org

Taylor, J. (2001). Paul Krugman Short Circuits. *Today's Commentary*, Cato Institute February 21, online at: http://www.cato.org

Taylor, J., & VanDoren, P. (2001a). California Screamin' ... About Deregulation. *Today's Commentary*, Cato Institute, January 17, online at: http://www.cato.org

Taylor, J., & VanDoren, P. (2001b). California's Electricity Crisis. Policy Analysis No. 406, Cato Institute, July 3.

Woolfolk, J. (2002). Consultant Says Utilities Helped Enron Manipulate Power Prices in California. *San Jose Mercury News*, June 6, online at: http://www.energycentral.com